REINVENTING BUSINESS MODELS

Praise for *Reinventing Business Models: How firms cope with disruption*

'A great book that de-mystifies business model innovation. In the first part, the authors explain the critical difference between replicating an existing business model to exploit past success and business model renewal that breaks new ground harnessing novel customer trends and new technologies. The authors identify why this separation of business model innovation into two paths is a novel but essential concept, and the organisational structures associated with effective results. The authors go further, in the second part they outline the leadership challenge associated with each path— identifying the agenda and roles of different actors, and the necessary culture and process that will make things happen. This book is a "must read" for CEOs and boards of directors, especially those of established companies in older industries.'

Charles Baden-Fuller, Centenary Professor of Strategy,
Cass Business School, City, University of London

'For CEOs operating in today's fast-paced world, the biggest challenge is knowing when and how to reinvent their business model—their formula for making money. This book, *Reinventing Business Models* provides the most detailed and compelling analysis to date of how to do this. Combining careful academic thinking with practical examples, it is a must-read guide for any educator, student or businessperson who wants to understand the secrets of corporate success in a disruptive world.'

Julian Birkinshaw, Deputy Dean and Professor of Strategy and
Entrepreneurship, London Business School

'This book provides an extensive and rigorous analysis of the imperatives and mechanisms for businesses to refresh their business models, building on numerous examples and case studies. For many companies this is a highly topical question as they face almost certain disruptions from technology development; the book reminds them to remain alert also to broader potential drivers of disruption, and to consider how responses must combine technology, management, organisation and partnerships to be most effective.'

Ruth Cairnie, Non-Executive Director at Rolls-Royce Holdings plc, Associated
British Foods plc and Keller Group plc and former Executive Vice
President for Strategy and Planning at Shell

'*Reinventing Business Models* provides significant research on business renewal and replication. This book provides unique thought provoking insights to the need to change and when and how to alter a firm's business model. It gives key requirements of management practices and the culture necessary to successfully alter a company's direction. Overall, the book is a great foundation for business model formulation in our rapidly changing business environment.'

Murray Deal, Vice-President EMEA, Asia Pacific and
Latin America at Eastman Chemical Company

'Business models go out of date increasingly fast. You really have to read this book to change your business model successfully.'

Guido Dierick, CEO, NXP Semiconductors Netherlands

'Business model innovation is a very challenging phenomenon. Practitioners agree that it is immensely important; yet, academic researchers have had little sound advice to offer on the subject. Volberda, Van den Bosch and Heij's new book means that this is changing: They offer clear conceptualizations, highly relevant theory, and numerous examples. A breakthrough and a milestone in a field that is crucially important, but still very much an emerging one!'

Nicolai Foss, Professor of Organization Theory and Human Resource Management, Bocconi University

'In today's economy, firms are confronted with disruptions in markets and technologies and erosion of their business models. The authors of *Reinventing Business Models* show perfectly that developing a new business model requires more than adopting new technologies. This inspiring book provides groundbreaking new insights for management scholars as well as new tools to help managers cope successfully with disruption in their industries.'

Vijay Govindarajan, Coxe Distinguished Professor at Tuck at Dartmouth & Marvin Bower Fellow at Harvard Business School

'In incomparable style, *Reinventing Business Models* shows what happens behind the scenes when you change your business model.'

Goof Hamers, Former CEO and President, Vanderlande Industries

'We all know the brands which were far ahead of competitors in their sector until a disruptor appeared on the market. This book will help you stay ahead of the game.'

Leon He, President Western Europe Enterprise Business Group, Huawei Technologies Co. Ltd.

'*Reinventing Business Models* is a thorough and academically-rigorous book that examines how a firm can reinvent its business model. It provides a clear and managerially focused roadmap on how to do this in practice and brings out several lessons of what works and what doesn't. In this age of disruption, organizations of any size and from any sector will find it required reading.'

Costas Markides, Professor of Strategy & Entrepreneurship, Holder of the Robert Bauman Chair of Strategic Leadership, London Business School

'*Reinventing Business Models* inspires and encourages managers to take action and to reflect.'

Hans Smits, CEO Janssen de Jong Groep, Non-Executive Director at Air France-KLM

'Adapting to a changing world ("survival of the fittest") calls for continual reinvention of your own business model and presents a major leadership challenge. This book can help you in this.'

Feike Sijbesma, CEO, DSM

'Highly recommended for managers who want to grow and develop their organizations.'

Jeffrey Tierie, Former CEO Claymount Technologies Group

'*Reinventing Business Models* is an important contribution to both academics as well as practicing managers. In this well researched, argued, and written book, Volberda, Van den Bosch, and Heij present a compelling point of view on how, when, and why organizations build capabilities to both replicate and renew. This book presents fresh data and induces fresh ideas on the roots of dynamic capabilities. It is one of those rare books that is both insightful and pragmatic. This book belongs on both the academic's desk and in the manager's office.'

Michael Tushman, Paul R. Lawrence, MBA Class of 1942 Professor of Business Administration, Harvard Business School

'The book gives a good picture of how managers can achieve the two variants of business model innovation: refining and renewing.'

Carlo van de Weijer, Vice-President Traffic Solutions, TomTom

REINVENTING BUSINESS MODELS

HOW FIRMS COPE WITH DISRUPTION

HENK VOLBERDA
FRANS VAN DEN BOSCH
KEVIN HEIJ

OXFORD
UNIVERSITY PRESS

OXFORD
UNIVERSITY PRESS

Great Clarendon Street, Oxford, OX2 6DP,
United Kingdom

Oxford University Press is a department of the University of Oxford.
It furthers the University's objective of excellence in research, scholarship,
and education by publishing worldwide. Oxford is a registered trade mark of
Oxford University Press in the UK and in certain other countries

© Henk Volberda, Frans van den Bosch, and Kevin Heij 2018

The moral rights of the authors have been asserted

First Edition published in 2018

Impression: 2

Published in the United States of America by Oxford University Press
198 Madison Avenue, New York, NY 10016, United States of America

British Library Cataloguing in Publication Data
Data available

Library of Congress Control Number: 2017942093

ISBN 978-0-19-879204-8

Printed in Great Britain by
Clays Ltd, St Ives plc

For Celine

This research was funded by the Foundation for Management Studies (VNO-NCW) in The Hague, the Netherlands.

Foreword

According to my fellow Dutchman Arie de Geus, a former strategist at Shell who wrote the book *The Living Company* in 1997, the average life of a larger (Fortune 500) firm at the end of the last century was between forty and fifty years. Richard Foster, Professor at Yale University, believes that this has now dropped to around fifteen years.

Whatever the right number is now, it is clear that firms face a huge task in surviving for a long time, especially in rapidly changing times. This often requires firms to rejuvenate themselves, renew themselves, or even reinvent themselves entirely. While some firms can keep going for many decades or even centuries, the vast majority are indeed granted only a shorter life, ending in split-up, takeover, or liquidation. Of the firms on the Dow Jones Industrial Average in 1896, only General Electric is still on the list. The Amsterdam Exchange index (AEX) shows a similar picture. Of the current twenty-five Dutch leading shares, only nine were part of the AEX in 1989. More than forty funds have left the AEX in the past twenty-five years, due to takeovers, liquidation, or other reasons.

There are people who say that it is not a disaster if firms go under. That it is part of the process of *creative destruction*. Rise and fall: that is the natural course of life, and the same is true of the business world. That keeps the economy thriving and innovative. Old business models have to make way for new ones so that the ever-changing demands of our modern world can be addressed.

As a biologist, I recognize the Darwinist image of the world in this. I also often use Darwin's maxim: '*to my own surprise: it is not the biggest, nor the strongest, nor the fastest, but the fittest who will survive*'. *Survival of the fittest*: not the 'healthiest', as people sometimes incorrectly translate it, but those that have adapted best to the changing surroundings. Adaptability—that is the key concept. Those who do not manage to adapt sufficiently when the environmental demands change will disappear. This can be a good thing for the larger whole, because it frees up space for 'fitter' rivals. But at the firm level—for its employees, other stakeholders, and the surrounding community—the loss of a firm can of course have significant ramifications. It is the duty of management to ensure continuity, in the short term and the long term. One of the most important strategic responsibilities of management is to adapt to changing circumstances.

Loss must be prevented by anticipating the changing circumstances in good time. The closure of the local coal mines, for instance, had a huge impact on the province of Limburg (in the south of the Netherlands) and its population. But it was an unavoidable government decision, especially once natural gas was discovered in the north of the country. Fortunately our firm, Royal DSM, had also developed a chemicals arm over the years. These chemical activities provided a platform which DSM could use to build a new, successful future in the bulk chemicals sector, based on gas and oil.

Around the mid-nineties we recognized that the firm needed to transform itself once again. In the first place, this was because competitive conditions in the industrial chemical sector were going to change significantly, partly due to the rise of players in the Middle East. But it was also because DSM itself wanted to switch to more innovative and sustainable activities which were less cyclical and had greater added value. This second transformation, into the present-day life sciences and materials sciences firm, took a good fifteen years. At DSM we are convinced that this has made the firm more future-proof, especially because the new activities anticipate the challenges that the world will encounter in times to come: challenges in health and wellness, climate change and energy supply, and sustainability.

Yet we also know that this does not mean the end of the changes within the firm. Quite the reverse: it is precisely *because* of this history that we recognize adaptation as being a continual process. DSM has totally reinvented itself twice now. Each time, over a period of around fifteen years, the firm has completely abandoned its core activities. This has been of fundamental importance for the longevity of our firm, which in 2017 reached its 115th anniversary.

In the transformation of an organization it is essential that the management should see (or want to see) on time that the environment is changing or, even better, that it is going to change. It is then important that management has the courage to take the right decisions in good time. Decisions taken too late will often mean that returns on activities that are to be dropped will decrease. Management itself is a factor which should not be neglected. It is the existing portfolio that has brought success for the top management of the firm. Transformation therefore requires them to undertake some important self-analysis, and to adjust the culture that has been part of the previous activities. Finally, I would like to emphasize the need for communication with all stakeholders, including shareholders and customers, but definitely also your own employees.

These experiences have taught me how essential it can be to renew, or if need be, reinvent a firm, but also how complicated that can be. I therefore see real value in this initiative to investigate the issue scientifically. And it is certainly good that this investigation should take place in the European context. Much of the literature in this field comes from America, so I welcome the fact this research gives us a fresh and different perspective.

The results are first class. To start with, this book provides a useful overview of the topic, and clarifies the many concepts. The model used by the researchers is an attractive one: it shows clearly how you can only escape the trap of an entrenched business model through directed innovation. Practical guidance is provided on how to reinvent your business model when facing disruption. Of course, no two firms or situations are the same. The cases in this book illustrate that. But the researchers have succeeded in bringing this diversity into a clear framework. They also exchanged ideas on their findings with a large number of managers and leaders. All in all, this has enabled them to end the book with a highly readable summary of the dos and don'ts of business model innovation. I am therefore very pleased to recommend the book to anyone wishing to gain a clearer view of this intractable subject.

Feike Sijbesma,
CEO, Royal DSM

Preface

This book is about how to reinvent your business model, and it focuses on the ways in which firms can innovate their business model when faced with disruption. Innovating your business model is a *must* for every living organization. Not just firms, but also semi-public and even public institutions need to subject their business models to very careful scrutiny. Clever business models of firms and institutions are one of the most important drivers of our contemporary economy. At a time of significant national and international challenges, having the right business model is crucial to the continued existence of many an organization. If it seemed for a short while as if business models adapted themselves automatically to economic growth, now that we are experiencing limited growth and even economic contraction, this has become a live issue once again for most firms and institutions around the world, and is high up everyone's agenda.

Business models say something about the revenue model, or rather the earning potential, of firms and institutions. In the study which forms the basis for this book, the researchers examine the different components of a business model, looking at the interrelationships between them, and how these align to the competitive strategy of the firm. They also analyse how value creation takes place for the various parties involved, and how that value is appropriated.

This book enlarges our insight into the business models of firms and institutions. It pays particular attention to the changing of existing business models, from moderate changes through to radical change. A survey of 590 respondents from firms and twelve case studies of well-known firms such as DSM, NXP Semiconductors, Randstad, Port of Rotterdam Authority, and Royal IHC enable the researchers to distinguish different forms of business model innovation: renewal, replication, and fixation. With these models they provide insight into how business models can be made more sustainable in the future. Renewal of a business model entails radical adaptation, while replication entails refinement and improvement. Fixation means that neither is applicable. Thus the business model of NXP—a producer of chips for televisions, smartphones, and car keys, among other things—is directed mainly towards replication. Thanks to its strong customer orientation and its focus on promising new niche markets, NXP has shown that it is capable of accelerating the replication of its business model and has become an important global player as a result.

It was a foregone conclusion for the board of the Foundation for Management Studies that a study like this one must come—and quickly, too, since there is a strong and growing need for it. The board is therefore proud of and grateful to the researchers, Henk Volberda, Frans van den Bosch, and Kevin Heij of the Erasmus Centre for Business Innovation at Rotterdam School of Management, Erasmus University, for undertaking this research. The supervisory committee, chaired by Mees Hartvelt, also made a tremendous contribution to the creation of this magnificent study.

As chairperson of the Foundation for Management Studies, I have great pleasure in presenting this challenging book to you. I wish you every success with changing and redesigning your business model.

Harry van de Kraats

Chairman of the Foundation for Management Studies, Managing Director of the General Employers' Association (AWVN), and Director Social Affairs of the Confederation of Netherlands Industry and Employers (VNO-NCW)

Acknowledgements

This book could only have come about thanks to the commitment and effort of a large number of people and organizations. We would therefore like to name and thank them. In the first place, we extend our thanks to the organization that commissioned this book, the Dutch Foundation for Management Studies. Here we would like to thank not only the supervisory committee and the programme committee, but also the general board which continually had faith in us. At the Foundation for Management Studies we would especially like to thank Mees Hartvelt, Nicolaas Weeda, and Marjan Roosenboom for the effort they put into this book. We would also like to express our gratitude to both David Musson, who recently retired, and Clare Kennedy of Oxford University Press, who pressed us to set priorities and assisted us with the difficult task of producing the final manuscript. In addition, we want to thank Catherine Walker for the great work she did in editing the text, and also in helping us to express our thoughts more clearly and improve our line of reasoning. We also want to thank Ruth Durbridge for carefully copy-editing the final manuscript and Subramaniam Vengatakrishnan for taking care of the production of our book.

A word of thanks to the organizations which collaborated with us in the survey and the case studies is also appropriate. The organizations and the individuals who took part are listed in the Appendices. The contributions made by members of our manager panel were important in helping to make the book more accessible and useful for managers. The panel consisted of Henk de Bruijn (Director of Corporate Strategy, Port of Rotterdam Authority), Goof Hamers (former CEO of Royal IHC), Erik van der Liet (labour market specialist at Randstad Netherlands), Charles Smit (Vice-President and General Counsel, EMEA, NXP), Jeffrey Tierie (CEO of Claymount Technologies Group), Robert Witvliet (director and founder of WIAR Workplace Performance), and Herman Wories (Vice-President, Global Business Incubator, DSM).

In addition, an enthusiastic team of research assistants and colleagues contributed to the realization of this book. Here we would like to thank Hajar El Amraoui, George Ankomah, Rick Hollen, Nadine Koerselman, Eline van der Lugt, Milos van Moorsel, Désirée Nieland, Diana Barbara Perra, Tatjana Schneidmüller, Arnoud Stok, and Benjamin Wörner. In particular, we would like to thank Menno Bosma for the support he gave us with the manager panel and Niels van der Weerdt for assisting us in the development of the business model innovation scan. We also owe a debt of gratitude to the Executive Board of the Erasmus University Rotterdam and the Erasmus Research Institute of Management (ERIM) for the support they have given to the Erasmus Centre for Business Innovation, which carried out the research.

Finally we would like to thank those closest to us: our families. We spent evenings, weekends, and even holidays getting this book into its final shape. That would not have been possible without the support, sympathy, and resilience of our loved ones.

The three of us would like to dedicate *Reinventing Business Models* to the seventeen-year-old Celine Volberda, who spent more than six weeks in hospital while we were doing our research on business model innovation and for whom recuperation was a personal experience of 'reinventing'. Celine, we are so glad that you were successful in coping with disruption, and that you are healthy and back on your feet again.

Henk Volberda
Frans van den Bosch
Kevin Heij

Contents

List of Figures

List of Tables

List of Cases

Executive Summary

When faced with increasing disruption, how do you reinvent your business model? Although research on business model innovation is flourishing internationally, many important questions on the 'how', 'what', and 'when' of this process remain largely unanswered, particularly in regard to the role of top management. This book answers some of those pressing questions by taking a deliberately managerial perspective. Most firms fail to innovate their business model because they continue to do the same things that have made them successful in the past. Managers in these firms listen carefully to customers, invest in existing businesses, and build distinctive capabilities, but tend to overlook disruptions in markets and technologies. Using new knowledge derived from a survey among firms from various industries and several case studies (including DSM, NXP Semiconductors, Randstad, and TomTom), this book seeks to give us a better understanding of 'how' firms can innovate their business model, 'what' kind of levers management should work on, and 'when' management should change the business model. We turn our attention particularly to one key question: is it better to replicate existing models or develop new ones? Business model renewal is regarded as being especially vital in highly competitive environments. Nonetheless, whatever the environment, high levels of both replication and renewal will be key for a firm to succeed.

We look at four levers that can be used by managers to innovate their business model: management itself, organizational form, technology, and co-creation with external parties. We will discuss the individual effects of these levers on business model replication and renewal. We also analyse specific combinations which strengthen business model innovation, including those which are technology oriented, internally oriented, externally oriented, and those which combine all levers in an integrated way.

To help firms avoid getting caught in one of the business model innovation traps, the book also explores the different factors that can either enable or inhibit business model innovation. By looking at replication versus renewal and at strategy-driven versus client-driven change, we identify four distinct modes of business model innovation:

- **exploit and improve** (replication which is strategy-driven): a directive management improves and perfects the existing business model
- **exploit and connect** (replication which is customer-driven): customer-oriented management strengthens the business model significantly by linking it more to existing customers
- **explore and connect** (renewal which is customer-driven): adaptive management upgrades the business model in response to completely new clients
- and **explore and dominate** (renewal which is strategy-driven): proactive management fundamentally renews the business model on the basis of an organization-wide transformation in which all levels of management are involved.

In particular, leadership is a vital factor in business model innovation. We end with a list of managerial dos and don'ts for business model innovation devised in conjunction with a panel of top managers from the firms that took part in the research.

I

Introduction

. . . .

ROLLS OF KODAK FILM: A MONEY-SPINNER FOR THE FIRM, BUT ALSO THE BASIS OF ITS DOWNFALL

Back in 1975 Kodak engineer Steven Sasson developed the electronic still camera. It was the precursor to the digital camera which decades later would all but wipe out the analogue camera. In 2012 Kodak applied for postponement of payment. In the digital era the firm that had invented the digital camera ended up in trouble. How could it have come to this?

The answer is to be found not with competitors, however, but with Kodak itself. Kodak decided to do nothing with the electronic still camera, because getting it on to the market would undermine the huge profits the firm was making from analogue photography. Two decades later, Kodak demonstrated how this defensive market approach was part of the firm's DNA. Despite extensive research and investment into mobile phones with inbuilt cameras, the firm chose to ignore that market as well. Yet again, the argument was that it would endanger Kodak's traditional activities.

Rivals Polaroid and Agfa also ran into problems. By contrast, Fuji, Kodak's other major competitor, flourished. Fuji stopped work on analogue camera technology and turned instead to cosmetics, medicines, and offset plates. All that seems to have little to do with photography. But there is a connection: these areas all require knowledge of molecular technology and coatings.

The story of Kodak shows that technological advantage does not guarantee commercial success. The determining factor is not whether a firm invents the right things in time, but whether it renews its business model in time. A business model—we will discuss its many definitions later—links technology to strategy and commerce. It determines what you do with those lovely new inventions. Do you leave them in the cupboard like Kodak did, because the margins on photographic film were so attractive? Or do you risk the leap into a new business, with all the associated uncertainties? And are your organization and your management ready for that?

. . . .

In the current turbulent environment, it is no longer relevant to ask *whether* firms should innovate their business model. Continuing to do what you have always done amounts to self-destruction (Hamel, 2000; McGrath, 2013; Nunes and Breene, 2011). Nobody can keep on making and selling rolls of film successfully for a century any more. These days it is about *how* you change your business model, *when,* and *the extent to which* you do that—questions which this book brings up for discussion. The business model has emerged relatively recently as a level of analysis (Foss and Saebi, 2017; Zott et al., 2011). Every organization has a business model—either explicit or implicit—but in today's rapidly changing business environments, business model innovation has become even more important (Amit and Zott, 2001; Schneider and Spieth, 2013) and is a crucial factor in explaining differences in firm performance. A business model reflects the outcome of a firm's strategic choices and how the firm executes its strategy (Casadesus-Masanell and Ricart, 2010; Richardson, 2008). It focuses specifically on creating and appropriating customer value (Baden-Fuller and Haefliger, 2013; Zott et al., 2011). Despite the increased attention being given to business model innovation, several important questions remain largely unanswered.

First, previous research has not differentiated sufficiently clearly between the various types of business model innovation. Research on business model innovation falls into two main streams, focusing either on *replication*, that is, leveraging an existing business model (e.g. Szulanski and Jensen, 2008; Winter and Szulanski, 2001), or on *renewal*, that is, introducing a new business model that is very different from the previous one (e.g. Johnson et al., 2008; Nunes and Breene, 2011).

Second, there has been relatively little empirical research—and few cross-industry surveys—on how these two basic types of business model innovation relate to firm performance, and in which particular environmental conditions different types of business model innovation are likely to be most effective. Most research on business models that seeks to explain how particular business models contribute to competitive advantage is either descriptive (Morris et al., 2005), conceptual (Lambert and Davidson, 2013), based on case studies (Baden-Fuller and Morgan, 2010; Lambert and Davidson, 2013), or focused on a specific firm, market, or industry context (Baden-Fuller and Mangematin, 2013; Casadesus-Masanell and Zhu, 2013; Schneider and Spieth, 2013).

This book seeks to give us a better understanding of *how* firms can innovate their business model, *what* kind of levers management should work on, and *when* management should change the business model. It provides management scholars and reflective practitioners with new insights and knowledge of the various types of business model innovation, the levers for changing business models, and the various paths open to firms to transform their business models. In addition, it shows managers how to outperform competitors and helps them to choose whether to improve their existing business model or to radically renew it. The conclusions are supported by quantitative research as well as in-depth case studies of firms that have undertaken business model innovation. We also asked a panel of top managers to formulate the *dos and don'ts* of business model innovation. With its focus on how business model innovation acts as a source of competitive advantage, this book is clearly embedded in the literature on strategic management and business model change.

In this opening chapter, we look at why business model innovation is needed, set out our research model and our key research questions, and outline the main elements to be discussed in subsequent chapters. These include: the changing competitive environment; business model innovation strategies; levers of business model innovation; catalysts and inhibitors in business model innovation; and competitive advantages of new business models. These elements form the basis of our research model. Chapter 1 sets out a series of questions that will be addressed in this book.

Chapter 2 focuses on what a business model is and what it adds to: it is a unique mix of activities that results in value creation and delivers value appropriation and competitive advantage. This competitive advantage can only be sustained for a limited time, so firms must innovate their business model. There are two ways of doing this: through replication or through renewal. With replication, firms scale up and improve their existing business model over time—as we can see, for instance, with McDonald's and IKEA. With renewal, firms bring in a new business model that is very different from their previous one. DSM and the temping agency Randstad are examples of companies that have done this. DSM, in particular, has reinvented itself several times as it moved from mining to petrochemicals, then to life sciences, and more recently to material sciences and sustainability. We also identify several levers of business model innovation. Most of the existing work focuses primarily on new technology as the main lever of business model innovation, but in this book we discuss a number of other complementary levers, including new managerial practices, new organizational forms, and co-creation with new partners.

Chapter 3 describes how firms tackle business model innovation in practice. Most firms replicate their successful business model, a few try to renew it fundamentally, but many firms are not capable of changing their business models. They suffer from what we term 'business model fixation'. There are also corporate entrepreneurs who replicate the existing business model in one part of the firm but develop a radical new business model in other parts (dual business models). When and why do firms choose replication, renewal, or dual business models—and what do each of these approaches deliver? Based on a survey conducted across a broad range of industries, we examine the extent to which firms and industries focus on these various types of business model innovation. We look in detail at how replication and renewal contribute to firm performance, and to what degree this depends on the level of environmental dynamism and competitiveness. What is perhaps striking is that one in three firms pays no attention to its business model and is in a permanent state of business model fixation. These firms are clearly ignoring any warning signs that they should change their business model. This is all the more surprising since we find that firms which engage in high levels of both business model replication and business model renewal perform on average 18 per cent better than firms trapped in business model fixation.

Chapter 4 shows how firms can use four different levers—technology, management, organizational forms, and co-creation—for business model innovation, and asks which combinations of levers will have the greatest effect on business model innovation. In this chapter, we start by showing how Polaroid's strong focus on developing technological skills was not accompanied by the development of new markets and distribution channels. The Polaroid case makes clear that paying attention exclusively to one lever (here primarily technology) is no guarantee of successful business model innovation. Mediocre technology with a superior business model can deliver more value than superior technology with a mediocre business model. In this chapter, therefore, we provide new insights into how our four levers contribute to business model replication and business model renewal. We also look at Ericsson, Oticon, Zara, and Muji to see how firms use these levers to innovate their business model. Of the four levers, adjusting management practices is the most important in both renewal and replication.

We also look in detail at how different combinations of levers can help in business model innovation. Firms might actually take four routes in the innovation of their business model: a route with a strong technological orientation, an internal route, an external route, and an integrated route.

We highlight, for example, TomTom's technologically oriented renewal (combining new technologies with new management practices), Ericsson's internally oriented renewal (through technology, management, and organizational forms), Procter & Gamble's externally oriented renewal (through co-creation, management, and organizational forms), and DSM's integrated renewal (using all four levers).

In Chapter 5 we discuss the different catalysts and inhibitors which firms encounter when they innovate their business model. We start by examining the various factors that prevented the Dutch telecoms company KPN from renewing its business model. We analyse how factors such as the organizational culture and style of leadership, the characteristics of the CEO, the degree of external orientation, organizational characteristics, and institutional stakeholders (e.g. shareholders, government, employees) can delay or speed up business model innovation. We look at the part played, for example, by transformational leadership, the length of the tenure of the CEO, the corporate governance regime, absorptive capacity, and innovative culture. We present case evidence from DSM, Randstad, Roche Diagnostics, and Shell to support our findings. For example, a study of business model innovation within Shell (Kwee et al., 2011) over a hundred-year period reveals that the closer we get to peak oil—when extraction reaches its peak—the more inclined the established players are to adhere stubbornly to their existing business model. Institutional factors such as the growing focus on shareholder value led Shell to withdraw its investment in solar and wind energy and other sources of renewable energy. If Shell continues to replicate its existing business model of extracting fossil fuels (oil and more recently gas), it might run into a business model trap. We also look at other journeys that firms may undertake in the transformation of their business model: from fixation to replication, from replication to renewal, and from renewal to replication.

In Chapter 6 we explore the dynamics of business model innovation by discussing the interactions between Sony and Apple over the minidisc and the MP3 player. It seems to be almost unavoidable that a period of business model renewal will be followed by business model replication. Both renewal and replication can be internally driven, that is, by strategy, or externally driven, that is, by customers. Combining types of business model innovation (replication versus renewal) with business model orientation (strategy-driven versus customer-driven) gives us four variations. Chapter 6 contains detailed case studies of these four variations of business model transformation: *exploit and improve* (strategy-driven replication in terms of improving and fine-tuning the existing business model), *explore and dominate* (strategy-driven renewal through an organization-wide transformation in which all levels of management are involved), *exploit and connect* (customer-driven replication through strengthening and expanding the firm's links with current customers), and *explore and connect* (customer-driven renewal by upgrading the business model in response to completely new clients). We look at four firms in illustration of these different approaches: DSM, the Port of Rotterdam Authority, NXP Semiconductors, and Royal IHC. Each approach has its own specific levers, environmental characteristics, and its enablers and inhibitors. If we think of these four approaches as quadrants in a matrix, these cases show how firms can change their position within that business model matrix over time.

In Chapter 7 we describe the decisive role of management in business model innovation. For each of the approaches in our business model innovation matrix, we examine the role played by top and middle managers. We look at how TomTom went through a recursive cycle of renewal and replication, with a visionary CEO as the main driver. We also identify a number of potential traps in business model innovation, and discuss how managers may avoid them. These traps include having too strong a focus on fixation, an overemphasis on financial performance, or a CEO and top management who are continuously developing a rapid succession of new business models, with the result that they miss out on the returns that come from replication. We also discuss various warning signs that might indicate to management that a change of business model is required.

We also examine the many different ways in which firms can combine replication and renewal—for example, by using a *dual* business model, an *oscillating* business model, or a *network* business model. In the dual business model, one part of the firm focuses on getting business model renewal underway and creating new added value, while another part focuses on replication and on making optimal use of established routines and competences. The basic principle of the dual business model is that the parent organization concentrates on business model replication while a separate subunit is assigned to work on business model renewal. The oscillating business model is based on alternating cycles of replication and renewal; here replication is characterized by refinements to existing technology, management, and organizational forms, while renewal is focused on the adoption of new technologies, new management practices, and new organizational forms. In the network business model, the firm itself develops a new business model and then outsources activities of the previous 'behind the scenes' model to a low-cost provider. These dual business models are illustrated by case examples from ASML Lithography, BMW, Dell, Ericsson, HP, and Randstad.

In our final chapter we summarize our main findings in the following areas: the two fundamental types of business model innovation, the levers of business model innovation, business model transformation, and the role of management. We also present a series of dos and don'ts for business model innovation, compiled from extensive discussions with a panel of senior managers who took part in our research and who have considerable experience in business model innovation.

The need for business model innovation

The speed with which technologies and strategies change forces firms to innovate their business model continually (e.g. Giesen et al., 2010; Teece, 2010; Voelpel et al., 2005). This is true of almost all industries. The oil and gas industries used to be relatively stable, and some sectors in packaged consumer goods remain so (Cliffe and McGrath, 2011). However, if a sector does not have very high barriers for newcomers, or if new technologies or regulations are introduced—and this applies to very many branches of industry—the existing players will definitely have to deal with new forms of competition. The introduction of new sharing business models (e.g. Uber, Airbnb, Helpling, Peerby, Taskrabbit) disrupted the existing taxi, hotel, and cleaning sectors and the DIY industry. Many established firms with bricks and mortar business models are finding themselves being superseded by new firms whose business models are based on the digital world. Online platforms such as Airbnb.com, Booking.com, Uber, and perhaps also Google Pay, make it easier for customers to get information about an offering without going through any traditional intermediary.

Venkatraman and Henderson (2008: 260) stated that 'it is no longer adequate to innovate in narrow domains—products, processes and services [...] we need to innovate more holistically—namely: the entire business model.' The business model has emerged in the literature as a relatively new level of analysis (e.g. Bjorkdahl and Holmen, 2013; Zott et al., 2011) for examining how a firm conducts its business (Hamel, 2000). In today's dynamic business environments, there has been an increasing focus on how to create distinctive business models and how to change them in order to sustain competitive advantage (e.g. McGrath, 2013; Schneider and Spieth, 2013).

The first sign that a business model is under pressure is often that new generations of products and services are not significantly better (Nunes and Breene, 2011). The new versions do not differ much from the old ones. Customers notice this, and either complain about it or look for alternative solutions. The business model is worn out and performance begins to dip.

In the relatively stable competitive environment which characterized much of the twentieth century, the traditional organizational forms and established strategies for limiting competition were highly satisfactory. They helped well-established firms like Shell, financial services firm ING, and the telecoms provider KPN become large and profitable. During long periods of relatively stable relationships between existing players, firms were able to continually extend and maintain their competitive advantage (Volberda, 2003; Volberda et al., 2011). The traditional strategies, based on top-down control, formal planning, and detailed industrial analysis, guaranteed that their business models would remain both distinctive and sustainable for some time (see Figure 1.1). There is only slow and gradual erosion of the business model and firms can anticipate in advance how to develop a new business model over time.

Not many enterprises still enjoy this luxury. Instead of long, stable periods with gradual erosion of the dominant business model, competition is now characterized by short periods of competitive advantage, alternating with frequent disturbances and disruption of the business model (see Figure 1.2) (Volberda et al., 2011). Market globalization, rapid technological change, shorter product life cycles, and increasing aggressiveness from competitors have changed the basic rules of competition. Stable competition has become

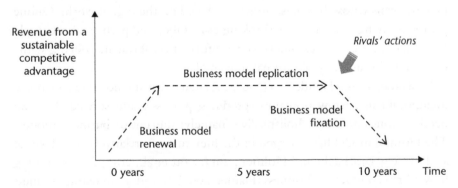

Figure 1.1 Gradual erosion of a business model

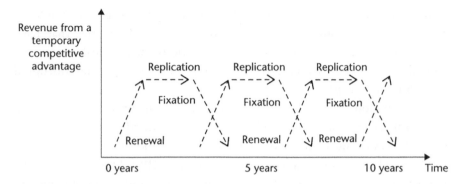

Figure 1.2 Business model innovation: frequent renewal and replication

hypercompetition, and there does not seem to be a way back (Govindarajan and Trimble, 2011; McGrath, 2013; Volberda, 1998). Consequently, no business will survive over the long term without reinventing itself (Bertolini et al., 2015). Firms will have to cope with frequent disruptions that are either demand-driven (new entrants finding unserved customer needs), supply-driven (emerging technologies that make the firm's business model redundant), or a combination of the two (Sood and Tellis, 2011). Supply-driven disruptions stem from new entrants introducing a fundamentally new technological architecture that cannot be copied by incumbents by simply improving elements of the existing technology (Henderson and Clark, 1990; Siggelkow, 2001; Gans, 2016). The iPhone, for example, was an architectural innovation in which software and hardware were integrated in a fundamentally new way that made it difficult for established mobile handset manufacturers to copy (Gans, 2016). Demand-driven disruptions occur when new entrants serve underserved market segments of incumbent firms using technologies that are initially inferior to the mainstream technologies used by incumbents. Although the new entrant's technology may at first underperform, it may do better on particular attributes which are valued by a new customer segment ('new-market foothold') or by a group of mainstream customers who are more price-sensitive ('low-end foothold') (Christensen et al., 2003). Over time, what was previously an inferior technology retains its initial advantage, but the new entrant also becomes able to meet the needs and demands of mainstream customers of the incumbent firm (Christensen et al., 2015; Govindarajan and Kopalle, 2006). There are many examples of industries that were transformed initially by supply-driven disruptions, ranging from steel mills (disrupted by mini-mills) and film photography (disrupted by digital imaging technology) to landline telephony (disrupted by smartphones). Industries that have been transformed by demand-driven disruptions include real estate (disrupted by collaborative connected platforms) and travel agencies (disrupted by online platforms).

Combinations of supply- and demand-driven disruptions often have a great impact on a sector as a whole. The huge growth in the market for smartphones changed the landscape not only for mobile phone manufacturers but also for infrastructure providers such as KPN. The revenue model that had been the bedrock of the sector since the introduction of commercial telephony—charging people according to the length of the call or later by messages sent—is now on the verge of collapse. Free message traffic via Internet telephony using Skype or FaceTime has caused the profits of traditional providers to evaporate.

The decline of Kodak and Polaroid following the advent of digital image technology illustrates how external changes can destroy a successful business model. A salient point is that neither firm was really surprised by the rise of digital image technology. They were both in an excellent position to develop new technological competences to exploit it. The point was not that the technology changed, but that the entire foundation supporting their growth eroded.

Kodak and Polaroid had for a long time profited from the *razor blade* business model. The essence of this is that one item (in this case the camera) is offered cheaply, or even for free, and a considerable margin is then achieved on another, related item (rolls of film) (Chesbrough and Rosenbloom, 2002). In the period up to the Second World War, Kodak sold 25 million cameras, Brownies, for one dollar apiece. The group later introduced another inexpensive and highly successful model, the Instamatic. The large profits were made on the rolls of film. In the mid-1970s, 90 per cent of all rolls of film sold in the United States were Kodak film. *That* was what Kodak did not dare to let go of.

The well-known management author Gary Hamel calls the current era the 'revolution era': instead of there being just more of the same, these days changes are abrupt, discontinuous, and seditious (Hamel, 2000). Change itself has changed, and enterprises have to cope with more and more turning points. Changing competitive environments force enterprises to keep examining their strategy and organizational form with a critical eye. However successful firms may be, competitive advantages can be imitated or even improved increasingly swiftly (Smith et al., 2010; Volberda, Van den

Bosch, Flier, and Gedajlovic, 2001). Products and services quickly turn into *commodities*; they become less distinctive, and consumers make their purchases more cleverly and cheaply. The result is what Prahalad and Ramaswamy (2004: 7) describe as the '*Walmartization*' of everything.

Managers and management authors are in agreement that the way to future success lies in moving away from traditional prescriptions for strategy. Merely defending a competitive advantage is tantamount to stagnation. Inventing something new does not guarantee success, but nor does imitating one's rival. This raises the question of how a firm is to stay on its feet in a swiftly changing competitive landscape.

A competitive race with only losers?

Firms can now only achieve temporary competitive advantages, because those advantages are being imitated or improved upon at an ever more rapid rate through business model innovation by other players in the market. This has brought greater competitive pressure and the need to change even faster (D'Aveni, 1994;Volberda, 1996, 2003).

The continuous interaction between changing and learning on the one hand, and greater forms of competition and selection on the other, has been dubbed the '*Red Queen race*', with reference to *Alice in Wonderland*. The players in a specific market are involved in a constant race against one another to incorporate new technologies and market approaches in their business model. Because everyone is running equally fast, nobody develops any real lead. Firms adapt faster and faster, but relatively speaking the players seem to be standing still because others are doing the same (Volberda, 1998).

In *Alice in Wonderland*, Alice is surprised to find that after running for a while she is actually still in the same place. '*In our country,*' she says, '*you'd generally get to somewhere else—if you run very fast for a long time, as we've been doing.*' To which the Red Queen replies: '*A slow sort of country! Now, here, you see, it takes all the running you can do, to keep in the same place. If you want to get somewhere else, you must run at least twice as fast as that!*' (Carroll, 1946).

It is not easy for firms entangled in this kind of Red Queen race to step out of it. In the course of their existence, organizations build up a reservoir of knowledge and routines. They develop core competences and highly specialized assets, and these form the basis of their success. But the very acquisition of those assets then makes those firms less able to renew their business model.

The decline of NCR (National Cash Register), established in the United States in 1884, is a case in point. The firm focused so strongly on its existing activities, electromechanical cash registers, and was so blind to the rise of electronic cash registers, that it lost as much as 80 per cent of the market to makers of electronic products between 1972 and 1976 (Rosenbloom, 2000).

GM (General Motors) is another example. Initially the American group was not willing to design and produce compact cars for fear of cannibalizing its own large-car segment (Schmidt and Druehl, 2008). IBM and Digital Equipment Corporation likewise ended up in this kind of competence trap. Deeply entrenched routines and extensive investments transformed products which were originally distinctive (mainframe computers and minicomputers) into a millstone (Tushman et al., 1997). Core competences became core rigidities, and the competence lead became a competence trap (D'Aveni, 1994).

A strong tendency to keep exploiting existing opportunities results in routines. These routines are institutionalized in rules, regulations, planning and control systems, and shared norms and values. Learning then only occurs within the existing standards and values (*single-loop learning*) and only results in small-scale improvements (Argyris and Schon, 1996; Nelson and Winter, 1982). Managers in these kinds of organization avoid risk, preferring stability (Benner and Tushman, 2002). The organization adapts fully to the existing environment (*fit*), making it highly vulnerable should the environment change unexpectedly (Giesen et al., 2010; Heij et al., 2014). The potential for change diminishes drastically, and the organization falls into a business model trap (see Table 1.1). Because of the fixation on the existing business model, the strength of the firm ultimately becomes the root of its failure.

Table 1.1 Business model trap versus business model innovation

Business model trap	Business model innovation
• fixation on existing technology	• investment in emerging technologies
• refining routines	• developing dynamic capabilities
• adapting to the existing environment (fit)	• anticipating new environment (stretch)
• small-scale improvements (single-loop learning)	• radical experimentation (double-loop learning)
• focus on existing customers (adapting to the market)	• focus on new customers (market creation)

The motivation of the players in the Red Queen race is '*how to do what you are currently doing better*'. That does not result in actual progress. What helps organizations leave the Red Queen race is not an established business model, but business model innovation. Organizations need to go in search of more dynamic sources of competitive advantage, setting their sights on '*how to be different*' (Hamel and Prahalad, 1994; Voelpel et al., 2005).

As the examples below show, all or any of the following can be a dynamic source of competitive advantage for firms:

- a challenging vision
- a forward-looking perspective on how an industry branch could develop
- a capacity to reflect on the learning system
- an innovative culture.

A challenging vision. For example, Tesla's vision is to 'accelerate the world's transition to sustainable transport' (Efron, 2017). Starbucks seeks to create an experience, rather than sell a product. And Apple's vision is to turn technologies into tools which are easy to use, and which can help people to realize their dreams and change the world.

A forward-looking perspective on how an industry branch could develop. We can see several game-changers that have disrupted the established logic of value creation and capture in their industry sectors (Sabatier et al., 2010). Amazon's idea of offering recommendations to customers based on their buying habits and search history transformed the entire retail industry, while IKEA's concept of making customers collect goods direct from the warehouse and assemble furniture themselves at home reshaped the furniture industry. Also Airbnb, an online platform which enables individuals to rent out rooms directly to travellers, disrupted the hotel industry. Its business model became a source of inspiration for other players in the industry and beyond, and in this way formed the new business model for the sharing economy. Other examples include Xerox's idea of a paperfree desk, or the notion of efficiency in aviation developed by Southwest Airlines.

A capacity to reflect on the learning system. Honda, for example, employed ingenious means to trigger self-questioning and learning within the company. In Honda's confrontational style, for example, hierarchy is discouraged and young employees are given more responsibility. Honda encourages employees to think independently, experiment, and learn (Volberda, 1998);

that is fundamental to organizations which are able to innovate their business model. Similarly, trial-and-error learning, unlearning of old routines, and experimenting with new retail stores enabled the dietary supplement shop Naturhouse to change its core logic. By opening its own retail stores it shifted from a primarily wholesale-oriented business model to a retail-oriented model (Sosna et al., 2010). Quite often new entrants are much better at this kind of higher-order learning, as demonstrated by the new start-up Bunq. Questioning established assumptions in the financial industry and only working with people from outside the industry is the hallmark of Bunq. The company considers itself to be not a bank, but an IT company with a banking. The founder and owner Ali Nikman deliberately moved away from the dominant logic in the banking industry of 'making money with money'. Saving and borrowing—an important part of the business models of established banks—are not part of Bunq's portfolio. Instead, it makes money only by providing services for customers: it facilitates real-time payments via an app, and telephone contacts rather than IBANs are used to facilitate those payments. Bunq can be considered as a kind of WhatsApp in the banking sector.

An innovative culture. Notable examples include 3M, with its commandment that 'Thou shalt not kill ideas for new products', and Google, with its policy of allowing employees to spend some of their working hours on new projects. Whirlpool also built a community of innovation experts as part of a move to encourage an innovative culture which would catalyse the company to come up with a series of new business models (Jay and Weintraub, 2013). Moreover, TomTom's culture of emphasizing diversity and openness encouraged employees to come up with new products, services, and solutions (maps, navigation software, mobility data). This helped the company to innovate its business model a number of times—for example, from software developer to producer of consumer electronics, and more recently to supplier to the automobile industry (business-to-business) and governments (business-to-government). Only organizations that promote a culture in which mistakes are tolerated are able to boost business model innovation. Creativity, employee empowerment, and happiness, for example, are pillars of the innovative culture at Zappos, one of the world's largest online shoe stores. At Zappos, core values explicitly encourage employees to 'embrace and drive change', 'create fun and a little weirdness', and 'be adventurous, creative, and open-minded' (Perschel, 2010). Zappos's CEO Tony Hsieh stated that 'we decided long ago that we didn't want our brand to be just about shoes, or clothing, or even online retailing [. . .] If you get the culture right, most of the other stuff—like great customer service [. . .] or passionate employees and customers—will happen naturally on its own' (quote adapted from Perschel, 2010: 28). The company considers its culture to be a vital weapon in dealing with the rise of e-businesses and the actions of its main competitors to offshore most of their operations to emerging economies. Instead of following the herd, Zappos does exactly the opposite. Its business model is based on keeping all operations in-house and expanding its portfolio with eyewear and handbags, for instance, to gain economies of scope (Vazquez Sampere, 2015).

Competing successfully in turbulent markets requires business model renewal, an approach which is essentially different to business model replication, which is needed in more stable markets (e.g. Heij et al., 2014; Osiyevskyy and Dewald, 2015a; Teece, 2010). Firms must continually build and exploit new business models. This means that management does not adapt fully to the existing environment, but creates room for flexibility in the organization and seeks to achieve objectives that may be unattainable (Hamel, 2000). This requires managers with a more entrepreneurial mindset (Hoskisson et al., 2011; Van Doorn et al., 2013). Using the flexibility created, the organization has to experiment (Argyris and Schon, 1996) and unlearn old routines (double-loop learning). Only this will make more radical business model innovation possible.

Sooner or later, the development of new capabilities and business models will come up for discussion in every firm. The big question is how established organizations can work on this while their existing models are still making a substantial contribution to sales and profit. Many former market leaders that failed to keep up with the accelerating pace of industry change have gone through large-scale strategic reorientations and experimented with new forms of organization. The metamorphoses of large enterprises such as Philips, KPN, Wolters Kluwer, TNT Express, and recently ABN Amro, have been only partially successful. Even in change programmes such as Philips's *Accelerate* or Air France-KLM's *Transform*, the emphasis is still on cutting down company expenditure. What firms do is still dictated to some extent by the restrictions of past business models. In some cases, firms will have to cannibalize their existing business models in order to introduce new, competitive models. It is not always possible for the new model to come into being alongside the old one, and that does not make the task for the mastodons any easier.

The research in brief

Our investigation concentrated on two questions concerning the strategies that managers use for business model innovation. First: what do they consider when choosing whether to exploit an existing business model (business model replication) or explore new business models (business model renewal)? Second: which levers do they use to innovate their business models successfully, and what role does management play in this?

The aim of our research was to identify the *best practices* and *next practices* of successful business model innovation. Both quantitative and qualitative methods were used. A survey of more than 590 managers provided new insights into the critical success factors for business model innovation strategies. Case studies threw more light on the underlying processes of business model innovation, factors that could inhibit the adoption of improved or new business models, and the role of management.

The research model can be divided into five parts (also see Figure 1.3):

1. *The changing competitive environment.* Managers are engaged in a perpetual race with the other players in the market, and also have to contend with newcomers to the market and rapidly changing technologies and strategies (hypercompetition).

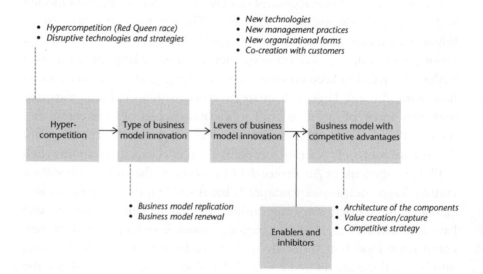

Figure 1.3 Research model

2. *Business model innovation strategies.* The increasing competitive pressure and environmental dynamism result in firms having to innovate their business models and to decide whether to replicate their existing models or renew those models fundamentally.

3. *Levers of business model innovation.* Firms use four levers to implement business model innovation: improvement of existing technologies or introduction of new technologies, different management practices, different organizational forms, and co-creation with customers. In business model replication, the firm further fine-tunes and strengthens the existing levers in order to improve the business model. In business model renewal, however, the firm invests in new technologies, introduces new management practices, creates new organizational forms, and collaborates with new partners in order to renew its business model.

4. *Enablers and inhibitors in business model innovation.* Various internal and external factors such as transformational leadership, an innovative culture, a strong identity, and the corporate governance system can strengthen or weaken the effect of the levers on business model innovation.

5. *Competitive advantages of new business models.* With the right enablers, these levers can, if used properly, result in new architectures, revenue models, and relationships with the environment, which deliver new competitive advantages.

The research specifically addressed the following questions (see also Figure 1.4):

• Which strategies for business model innovation do firms use, and what drives their choice? How do they weigh up the pros and cons of replication and renewal?

• How urgent is the need for business model innovation in firms, and in what sectors and markets is it most essential?

• Which levers do managers use for business model replication and renewal? Do they use several levers at once, or one after another? Which combination offers the greatest return?

• What effects do the levers of business model innovation have on the performance of firms? In which context will a specific strategy actually result in a sustainable lead over one's rivals?

• Which inhibitors and enablers weaken or strengthen the effect of these levers on business model innovation? Which factors support the replication and/or renewal of a business model?

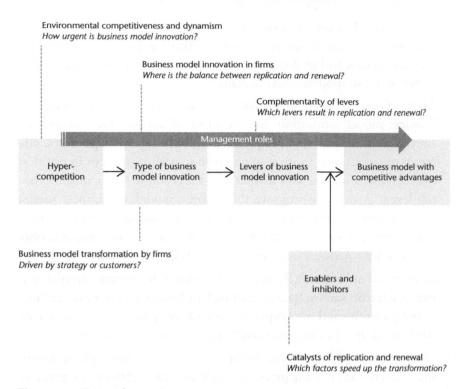

Figure 1.4 Research questions

- How do firms change their business model over time? How do firms know whether they have held on to their business model for too long (fixation), and how do they make the change to replication or renewal? What are the various stages in transforming a firm's business model? Are firms guided by existing or new customers (external influences) or is the renewal driven more by strategy (internal influences)?
- What roles do top, middle, and frontline management play? What are the dos and don'ts of business model innovation?

Research approach

In this research we used a multi-method approach. A quantitative survey enabled us to make a comparative analysis of Dutch firms. In addition, qualitative case studies revealed how the process of business model innovation

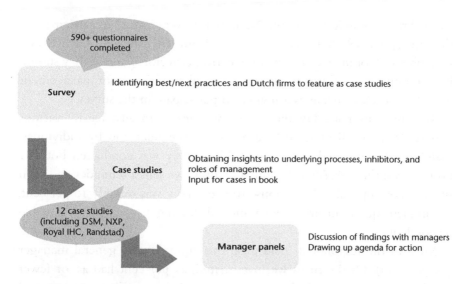

Figure 1.5 The research approach

unfolded over time. When we compared the findings from the two types of research, we found that they were in line with one another.

The survey included large, medium-sized, and small firms from various sectors in the Netherlands. The survey gave us new insights into what the critical success factors are for business model innovation, and helped us to select the sectors and firms for the qualitative investigation.

In the qualitative phase of the research, we developed a number of case studies, using publicly available material such as annual reports, together with internal company documents and interviews with managers from the selected firms. The interviews provided insights into the underlying processes, inhibitors, and the role of management. We draw on material from some of those interviews in the cases presented in this book. In the final stage of our research, we worked with a panel of managers who had taken part in the project to draw up a list of dos and don'ts for business innovation and explore the critical success factors in more depth. Figure 1.5 illustrates the research approach.

The quantitative research

The quantitative element consisted of a survey for which we used existing scales from academic literature. Approximately 10,000 organizations from a broad range of industries in the Netherlands were invited to participate in this survey. We selected them at random from the database of the Dutch Chamber of Commerce. The main selection criterion was that they should have a minimum of thirty employees. A member of the senior management team from each company was invited to participate in the survey.

To ensure its reliability, the survey was tested in advance by various experts from the Rotterdam School of Management and by individuals matching the intended target group. The survey was conducted both by post and via the web. After the initial mailing, we sent a reminder and then made follow-up calls. The response to the survey was roughly 10 per cent. Incomplete questionnaires were removed, leaving more than 590 usable respondents.

Most of the respondents held positions equivalent to general manager (65 per cent). Of the firms we investigated, 25 per cent had 41 or fewer employees, 50 per cent had 90 or fewer employees, and 75 per cent had 306 or fewer employees. The average number of employees was 1,773. The average tenure of the respondents was just under thirteen years. This included the years they had worked in the firm before reaching executive level. The organizations represented had an average age of 56 years. Various characteristics of the respondents are shown in Table 1.2.

Business services and other services made up almost half of responses to the survey. Twenty-three per cent of the firms included were from business services such as financial service providers, and 20 per cent from other services (see Figure 1.6). Examples of other services are the government, government-related, and energy providers. The manufacturing industry, which included sectors such as construction and the food industry, accounted for 32 per cent of our sample. Firms classified as 'other' represented around 20 per cent of the respondents.

Table 1.2 Various characteristics of the respondents' organizations

Characteristic	Value
Average age of organization	56 years
Average number of employees	1,773
Organizations with fewer than one hundred employees	54.6%
Organizations with headquarters in the Netherlands	80%
Average tenure of respondents	13 years

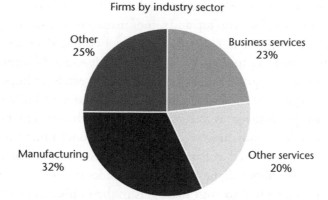

Figure 1.6 Participating organizations by sector

The qualitative research

The case studies in this stage of the research enabled us to explore in more depth why business model innovation takes place, and precisely what role is played by the critical success factors identified through our survey. We built up case studies of more than fifteen firms, using semi-structured interviews with managers. All the firms were selected on the basis of their results in the survey. We return to these case studies at various points in the book. DSM, the Port of Rotterdam Authority, NXP, and Royal IHC are discussed in detail in Chapter 6. Other case studies such as Randstad and TomTom are used at the start of chapters to introduce and illustrate the subject matter in question. Findings from the case studies are also woven through the text. The cases come from different sectors, ranging from healthcare to mobile navigation, and include both large firms and small firms.

Before undertaking each case study, we developed a case protocol for the firm. An important part of this was the case study report made specifically for that firm, containing detailed information about its activities and the sector in which it operated. This enabled us to make rapid connections between the variables we were investigating and the firm in question, and made it possible for us to ask more specific questions.

Manager panel

At the end of this book, we present the lessons learned regarding business model innovation and we provide a list of dos and don'ts which managers can use in innovating their business model. The dos and don'ts were drawn up in close collaboration with top and senior managers in order to guarantee their relevance to practice. This manager panel consisted of seven senior managers from firms featured in the case studies developed for this book.

We hope that our qualitative and quantitative research findings together with the managerial lessons will enrich the knowledge of business model innovation for practitioners as well as management scholars. This book contains not only important insights into business model innovation which were developed and tested at firms, but also accessible practical examples, best practices, and, above all, next practices. Besides the book, we have also developed an online tool to assist managers in their effort to innovate their firm's business model. This Business Model Innovation scan can be found at www.reinventingbusinessmodels.com.

In Chapter 2 we will further explore the business model concept and examine various strategies to innovate business models.

2

Know Your Business Model

DSM SWITCHED FROM PETROCHEMICALS TO LIFE SCIENCES AND MATERIALS, INCLUDING THE MANUFACTURE OF COATINGS FOR SOLAR PANELS

In less than half a century, DSM has succeeded in switching from mining to life sciences and materials, via a series of steps. The group could have chosen to retain or even strengthen the position it had established in the petrochemical industry. Instead, DSM chose to turn the peripheral technology of life sciences into its core technology and to abandon the petrochemical industry, its old core technology. This decision was motivated in large part by the appealing opportunities and profit margins in life sciences. Moving from petrochemicals to life sciences was a clear example of business model renewal. DSM had been practising replication for a while in its petrochemical phase. What the company is now doing in its life science activities is also a form of replication (see Chapter 6 for more details).

RANDSTAD MOVED FROM INTERMEDIATION TO INTEGRATED HR SERVICES

Randstad, a market leader in several European countries, had traditionally earned its money by supplying temporary agency workers. As long as the firm concentrated on its traditional intermediation role, it was practising replication. These days Randstad offers its customers extra services. Through outplacement, recruitment, and selection it can take over all or part of a client's HR functions, for instance, and it can provide planning. This kind of cross-selling makes it possible to increase back-office efficiency, for example, in the area of ICT. Randstad now offers this concept of integrated HR services to other organizations as well. For the time being, the group is targeting the manufacturing industry, but it also wants to serve service sectors such as healthcare, and ultimately even to venture abroad. Randstad is thus shifting from replication to renewal.

Introduction

In Chapter 1 it became clear that changing competitive environments force firms to innovate their business models. This can go in two directions (see Figure 2.1): replication (improving and reproducing the existing business model) or renewal (overhauling the business model fundamentally). As DSM and Randstad demonstrate, replication and renewal are not static conditions. Neither is a firm destined to change its business model in only one way. Firms can apply different business model innovation strategies in different phases of development. It is usually a strategic choice which determines whether this will be replication or renewal. In principle, a firm can go in either direction, although doing that successfully, as we shall see, requires certain steps.

The concept of a 'business model' has been subject to much debate, but within this book we will confine ourselves to exploring the common characteristics (e.g. Massa et al., 2017; Foss and Saebi, 2017; Spieth et al., 2014; Zott et al., 2011). We will then examine various business model innovation strategies. Finally, we identify the four levers of business model innovation: technology, management, organizational forms, and co-creation with customers.

Elements of a business model

Firms use business models to commercialize new ideas and technologies (Chesbrough and Rosenbloom, 2002). It is crucial to choose the right business model: even when the idea taken to the market is the same, different business models can result in very different company performance and competitive positioning (Chesbrough, 2007). According to innovation guru Henry Chesbrough, commercializing a mediocre technology with a superior business model may well prove more successful than

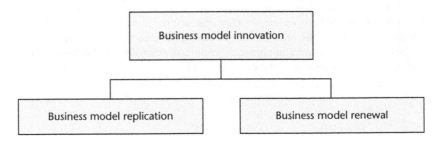

Figure 2.1 Two types of business model innovation: replication and renewal

commercializing a superior technology with a mediocre business model (Chesbrough, 2010: 354).

The concept of 'business model' has been receiving a lot of attention since the mid-1990s, and is widely used in discussions on matters such as technological and social innovation, co-creation with customers, sustainability, and deregulation (Foss and Saebi, 2017; Massa et al., 2017). Yet despite many academic and management books on the subject, there has never been a truly clear, unambiguous definition of the concept—indeed, rather the reverse (see the Appendices for various definitions). The business model has been described at various levels of abstraction, ranging from a narrative to activity systems (Massa and Tucci, 2014). Gary Hamel (2000) has provided what is possibly the simplest definition, describing a business model as a 'way of doing business', or a 'business concept'. Raphael Amit and Christoph Zott (2001: 493) give a more complicated definition. They describe a business model as a bundle of specific activities designed 'to create value through the exploitation of business opportunities' by highlighting 'the content, structure and governance of transactions'. Within these many definitions, we can distinguish three common elements.

. . . .

COMMON ELEMENTS IN DEFINITIONS OF A BUSINESS MODEL

1. A business model is made up of various *components* and describes the *relationships* between them ('architecture') (e.g. Heij et al., 2014; Johnson et al., 2008). It also describes the relationships with external parties such as customers. Business model components include an economic model, internal infrastructure, target market, partner network, and value offering (e.g. Morris et al., 2005; Osterwalder and Pigneur, 2009).

2. A business model embodies how *value creation* occurs, and for which parties, and how the firm *appropriates value* (e.g. Amit and Zott, 2001; McGrath, 2010).

3. A business model provides insight into how the various components and the relationships between them contribute to the *competitive strategy* (e.g. Casadesus-Masanell and Ricart, 2010; Klang et al., 2014).

. . . .

A business model describes the architecture of a number of components

Business models have been conceptualized as an architecture or a template (Baden-Fuller and Mangematin, 2013; Zott et al., 2011). The 'architecture' of an enterprise includes the internal and external actors, information flows, products, and services which the enterprise uses to create value for one or more target groups. In a way, the business model describes the structure of the value chain which is needed to create and distribute a value proposition, as well as the extra assets required for this process (Foss and Saebi, 2015). An architecture of this kind is not restricted to the firm: the boundaries of a business model extend beyond those of the enterprise itself (Zott and Amit, 2010). The success of a business model is dependent partly on how it relates to the business models of external players, whether they be partners or rivals (Casadesus-Masanell and Ricart, 2011; Teece, 2010).

Over the last couple of years there has been greater emphasis on understanding which components are fundamental to a business model, and how they contribute to competitive advantage and performance (Morris et al., 2013). Components that are often mentioned include a firm's value offering, economic model, partner network, internal infrastructure, and target market (e.g. Cortimiglia et al., 2016; Morris et al., 2005). The *business model canvas* developed by Osterwalder and Pigneur (2009) describes various components of a business model—including both the production side and the market side—and extends to partners, distribution channels, and target groups in the market. Breaking down a business model into its component parts reveals that there are interdependencies between those various components, including some complementary effects (Demil and Lecocq, 2010; Massa and Tucci, 2014).

One element central to a business model is the operational model. This is about how key resources, capabilities, activities, and processes (Demil and Lecocq, 2010; Johnson et al., 2008; Kaplan, 2012) and their interdependencies (Baden-Fuller and Morgan, 2010; Kaplan, 2012), ranging from a firm's input through to its output (Chesbrough, 2007), are deployed in order to realize operational and process advantages (McGrath, 2010). Some scholars also refer to an operational model as a firm's position in, and its linkages within, its industry value chain (Baden-Fuller and Mangematin, 2013; Chesbrough, 2007; Margretta, 2002). It can also be broken down further into elements such as an investment model (Mullins and Komisar, 2009) or a production and distribution model (Yoon and Deeken, 2013).

A business model represents how value is created and how the firm appropriates that value

A second element common to definitions of business models is *value creation* and *value capture* (e.g. Amit and Zott, 2001; Morris et al., 2005; Spieth et al., 2014).

The value proposition describes how value is realized for specific target groups and markets. A business model can create different kinds of benefits for customers. For example, it can provide cost advantages, meet previously unmet needs with new products and services, offer greater information and choice, or confer status associated with a brand (Mitchell and Coles, 2003; Osterwalder and Pigneur, 2009). Some scholars (e.g. Baden-Fuller and Haefliger, 2013; Baden-Fuller and Mangematin, 2013) have also described firms as being either 'buses' or 'taxis', depending on whether they provide their customers with more standardized, large-scale, and predesigned solutions, or whether they offer more project-based solutions.

One element that is fundamental to any concept of a business model is the economic model: the cost structure and the mechanism by which the firm generates revenue and makes a profit (Baden-Fuller and Haefliger, 2013; Morris et al., 2005). For whom does the firm create value, and how does it make money? This is also referred to as a 'financial model' (e.g. Pohle and Chapman, 2006; Richardson, 2008) or 'monetization' (e.g. Baden-Fuller and Haefliger, 2013; Baden-Fuller and Mangematin, 2013), and can be further divided into a 'revenue model' (e.g. Giesen et al., 2007; Zott and Amit, 2010) and a cost structure (e.g. Johnson et al., 2008; Kaplan, 2012; Osterwalder and Pigneur, 2009). A firm needs to decide who should pay for the value that is created (Kaplan, 2012; McGrath, 2010) and which pricing strategy to apply—auctioning, fixed price, according to delivered value, etc. (e.g. Baden-Fuller and Haefliger, 2013; Zott and Amit, 2010). It also needs to decide how often one should pay. Should it be a one-off payment, as with the sale of a product, or should the payment be spread, as when a product is leased (Chesbrough and Rosenbloom, 2002; Johnson et al., 2008; Osterwalder and Pigneur, 2009)? Additionally, a firm needs to choose when it does and does not charge for the value created. Adobe, for example, uses a so-called 'free-mium' model (a combination of 'free' and 'premium') (Itami and Nishino, 2010; Kaplan, 2012), where certain features are provided for free and others are charged at a premium rate. In the case of Google and Metro it is only the advertisers who are charged for taking online space. Similarly, traditional firms such as Kodak and Polaroid have been, in the past, very successful with their *razor blade* profit model. The concept springs from the shaving industry, which obtains its profits mainly from the sale of razor blades and much less from the sale of the razors themselves. Kodak and Polaroid were dependent not so much on selling cameras but on selling *consumables*: the rolls of film and, for Polaroid, the instant photographic materials. Senseo and Nespresso are more recent successful examples of the *razor blade* business model; they made large profits on the coffee pads or capsules, not on the coffee machines. As long as these pads and capsules were patented, they were able to fully capture the value, but when the patent expired, many competitors stepped in.

These questions of value creation and value capture are of fundamental importance. After all, without an economic model which delivers revenue, a commercial enterprise cannot exist. A business model should create some level of value for customers and stakeholders, but also 'entices customers to pay for value, and converts those payments to profit through the proper design and operation of the various elements of the value chain' (Teece, 2010: 179). Capturing enough of the value created is vital. If a firm captures hardly any of the value it creates, the survival of the firm will be threatened as there will be insufficient revenues. However, if a firm captures too much of that value, then customers are unlikely to buy its goods, because the prices, for example, may be too high. This also threatens a firm's survival (Chesbrough, 2007).

A business model sets out the competitive strategy by which larger or new competitive advantages are achieved

A business model answers questions such as how can the firm position itself on the market? Which core competences underlie this positioning? What limits the *scope* of the enterprise, and within this scope how can advantages be gained over rivals?

Amit and Zott (2001) identified four factors which make a business model successful. A business model results in substantial added value if it makes new combinations possible, involves greater switching costs for customers (*lock-in* effects), creates a strong interdependency between activities, and delivers substantial cost savings as a result. Clearly identifying stakeholders, differentiating one's offerings, and having a clear vision are all important elements.

If a business model does not result in a competitive advantage which is sustainable (at least temporarily), it has no value. That is why the strategy behind business model innovation must make explicit how innovation leads to a position which rivals cannot imitate quickly (Teece, 2010). It is essential to assess the reaction of rivals; after all, a business model does not work in a vacuum. The success or failure of a business model depends to a large extent on how it compares to business models of other players in the industry (Casadesus-Masanell and Ricart, 2011). As such, a business model itself also needs to be differentiated from other industry players in order to act as a source of competitive advantage (Teece, 2010).

Now we turn our attention to the essence of this research; which business model innovation strategies do firms use, and how do they use these models to achieve success?

Business model innovation

Changing the business model is on the agenda of almost every top manager, even if only implicitly. A biennial study of CEOs carried out by the IBM Institute for Business Value reported in 2006 that top managers in all kinds of industries consider the development of innovative business models to be a top priority (Giesen et al., 2007; Pohle and Chapman, 2006). A follow-up study in 2009 revealed that seven out of ten firms are involved in business model innovation. No less than 98 per cent of the managers surveyed stated that they modified their business models to a certain extent (Matzler et al., 2013). Innovation of a business model occurs not only when the components of the model change, but also when those components are combined in different ways (Amit and Zott, 2012; Björkdahl and Holmén, 2013; Zott and Amit, 2010). We now look in more detail at our two main types of business model innovation: renewal and replication (cf. Aspara et al., 2010; Heij et al., 2014; Osiyevskyy and Dewald, 2015a).

Business model renewal

Business model renewal can be defined as the introduction of new business model components or new interdependencies between those various components which go beyond the framework of an existing model in order to create and capture new value (e.g. Morris et al., 2005; Schneider and Spieth, 2013). It involves a radical appraisal of a firm's current business model (e.g. Amit and Zott, 2001; Eyring et al., 2011) in order to arrive at a new or more sustainable competitive position for the firm (Giesen et al., 2010; Markides and Oyon, 2010). There are two key characteristics of business model renewal. First, a firm obtains new business model components (Morris et al., 2005), either by developing them itself (making), acquiring them (buying), or accessing external components (e.g. making alliances). Next, new interdependencies are created among business model components (e.g. Johnson et al., 2008; Morris et al., 2005). This is done either by fundamentally revising the existing model (Cavalcante et al., 2011), or by developing a new model 'from scratch' (e.g. Govindarajan and Trimble, 2011).

Business model renewal increases a firm's chances of survival in the longer run (Andries et al., 2013), but it is a risky process. It requires experimentation, and this can often result in failure (McGrath, 2010) as few companies understand their business model well enough, including its interdependencies, strengths, weaknesses, and underlying assumptions (Johnson et al., 2008). Renewal also involves more challenges and barriers than replication, due to organizational inertia, political forces (Cavalcante et al., 2011; Chesbrough, 2010; Doz and Kosonen, 2010), or fear of cannibalization, for example (Voelpel et al., 2005).

Firms that introduce new-to-the-industry business models face particularly high risks, because they have no proof of whether those new models will be viable (Casadesus-Masanell and Zhu, 2013). The new business model created is not only new for the firm but also for the sector as a whole (Casadesus-Masanell and Zhu, 2013; Gambardella and McGahan, 2010). Here we can talk of the reconceptualization of an entire business. Sometimes a new business model of this kind can turn the competitive relationships in a sector completely upside down. This happened when Apple launched iTunes, and when Ryanair and EasyJet introduced budget air travel into the European market. Other examples of disruptive business models include Airbnb, Booking.com, Netflix, Peerby, Spotify, and Uber. These online platforms changed the rules within a sector, and resulted in a completely new value proposition. Moves of this kind make it possible for the initiating firm to create a disproportionate level of value and to grow strongly (the 'winner-takes-all' effect). Renewal can thus be a powerful means of escaping a competitive race and developing a new and possibly more sustainable competitive advantage.

Radical disruption is essential to business model renewal. This is not solely about firms renewing their products as a result of disruptive technologies. Business model renewal can enable a firm to make an aggressive move in existing markets (e.g. Casadesus-Masanell and Tarziján, 2012; Markides and Oyon, 2010) or to enter new markets (e.g. Eyring et al., 2011; Johnson et al., 2008). For instance, Virgin expanded from retail and music into new industries such as airlines and financial services (Giesen et al., 2007), and Singapore Airlines took on the competition within its own industry by introducing a low-cost carrier airline, Silkair (Markides and Chariou, 2004). Business model renewal can also mean the penetration of niche markets which were not being served, the redefinition of customer sectors and customer needs, and new methods of delivery and distribution, or combinations of these (Johnson et al., 2008; Markides and Charitou, 2004).

Renewal is not reserved only for small start-ups or ICT firms. Large corporate groups can also follow totally new avenues. Consider Philips, which has turned to health and lifestyle, or Ricoh, which is now moving from printing to documents service and 3D printing. Renewal can also be found in the high-value professional services sector. The world in which accountants, lawyers, and consultants operate is undergoing dramatic change. New information and communications technologies enable new ways of working. New generations of professionals are introducing greater creativity and entrepreneurship but also bring their own demands, wanting to forge their career according to their own rules. New boutique firms capitalize on these trends by offering focused services and start working together in new networks. They present a growing competitive threat to major global players.

A recent study we carried out in small Dutch accountancy firms who worked mostly with SME (small and medium enterprise) clients provides a clear example of business model renewal in high-value professional services. Due to competitive pressures from the 'big four' accountancy firms (PwC, Deloitte, EY, and KPMG), the smaller accountancy firms were facing decreasing margins. Most of these SME accountants chose the same business model (see the average business model components of 212 SME accountancy firms in Figure 2.2). That is, they all focused on a niche market, and experimented to some extent with digital channels in addition to their traditional physical channels. And they all tried to achieve a balance between advisory and production activities, between people and ICT as key resources, and, in their revenue model, between charging by hourly rate or by subscription. The lack of distinctiveness in their business model led to fierce competition on price and to the closure of many accountancy firms.

More distinctive business models of SME accountants that resulted in more profitable market positions can be clustered into three categories (see also Figure 2.3):

- the *specialist*, which focuses on a specific market niche or specializes in a single service or a small range of services
- the *house of service*, which tries to create the best of both worlds: it combines standard services with tailor-made advice
- the *digital accountant* (or 'digi-countant'), which combines accountancy and automation solutions in a small number of standard online services (administrative support, bookkeeping, and real-time financial dashboard).

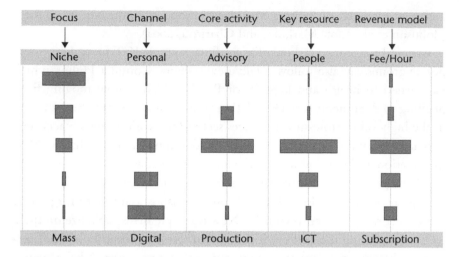

Figure 2.2 The business model components of SME accountants

Source: Volberda et al. (2015)

N.B. The size of each box represents the number of small accountancy firms.

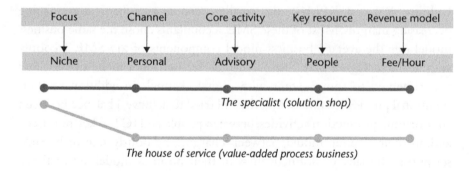

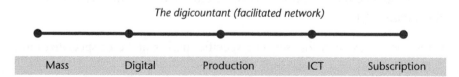

Figure 2.3 Three distinctive business models for SME accountants

Source: Volberda et al. (2015)

Firms in the first two categories focus on a particular niche, use personal rather than digital channels, provide advisory activities, and have people, not ICT, as their key resources. Firms in both these categories use business models in which they still charge an hourly rate rather than a subscription fee (Volberda et al., 2015).

Business model renewal is not always driven by increased competition, however—it can also be prompted by regulatory change. For instance, legislative changes forced Dutch financial advisors to abandon their commission-based business model. Their traditional brokerage model was based on pushing attractive financial products from large insurance companies and minimizing the amount of activities performed for the client. The profit for the financial advisor was based on bonuses from insurance companies and on high commissions on the type of financial products delivered. The result was that advisors did not actually serve the interests of the client but simply sold whichever financial products gave them the highest commissions. Now it is the other way around. The new, more transparent business models employed by Dutch financial services firms have a greater focus on adding value and do this in various ways. It may be by forming alliances with other financial advisors to create advantages of scale and scope, or by specializing in particular financial services such as pensions or insurance. The models may also be based on co-creation with new partners such as fitness companies or labour unions, or on serving and tying in more

Table 2.1 Characteristics of business model renewal

Aim	• reach a new, more sustainable competitive position
Focus	• new methods of value creation through radical renewal of existing business model
Levers of change	– new technologies – new management practices – new organizational forms – new relationships with customers: co-creation
Business model components	• obtain new business model components
Business model complementarities	• create new complementary effects among business model components
Outcomes	• aggressive move in existing markets or entering new markets
Risks	• very high risk for first firm in the sector • high risk for imitators

closely to specific customer segments such as the agricultural or the transport sectors (Volberda and Heij, 2014).

In Table 2.1, we can see the central characteristics of business model renewal.

Business model replication

As an alternative to radically renewing a business model, firms can also employ a strategy of improving or replicating a business model. McDonald's and IKEA have elevated the expansion and perfection of their existing business models to an art, and achieved global success as a result (e.g. Winter and Szulanski, 2001). Since these firms originally worked on the basis of renewal, they provide powerful examples of how renewal and replication can be used effectively in succession. Less well-known examples of firms that employ replication are Vopak and NXP Semiconductors (see Chapter 6).

Business model replication can be described as the 're-creation of a successful model' (Szulanski and Jensen, 2008: 1738) in which a firm develops or upscales components of its existing business model so as to create and capture more value. That is, it leverages those existing components (Baden-Fuller and Winter, 2007)—and the interdependencies between them—by refining and adjusting its current model (Schneider and Spieth, 2013), or by using the model more widely across different parts of the firm (Jonsson and Foss, 2011; Szulanski, 1996). Replication is not about cloning the original model, but creating a model that is broadly similar (Baden-Fuller and Winter, 2007). The focus is on improving existing methods of value creation and appropriation by making incremental changes to an existing business model (e.g. Baden-Fuller and Winter, 2007; Casadesus-Masanell and Ricart, 2011). Replication involves the reconstruction of a system of activities and processes that are often imperfectly understood, causally ambiguous, complex, and interdependent (Szulanski and Jensen, 2008; Winter and Szulanski, 2001). It is a dynamic and evolving process (Dunford et al., 2010) that requires the right balance between learning, change, and precise replication (Winter et al., 2012). Business model replication offers a comparatively safe route to short-term success (Szulanski and Jensen, 2008; Voelpel et al., 2005), but it lacks variety, and this can threaten a firm's survival in the longer run (Andries et al., 2013). The more proficiently a firm replicates a business model elsewhere, the more effectively it can reap the rewards of that replication (Heij et al., 2014).

Table 2.2 summarizes the features of business model replication. Two key characteristics of business model replication stand out. First, business model

Table 2.2 Characteristics of business model replication

Aim	• maintain or improve existing competitive position
Focus	• improving current methods of value creation through incremental innovation of the existing business model
Levers of change	• perfecting and deepening existing technologies, management practices, organizational forms, and customer relations
Business model components	• refining current business model components
Business model complementarities	• strengthening complementarities between current business model components
Outcomes	• remaining active in existing markets, or entering similar, but geographically different markets
Risks	• limited risk in the short term • high risk in the longer term

replication is about leveraging the components of a firm's existing business model (Baden-Fuller and Winter, 2007; Szulanski and Jensen, 2008). Second, internal fit between business model components is needed to create or reinforce consistency between those components (Demil and Lecocq, 2010); business model components 'need to be co-specialized to each other, and work together well as a system' (Teece, 2010: 180) so that firms can benefit from the complementary effects of different sources of competitive advantage (Winter and Szulanski, 2001).

There are various ways to replicate a business model. An existing business model can be applied in a different context. In geographical replication, for example, an existing business model is applied in a different country or region (Baden-Fuller and Winter, 2007; Dunford et al., 2010). One example of this is the way IKEA continually opens new branches on different continents (Jonsson and Foss, 2011). Enriched knowledge of operations, products, services, and markets, gathered over time, enables the company to refine its existing business model (Baden-Fuller and Volberda, 2003; Baden-Fuller and Winter, 2007).

. . . .

IKEA CONQUERS THE WORLD

Until the 1960s, there was no international market for furniture. A major reason for this was that furniture takes up a large amount of space in relation to its value and is easily damaged, so the costs of transportation were high. IKEA circumvented this problem by involving the customer in the assembly and transportation; flat-pack and home assembly is central to their approach. In 1963 the Swedish group took the plunge and expanded into Norway, and then into Switzerland in 1973. Other European countries followed, as well as Australia and Canada. When IKEA made the jump to the United States in 1985, it discovered that Americans have different tastes. It was able to solve this problem by engaging local suppliers. Expansion into Eastern Europe was next. Although there is a different perception of IKEA in different countries—in Singapore and Malaysia, for example, it is regarded as a prestigious brand and customers prefer not to do the assembly themselves—it is one of the few corporate groups to succeed in replicating a business model almost unchanged throughout the world.

Source: Volberda et al. (2011)

Replication can also be applied over time (Baden-Fuller and Volberda, 2003; Bowman and Ambrosini, 2003). Improving an existing business model over a certain period of time is known as longitudinal replication. Most firms do this: they improve their existing business models by enriching their existing knowledge of the market and of production processes (Baden-Fuller and Volberda, 2003).

Improvement in replication takes place using existing knowledge and experience, mainly from within the firm itself. It is a case of exploitative learning, deepening the existing knowledge base of the firm (Winter et al., 2012). It is important in this connection to point out that business model replication means not only replicating repeatedly, but also discovering and learning from complex, and partly implicit routines that are interdependent (Szulanski and Jensen, 2008; Winter and Szulanski, 2001). So replication does not lead to stagnation: you can learn once again from the process itself. Experience of using a particular business model (Demil and Lecocq, 2010; Teece, 2010) enables a firm to improve on that model by rectifying mistakes and getting rid of inefficiencies (Schneider and Spieth, 2013; Szulanski and Jensen, 2008). It can also remove particular components or change the priority given to them (Demil and Lecocq, 2010). Business model replication can increase a firm's profit in two ways. First, it provides cost advantages because it allows the firm to operate more efficiently (Szulanski and Jensen, 2008; Zott and Amit, 2007) and exploit economies of scale (Baden-Fuller and Winter, 2007; Contractor, 2007). Firms with more experience of business model replication can thus replicate at lower cost (Contractor, 2007). Second, replication can also increase revenue, because by increasing its competitive advantage or overcoming previous limitations (Schneider and Spieth, 2013;

Voelpel et al., 2005), the firm is able to capture more value from its existing business model (Jonsson and Foss, 2011; Szulanski and Jensen, 2008).

Sustained replication also results in stronger interactions, tighter links, and more synergies between the various components of a business model (Demil and Lecocq, 2010; Teece, 2010). This makes it harder for competitors to identify the precise components of a firm's business model or the source of its success, and the model becomes more difficult for outsiders to imitate (Teece, 2010). Business model replication is clearly a path-dependent process of learning (e.g. McGrath, 2010), in which the strengthening of combinations of components differentiates a firm's business model from those of its competitors (Demil and Lecocq, 2010). A business model that is more differentiated and more difficult to imitate increases a firm's competitive advantage (Barney, 1991), and thereby its performance.

Business model renewal, or replication after all?

Over the years, management and innovation authors have come out strongly in favour of business model renewal as the best way of achieving success. Well-known examples are Kim and Mauborgne (2005), who argue for the creation of new markets through their *Blue Ocean Strategy*.

This preference for business model renewal is not altogether justifiable. There are arguably fewer risks with business model replication than with business model renewal, though the gains can be just as great (Andries et al., 2013; Casadesus-Masanell and Zhu, 2013). After fifteen years of investigating successful firms, Zook and Allen (2011) came to the conclusion that the ones that are most successful elaborate continuously on their fundamental basis of differentiation; they literally go from strength to strength. These firms learn how to bring their value proposition to the market and build organizations which live the competitive advantages, day in, day out. They learn how to change their business models, not radically but incrementally, by adapting constantly to changes in the market. In the meantime they resist the whims of the market better than rivals whose focus is not as sharp. The result is a simple, scalable, and repeatable business model which the firm can apply again and again, including to adjacent products and markets, in order to realize sustainable growth.

What Zook and Allen found was that the most successful firms do not give in to intermittent radical revolutions, but concentrate on replicating their current business model. Sometimes radical revolutions do help firms to discover the value of replication. Vopak, the world's largest independent tank terminal operator (with seventy-eight terminals, across twenty-eight countries), is a good illustration of this. Vopak resulted from the merger of two traditional Dutch warehousing firms, Pakhoed and Van Ommeren. For a while it threw itself into air transport, shipping, road transport, containers, real estate, and chemical storage (see Figure 2.4). After countless failures in those activities which were alien to the sector, the firm concluded that it could only replicate and refine the traditional business model of storing oil in many ports, and that this would form the basis of a unique competitive advantage. Shipping, road transport, and even chemical storage turned out to require a completely different business model which was not compatible with the firm's existing technology, know-how, organizational form, and culture (Volberda, 1998; Van Driel et al., 2015).

Developing new business models needs a great deal of stretch or flexibility in technology, management, and organization, and some firms apparently

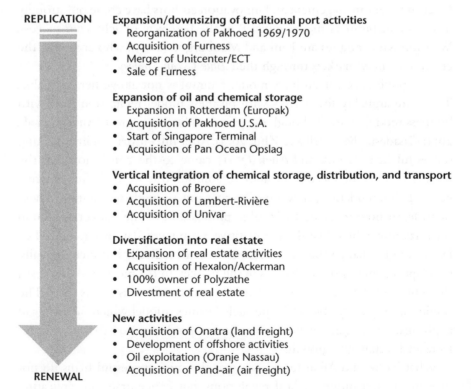

REPLICATION

Expansion/downsizing of traditional port activities
- Reorganization of Pakhoed 1969/1970
- Acquisition of Furness
- Merger of Unitcenter/ECT
- Sale of Furness

Expansion of oil and chemical storage
- Expansion in Rotterdam (Europak)
- Acquisition of Pakhoed U.S.A.
- Start of Singapore Terminal
- Acquisition of Pan Ocean Opslag

Vertical integration of chemical storage, distribution, and transport
- Acquisition of Broere
- Acquisition of Lambert-Rivière
- Acquisition of Univar

Diversification into real estate
- Expansion of real estate activities
- Acquisition of Hexalon/Ackerman
- 100% owner of Polyzathe
- Divestment of real estate

New activities
- Acquisition of Onatra (land freight)
- Development of offshore activities
- Oil exploitation (Oranje Nassau)
- Acquisition of Pand-air (air freight)

RENEWAL

Figure 2.4 Strategic actions of Vopak: replication and renewal

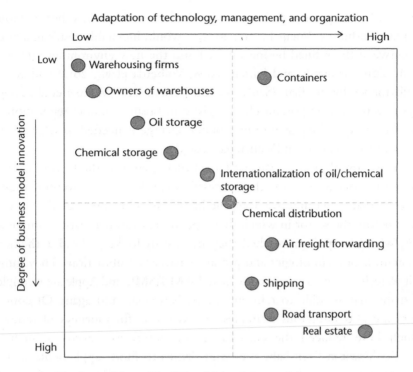

Figure 2.5 The limited 'stretch' of Vopak's business model

only have a limited amount of that flexibility (see Figure 2.5). Changing business model requires not only a strategic choice but also control of the levers which make that change possible.

Discussing the relative merits of replication and renewal does not give us a definitive answer as to which may be the best strategy for firms. That will naturally depend on the particular circumstances of the firm. Business model renewal is needed to respond to threats to the existing business model (Cavalcante et al., 2011; Giesen et al., 2010) and to adapt to changing environmental conditions (Casadesus-Masanell and Ricart, 2010; Schneider and Spieth, 2013). It enables a firm to create a fit with the new environment (Giesen et al., 2010) and helps to ensure its longer-term survival (Hamel and Välikangas, 2003; Voelpel et al., 2005). Leaving it too late to reinvent the business model results in a decline in firm performance (Nunes and Breene, 2011), and if a firm undertakes little or no business model renewal, then it will not be able to replace its existing business model. Such inability to adapt to fundamental environmental changes threatens the very existence of a firm (Wirtz et al., 2010). In this type of situation, replication—which involves building on a business model that has worked in other environmental conditions (Voelpel et al., 2005)—would inevitably result in a poor fit between the refined business model and the new environment (Giesen et al., 2010; Szulanski and Jensen, 2008; Volberda et al., 2012) and worse performance by the firm (Szulanski and Jensen, 2008;Voelpel et al., 2005). Optimization, an important characteristic of business model replication, is adequate only as long as no fundamental change is needed in what has to be optimized (Hamel and Välikangas, 2003).

A study by Nunes and Breene (2011) that examined the basis of above-average performance proves that successful firms keep on reinventing themselves so that they can move from one life cycle to the next (see Figure 2.6). Even before the sector in which they operate reaches maturity, or immediately when that point is reached, they are already looking ahead to the next generation of technologies and product/market combinations. They jump, as it were, from one S-curve to the next. DSM, ASML, and Apple are examples of firms that are able to reinvent themselves again and again. Of course, there are also numerous examples of less successful journeys of renewal which have reduced the chances of the enterprise surviving, such as Numico's switch from baby food and drinks to food supplements, or the transformation of the French state-run water company Compagnie Générale des Eaux into the mass media and digital entertainment group Vivendi.

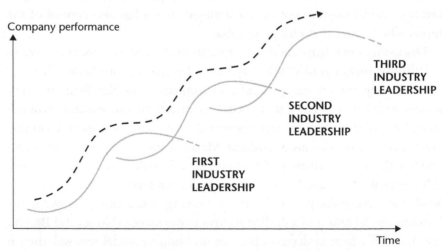

Successful firms are already growing with new business models by the time their existing business models start to fail.

Figure 2.6 Jump on the S-curve
Source: adapted from Nunes and Breene (2011)

Likewise, successful business model renewal in the past is no guarantee of similar future success (Govindarajan and Trimble, 2011). Nokia had always been praised as an organization which had reinvented itself several times: the Finnish firm moved from paper production via rubber into cables and telecommunications towers, and finally into mobile phones. For the time being, that is where it remains: Nokia does not seem able to make the jump to a new S-curve. Renewal is not an inherent ability that can be called upon at will. Compare it to sport: you need the talent but you have to train.

. . . .

NOKIA: SUCCESSFUL BUSINESS MODEL RENEWAL IN THE PAST DOES NOT GUARANTEE FUTURE SUCCESS

The most celebrated example of a corporate group which has already renewed its business model successfully several times is the Finnish mobile phone manufacturer Nokia. The firm was established in 1865 as a paper mill, with the vast Finnish conifer forests providing the raw materials. A new activity was added at the end of the nineteenth century: generating electricity by means of hydropower, also something in plentiful supply in the Finnish countryside. In 1920 Finnish Rubber Works (FRW), a pioneer in rubber production (providing boots and car tyres), acquired a controlling stake in Nokia. Two years later FRW also acquired a controlling stake in Finnish Cable Works.

The three-headed group was then the country's market leader in all of its activities—paper pulp, rubber, and cables. The cable activities would remain the backbone of the firm's growth until 1960. In addition, as a spin-off Nokia set up a company unit to produce telephone equipment. The group was becoming increasingly dependent on export to the Soviet Union. Those at the top wanted to turn it into a modern, competitive firm. Nokia therefore embraced consumer electronics such as televisions and video recorders. A new growth market was also found in the interface between electronics and telephony: digital switches which made telephone networks both much more advanced and less expensive. Nokia sold off its paper and rubber activities and acquired firms in consumer electronics, positioning itself more and more as a European electronics giant.

The firm was a pioneer in mobile telephony in the business-to-business market (car phones for business use). With the new standard for mobile telephony (Global System for Mobile Communications) approaching, the newly appointed CEO, Jorna Ollila, saw that mobile telephony for consumers was the new growth market. Helped by the fact that the Finns embraced digital technologies quickly and enthusiastically, by 2006 Nokia had been able to develop into the global market leader in mobile phones. At the time there was also more than enough space for other players, such as LG, Sony Ericsson, the Taiwanese firm HTC, and Motorola. Samsung also had reasonable success lower down the market. None of these players believed it possible that an outsider like Apple could break this power bloc. Yet in 2007 Apple disrupted Nokia's business model by introducing its iPhone. As a result, there was a proliferation of movie uploads, music exchange, photo files, and traffic from free chat and Facebook. Countless different business models were trampled with this wholesale infringement of data protocols (Volberda et al., 2011).

. . . .

Whether *jumping the S-curve* is a gradual form of renewal or an extreme form of replication can be discussed at length. But that is less interesting than the question of how firms can foster both replication and renewal. How can a firm adopt two different business models for the same market? This is becoming an increasingly urgent issue for a growing group of established enterprises which have come under fire from *strategic innovators*— firms which disrupt the established order by introducing radically new business models (e.g. Markides and Oyon, 2010).

The growth in market share of these strategic innovators creates a huge dilemma for established enterprises. On the one hand, there are enormous growth opportunities to be gained if the new business model is embraced. But should that then mean dumping the existing model completely? New business models often conflict with existing models, so by choosing both models firms run the risk that these will not be managed well and value will be lost. How can established firms adopt a new business model without neglecting or cannibalizing their existing business model?

Markides and Charitou (2004) offer a solution to this problem. They believe that the challenge lies in developing the two business models in tandem (to prevent potential conflicts) and, at the same time, seeking a sufficient degree of integration between them so that synergies can be exploited. Introducing a second business model can also be an effective strategy for countering a strategic innovator, provided that this model is clearly different from both the existing model and that of the strategic innovator, and that a good balance can be found between structural separation and integration (Markides and Charitou, 2004).

Developing fundamentally new business models goes hand in hand with experimentation, and not every organization is immediately capable of developing more than one business model. For example, KLM set up the low-cost carrier Buzz in 1999 to compete with Ryanair and EasyJet (Markides and Oyon, 2010). It was not successful. A salient detail: after Buzz was closed down, its Boeing 737-800 aircraft were taken over by Ryanair, which now uses them as standard.

KLM had more success in its takeover of Transavia. Experimenting under the name Basiq Air, Transavia gradually shifted to selling over the internet and serving the low-cost, low-fare market. In around 2009 KLM started searching more intensively for synergy between its different business models: KLM, Martinair (cargo airline), and Transavia.com. After various failures, the company was able to set up a new business model for the growing low-budget market under the separate Transavia label.

Four levers of business model renewal and replication

More important than the precise definition of a business model is knowing *how* firms can *develop* a business model. What levers does an organization have at its disposal to improve an existing business model (replication) or develop a new model (renewal)?

There are four key levers that can be used: new technologies, new management practices, new organizational forms, and co-creation with customers or partners (Chesbrough, 2007; Itami and Nishino, 2010; Teece, 2010). The interaction between the levers is also very important. For example, the changing of a number of levers simultaneously can affect the speed of business model innovation.

Lever 1: technology

Technology is essential in every business model, and helps transform *inputs* into relevant *output* (Daft, 1978). Business model innovation through the introduction of new or improved technologies is thus an obvious lever for changing the business model (Baden-Fuller and Haefliger, 2013). There have been successive waves of technology that have given rise to new business models. During the industrial revolution, the arrival of steam made it possible to mechanize production. This saw the rise of companies that provided and used steam engines, such as steam mills and locomotives. There was arguably a second similar revolution roughly a century ago, driven by the invention of electricity and other technologies such as the combustion engine, aeroplanes, and moving pictures. The use of electricity led to mass production. A third wave of industrial development came with the rise of the personal computer, digital technology, and the internet, which led to greater automation of production through the use of ICT. The most recent wave is based on a fusion of technologies that fully integrate digital, physical, and biological environments (Schwab, 2016). Technologies that were previously separate, such as artificial intelligence and machine learning, robotics, nanotechnology, 3D printing, genetics, and biotechnology, have come together to build on one another. Developments such as the internet of things, big data, portable and implantable technologies, and driverless cars have brought about completely new and unexpected business models. For instance, companies such as TomTom, Vodafone, and various car manufacturers have business models that are about navigating and providing mobile solutions, but because the technologies used are based on geolocation, this enables them to sell other services to customers. Drone technology is allowing Amazon.com to experiment with new and potentially faster logistical services so that established parcel delivery companies now risk being pushed out of Amazon's value chain for regional transportation.

Business model innovation can also enable a firm to come up with new ways of commercializing its existing technologies and activities (e.g. Chesbrough and Rosenbloom, 2002). For example, companies like Deutsche Post DHL Group, Lufthansa, and Porsche have created consultancy branches that allow them to make more commercial use of their knowledge and expertise.

On the one hand, technology is a lever that involves the capacity to encourage technological innovation within the firm itself by acquiring additional knowledge and increasing investment in R&D (Chesbrough et al., 2013). On the other hand, it concerns the capacity to absorb new technologies and knowledge from outside the organization (Cohen and Levinthal, 1990).

Technological innovations are making the boundaries of branches of industry increasingly diffuse and porous. We are seeing the emergence of overlapping branches of industry—for example, in the multimedia, telecommunications, and financial sectors (e.g. De Boer et al., 1999; Prahalad and Ramaswamy, 2004). Traditional players such as publishers, telecom operators, and banks are being confronted with new and dynamic competitors. To compete successfully, they have to absorb and combine unfamiliar technologies and new areas of knowledge. For instance, the rise of financial technology (fintech) and various new entrants with banking licences—such as Google, Apple, and Amazon—blur the boundaries of the banking industry, eroding the competitive advantage of many established banks. As a result, the expectation is that banks will become more and more ICT-based in the future.

Ericsson is an illustration of how new or improved technology can facilitate the switch to a new business model. Fast internet connections have now made it possible for the calculation capacity of large computers to be separated from the interfaces, such as desktop computers, at customers' workplaces. Ericsson made use of this when it used cloud computing to introduce a new business model in the telecom infrastructure (Khanagha et al., 2013, 2014). In addition to a production-based model, the firm also had a service-based model (see Figure 2.7), and now sells hardware, software, *and* services. But business model innovation can also occur without technology development (Baden-Fuller and Haefliger, 2013), as we will discuss in the next sections.

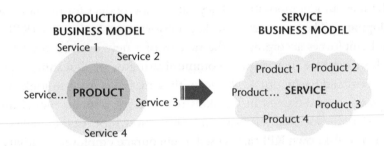

	Existing telecom technology and complementary assets	Features of cloud computing
1	Customers buy off-the-shelf products and services which are developed, sold, and implemented by the seller	On-demand self-service—Customers have at their disposal services such as server time and network storage which involve no human interaction with the service provider
2	Functionalities are packaged in products which are brought by customers	Wide network access—Capacity is available via the network and can be accessed via the customer's platform
3	Resources are distributed and sold to individual customers	Resource pooling—Bundled physical and virtual capacity of provider is assigned dynamically on the basis of market demand
4	Products are sold on the basis of their whole life cycle, and customers pay, even if they do not use the product	Rapid elasticity—Capacity is offered 'elastically', sometimes automatically, to enable rapid outward and inward scaling according to the customer demand
5	Physical product is the core unit sold, and supplies the revenue	Product as a service—Service provider sells access to bundled resources without selling a physical product

Figure 2.7 Ericsson's new business model
Source: adapted from Khanagha et al. (2013)

Lever 2: management

A seemingly less obvious lever is management. This involves the application of new management practices in order to innovate the firm's business model (see Figure 2.8). The management lever covers changes in *what* managers do as well as the *way* that they do it (Birkinshaw, Hamel, and Mol, 2008; Hamel, 2006; Volberda et al., 2013). For example: how do managers take decisions, and how do they set goals? How do they coordinate activities, and how do they motivate people? These changes reveal themselves through new management practices, processes, or techniques, often referred to as management innovation.

A number of different management interventions can be used to stimulate business model innovation. They can release budget for business model development. They can set new key performance indicators (KPIs), or reward employees according to the success of a new business model. They can also introduce new ways of communicating or of allocating responsibility (Foss and Saebi, 2015). Not least, they may also want to look at how employees can be trained in the skills required for business model innovation, and at associated selection and promotion processes. Google's '20% time' is a well-known KPI that is used to encourage employee creativity and innovativeness rather than mere productivity. This has enabled the company to develop its AdSense business model, whereby it acts as a broker between

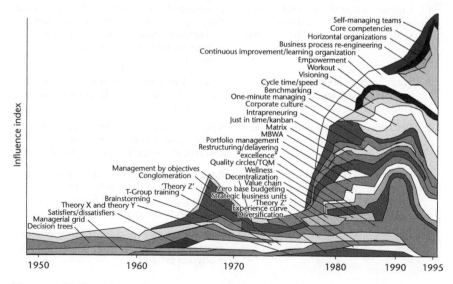

Figure 2.8 Overview of management practices, 1950–2000
Source: Copyright © 2017 by Pascale (1990). Used by Permission. All rights reserved.

publishers who offer advertising space on their websites and companies who want to place their ad on targeted external websites that are particularly relevant in terms of their content. Google receives a fee each time a visitor to that website clicks on the ad.

The less visible management processes of decision-making, coordination, and implementation within the organization should also tie in to the new business model. For instance, 'Dell and Wal-Mart's business models were different, superior, and required supporting processes that were hard for competitors to replicate' (Teece, 2010: 180). New management practices under the label 'lean retailing' were required to execute Walmart's business model (Teece, 2010). Entrepreneur Sam Walton built a retail juggernaut that began with thirty-nine stores in 1971 and grew out to almost three thousand. He did so by insisting that suppliers implement information technologies for exchanging sales data, adopt standards for product labelling, and use modern methods of material handling which assured customers a high variety of products at low prices. Because lean management works in an entirely new way, retailers had to reshape their planning methods, cost models, inventory practices, workforce utilization, and sourcing strategies. Retailers that adopted these new management practices were the ones with the strongest performance—not those that had simply invested in ICT.

New business models can also be created by applying a new management technique involving a new tool, approach, or technique which is adopted in a business framework (Waddell and Mallen, 2001). One such new management technique is the balanced score card (Birkinshaw et al., 2008). Setting goals by introducing the *balanced scorecard* method can stimulate an organization to develop new business models. Here management steers not only by offering short-term financial incentives but also through feedback from customers, internal company processes, and the capacity of the firm to learn and grow. Taking into consideration the shareholder (financial perspective), the point of view of the customer (customer value), the processes which need to be optimized in order to realize this (internal perspective), and the future growth capacity (learning and growing perspective) leads to a more balanced process of business model innovation.

Another example would be the introduction of self-managing teams, as used by DSM, a global market leader in products such as antibiotics and vitamins, and the Fortune 500 company Procter & Gamble (see case illustrations below). The way these organizations set goals, motivate employees intrinsically, and coordinate activities has given enormous momentum to their business model innovation process (Vaccaro et al., 2012a). Even though management practices do not always spring readily to mind when we talk of business model innovation, management innovation can in fact bring about dramatic change to a firm's competitive position (Birkinshaw et al., 2008; Damanpour and Aravind, 2012). It is precisely because management innovations are often company-specific and not readily 'visible' that they are more difficult for rivals to imitate (Mol and Birkinshaw, 2006; Walker, 2008). Indeed, Gary Hamel (2006) believes that management innovation, more than any other form of innovation over the past century, has enabled firms to achieve higher levels of performance and to develop distinctive business models. Moreover, the findings of the Erasmus Innovation Monitor covering the years 2006 to 2014 (Volberda et al., 2014) indicate that management innovations are of great importance and explain about 50–75 per cent of the variation in innovation performance between Dutch firms. Furthermore, in controlled experiments on management innovations in firms, TNO—a Dutch institute for applied research—reported productivity increases of firms that implemented management innovations (such as lean, self-managing teams) of up to 16 per cent and a substantial reduction of throughput times (cf. Totterdill et al., 2002).

. . . .

MANAGEMENT INNOVATION AT DSM ANTI-INFECTIVES, DELFT: FACILITATING LEADERSHIP

Several years after opening its new Zor-f factory for penicillin production in Delft, DSM was faced with the rapid rise of Chinese manufacturers, which led to strong downward pressure on prices. The situation was so serious that top management considered moving production to China, where DSM already had a joint venture with a local manufacturer. The factory in Delft would consequently have to close.

The management decided to try something else first. To start with, they applied a new technology (biotechnology) which cut the number of production phases and reduced losses. This technology is now being copied by the Chinese rivals. In addition to this technological innovation, DSM also focused on management innovation. The company decided that the Zor-f factory could be retained if productivity and efficiency were boosted through smaller teams, better cooperation, and greater commitment to maintenance.

Five self-managing teams were established, each with five operators who kept the factory running round the clock in eight-hour shifts. Although there is no formal supervisor, an operations expert acts as an interface between the teams and the management. Maintenance is taken care of through a joint venture between DSM and two maintenance firms. The success of this approach has led to the factory being preserved for Delft and for the employees. The adoption of self-managing teams within DSM Anti-Infectives resulted in increased productivity (12 per cent), improvements in process technology, savings in maintenance and operation, lower costs, and better accomplishment of targets. Moreover, it resulted in a greater sense of mission, more trust, better interaction between different constituencies, more exchange of knowledge, and a highly motivated and engaged workforce.

Source: Vaccaro et al. (2012b)

. . . .

. . . .

MANAGEMENT INNOVATION AT PROCTER & GAMBLE: SELF–MANAGING TEAMS

The introduction of self-managing teams at Procter & Gamble affected the practices, processes, and structures of management. The management practice changed in that senior management specified frameworks within which employees themselves would be responsible for setting goals and for determining when and how duties would be carried out. In addition, there were also changes to the method of remuneration, as the remuneration level now depends on the skills level of employees. This then serves as the basis for promotion, which is determined by fellow team members. Because hierarchical layers were removed to make space for the self-managing teams, the management structure was also changed.

Source: Vaccaro et al. (2012a)

. . . .

Classic examples of management innovations are Ford's introduction of the assembly line and Toyota's total quality management, an approach adopted by many firms (Vaccaro, 2010). The complexity of management innovations makes them very ambiguous and difficult to imitate. It took many years before Western car manufacturers managed to copy the way that Toyota used the intelligence of employees to reach very high levels of efficiency (Ward et al., 1995). However, once achieved, management innovations provide a sustainable source of competitive advantage and fertile ground for business model innovation.

Lever 3: organizational forms

In the relatively stable environments of the past decades, traditional organizational forms were perfectly adequate. Market globalization, swift technological change, shorter product life cycles, and increasing aggressiveness from competitors have drastically changed the basic rules of competition. This means that companies are forced to review their business model at shorter intervals.

That requires totally different organizational forms which support new business models by allowing the firm to protect experimentation and to develop new competencies from its ongoing operations (Gilbert, 2006; Volberda, 1997). Implementing new organizational forms within a firm is a third lever of business model innovation. It is still not entirely clear, however, whether organizational forms enable business model innovation or whether it is the other way around (George and Bock, 2011). Following prior research (e.g. Foss and Saebi, 2015; Markides and Oyon, 2010) we consider the implementation of new organizational forms in a firm to be a third lever for realizing business model innovation.

What we mean by organizational forms is how work is divided into tasks and how those tasks are coordinated (Volberda, 1998; Hamel, 2007). The development of an appropriate organizational structure is needed to coordinate a firm's activities (Cavalcante et al., 2011), and the organizational form can be modified or renewed in order to promote the development of new business models (Foss, 2002; Foss et al., 2009). For instance, bringing in a new, more service-based model requires changes to a firm's organizational forms (Foss and Saebi, 2015; Khanagha et al., 2013; Kindström and Kowalkowski, 2014). Jeff Bezos, founder and CEO of Amazon, believes in the 'two pizza rule', suggesting that a team should comprise no more people than can be fed with two pizzas—namely, between five and seven. Such two-pizza teams came up with the Gold Box feature (deal of the day, best deal). The creation of new organizational units or subunits enabled companies like ING, Singapore Airlines, and USA Today to introduce new business models (Dunford et al., 2010; Markides and Oyon, 2010; Smith et al., 2010).

Change in organizational structure may involve reconfiguration, simplification, and expansion by means of delegation, elimination, or consolidation. Simplifying the organizational structure, for instance, makes managers more responsive to opportunities in the external environment (Bock et al., 2012). A firm's capacity for change is crucial to the implementation of new organizational forms. This capacity depends on the organizational structure and the underlying planning and control systems. Can the firm react at the right time and go in the direction required? Multifunctional teams, few hierarchical levels, and few process rules increase a firm's capacity for change.

The interest in innovative organizational forms has increased enormously since the end of the 1990s. Some management authors have suggested that there have been major changes to the shape, character, and processes of contemporary firms. In attempting to capture the essence of those changes, they have developed various names. These refer mainly to new basic organizational forms, but also include new processes and systems. For example, they talk of network enterprises, the cellular organization, the federal enterprise (see also the ABB case), and the post-modern flexible enterprise.

. . . .

NEW ORGANIZATIONAL FORMS AT ABB IN THE EARLY 1990s

ABB (Asea Brown Boveri), a market leader in power and automation technologies, is a good example of the impact that structural change can have on the development of new business models. The group originally had the classic M form, or multi-divisional organizational form. In an M form organization, most business assets are allocated at the corporate level, which is where responsibility for strategy-making also lies. The enterprise split in the 1990s into a federation of around 1,300 firms, each with responsibility for their own profit and loss. These decentralized units were held together by new horizontal and vertical processes. On the horizontal axis there was more focus on communication and collaboration across the firm, with other units at the same level. The units, which each had around two hundred employees, were very dependent on one another and shared a great deal of knowledge and resources. It was no longer necessary to communicate instructions or share resources via the vertical hierarchy; instead they were able to focus on promoting unity and a shared company mission. This structure of small 'independent' enterprising business units, with bottom-up dynamics rather than top-down processes, increased ABB's capacity to develop new business models and replicate them elsewhere in the enterprise.

. . . .

The most distinctive feature of these dynamic new forms is that they can develop and change in structure. This facilitates the development of skills across all the different hierarchical levels, positions, and divisions. These skills are the basis of successful development and implementation of new business models. Large organizations like Philips and Unilever have changed their existing organizational forms fundamentally so that they can react better to market developments. Unilever created divisions with self-organizing teams and developed new systems of assessment and remuneration. The group is now able to put its superior innovation and market skills to better use (Volberda et al., 2011).

A hybrid organizational form is often used in the development of a new business model. In hybrid organizational forms one sees asymmetry between high-growth businesses and older, mature operations. Mature divisions that are experiencing moderate competition aim to replicate activities, while new divisions which need to create or react to hypercompetitive disruption work on business model renewal.

Many researchers (e.g. Markides, 2013; Smith et al., 2010) have considered how new business models can be created within large, established enterprises. How should you organize new flexible units which promote business model renewal, and what is their relationship with the other units of the organization? Van de Ven (1986) points out the structural problems of managing relationships between the part and the whole. Drucker (1985) finds that new units need to be organized separately for business model disruption and awarded a considerable degree of autonomy compared to the rest of the organization, especially with respect to the operational units. Galbraith (1982) emphasizes the importance of 'reserves' which are totally devoted to the creation of new ideas, while Peters and Waterman (1982) use the term 'skunk works' for this phenomenon. Kanter (1988) makes a distinction between generating a new business model, which requires frequent contact and close integration with other parts of the organization, and realizing that model, for which isolation, on the contrary, is useful.

Firms sometimes isolate a flexible unit of the existing business model (Hill and Rothaermel, 2003; Orton and Weick, 1990). IBM applied this principle when developing the personal computer. The mainframe logic which was strongly preserved in IBM's dominant business model prevented the firm from entering the new PC market. This isolation strategy initially worked very successfully for IBM. However, the firm later found it very difficult to transfer the new skills to the existing business model as it lacked the necessary communication channels and a common way of thinking. Kodak, Philips, and Xerox likewise had only limited success with their internal programmes for developing new business models (Chesbrough and Davies, 2010).

A more complicated organizational form is the continuous splitting-off of groups to form separate organizations. Hewlett-Packard, Johnson & Johnson, and Atos developed a system in which small, semi-autonomous units allowed entrepreneurs to realize their ideas, while older, established divisions took care of the continuity and replication of the existing business model. This process is comparable to regular cell division. As long as new units keep emerging, such organizations seem to be in an everlasting state of business model renewal. The downside of this cell structure is that if too many cells are being spun off from the old ones such enterprises have difficulty in exploiting the synergies between the various business models (Markides and Oyon, 2010). They lose their identity through the continual division and become uncontrollable.

Organizations such as 3M, HP, and Motorola have developed structures and systems to renew their business models in a structural way. To prevent the organization from getting stuck in its existing model, there is a formal objective at 3M that 30 per cent of the sales must consist of new products or products which have been revised significantly in the last four years. Fifteen per cent of the research budget is reserved for discretionary spending. Like HP and Motorola, 3M delegated decision-making to team and divisional levels, and the firm encourages new projects. Employees are forbidden to think in fixed structures or to put structures down on paper. In contrast to this absence of structures, there is a strong shared culture which is dominated by values such as trust, respect, integrity, and teamwork.

Several hybrid forms of enterprise have emerged in recent times. These include the heterarchy (as opposed to hierarchy), in which assets and leadership are dispersed, communication is mainly horizontal, and coordination is largely informal; the platform organization, whose shape is constantly evolving through frequent recombination of existing elements; and the hypertext organization (Nonaka et al., 2006). The last form, found in successful Japanese firms, combines a hierarchical bureaucracy with a flat, cross-functional task group which works on the new business model. Sharp is one firm which operates in this way. If rapid product development is required, the firm sets up a project organization. Top management can release managers from their line responsibilities for a certain period so that they can concentrate fully on a specific task. These 'golden' managers are temporarily their own boss, and can bring in people from various functional divisions to the project organization. What is different here from the matrix organization is that the project organization is fully autonomous, and the golden manager is not accountable to functional or line managers. Philips used Tiger Teams which operated across its various divisions to speed up business model innovation.

· ·

TOWARDS ONE PHILIPS: SIMPLIFYING THE ORGANIZATIONAL STRUCTURE

Gerard Kleisterlee, who took up the position of chief executive of Philips in 2001, shifted the direction of the electronics group towards health and lifestyle products. From 2004 this was accompanied by a global marketing campaign: Sense and Simplicity. Kleisterlee also enforced simplification internally. Under the 'One Philips' slogan, he trimmed down the organizational structure of the multinational. The number of product divisions was reduced from fourteen to four, and later to three.

The chip arm, which continued as NXP, was sold, as were other units with few prospects. In contrast, Kleisterlee strengthened the weak medical arm with several takeovers. The simplified and better-focused Philips survived the subsequent economic crisis relatively well. Kleisterlee's successor, Frans van Houten, launched Accelerate, a cost-saving programme which included further streamlining of the organization and was designed to create a more enterprising and more innovative organizational culture.

Source: Volberda et al. (2011)

Lever 4: co-creation

Firms are increasingly obliged to look for innovation outside the boundaries of their own organizations. In the telecoms sector, European firms such as Ericsson and KPN initially continued to focus on improving their existing business models which were based on developing their own technologies and their own in-house engineering teams. They then discovered that the big innovations in their industry actually came from small start-ups.

Firms which are strongly focused on their core competences are often not capable of performing all the innovation activities themselves. Innovation is increasingly becoming an inter-organizational activity: the firm works with one or more partners in the value chain to develop a new or improved business model (Chesbrough, 2003; Vanhaverbeke et al., 2008). In Europe, BT, Siemens, Nokia, and Ericsson all now engage in co-creation. They realize that you often get better ideas if you examine a problem together with others. The old *not invented here* mentality is giving way to *proudly found elsewhere*.

Chesbrough (2011a, 2011b) cites two factors which explain the growth of open innovation business models: the growing costs of R&D and the shortening life cycles of many products. Developing a production facility for semiconductors cost Intel as much as $3 billion in 2006, while twenty years earlier it was investing less than 1 per cent of that amount. The development costs of new products in the pharmaceutical industry have increased tenfold in a decade. Even the fast-moving consumer goods sector is feeling the pressure. Procter & Gamble estimates that developing a new product has become two to five times more expensive over the same period. We can see similar changes elsewhere. For example, in the early 1980s a generation of hard disk drives had a lifetime of four to six years. By the 1990s it was no more than six to nine months. The advantage conferred by a patent in the pharmaceutical sector is also much more short-lived, because test procedures take longer and rivals enter the market faster with generic medicines.

The benefits of scale can by no means always compensate for the increase in development costs and the shorter life cycles.

These trends make it increasingly difficult to justify investments in R&D. Open innovation offers some consolation. It tackles the cost side by making use of external research and development resources, and the revenue side by generating new revenues from new business models (see Figure 2.9). Thus Procter & Gamble creates new brands by taking out licences for technologies from firms all around the world. This has resulted in products such as the Spin brush, a battery-operated toothbrush which brought the company $200 million in sales in its first year. In addition, the firm earns revenue from selling licences for technology for which it cannot create a cost-effective business model itself (Chesbrough, 2011a). Figure 2.9 shows the revenues and costs of innovation in closed and open innovation models.

Although the phenomenon has been around longer, the concept of co-creation is generally ascribed to Prahalad. The now deceased management guru wrote the book *The Future of Competition* with Ramaswamy in 2004. Several definitions have been provided since then to clarify the concept. Co-creation is a form of innovation where markets are regarded as forums in which firms and customers share, combine, and renew their ideas. Dialogue plays an important part in this process. The main focus has been on co-creation in inter-organizational (Chatterji and Fabrizio, 2014) and

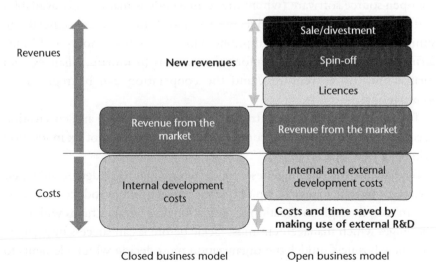

Figure 2.9 Revenues and costs of innovation in closed and open innovation models
Source: adapted from Chesbrough (2011a)

manufacturing settings (Mention, 2011). Markets are also regarded as a series of conversations between customers and the firm. Co-creation enables customers to participate in the development process, adapt it to their own context, and define and solve shared problems. Developing solutions and selling them to customers has given way to a stronger emphasis on developing solutions *with* customers (Teece, 2010; Vargo and Lusch, 2008). For instance, Apple's business model is designed to 'own the customer' (Montgomerie and Roscoe, 2013). Lego has created the 'Ambassador Program' to improve both its interaction with customers and interaction between customers. This has given the Danish company access to new ideas and business partnerships, while the more adult Lego fans have influenced the company's decisions to come up with products for other parts of their market (Antorini et al., 2012).

Co-creation means opening up the organization to customers, suppliers, complementary players in the value chain, and even rivals. Innovation can also be advanced through cooperation with universities and training institutes, industry bodies, or the government (e.g. Brandenburger and Nalebuff, 2011; Ritter et al., 2004).

Co-creation can take various forms, from developing new products with one or more large customers to opening up the innovation process completely. That is open innovation. Examples of far-reaching co-creation are open source software (where the source code is made freely available) and the development of products with and for lead users whose needs are similar to those of the general public. This can involve short- and long-term cooperation. There are informal variations (platforms, alliances) and formal ones (joint ventures), and the cooperation can be regional or international.

The difference between the traditional closed innovation and co-creation becomes especially clear if we compare the two on the basis of six innovation principles (see Table 2.3).

By drawing from the huge reservoir of ideas and knowledge outside their own organization, firms can rapidly develop, select, and introduce new business models through co-creation. Co-creation does present firms with three challenges which management must tackle before it can successfully generate a new business model: the organization must decide which elements to keep closed, and which to open up; it must be able to select and absorb new knowledge; and it must be able to adapt the routines to fit the new model of the organization (e.g. Berchicci, 2013; Cassiman and Veugelers, 2006).

Table 2.3 Six principles of closed and open innovation

	Closed innovation principles	Open innovation principles
1	The cleverest people in our field work for us.	Not all clever people work for us, so we have to obtain knowledge from clever people from outside.
2	In order to make R&D investments cost-effective we have to do the development, production, and marketing ourselves.	External R&D can realize significant value; internal R&D is needed for us to appropriate a part of that value.
3	If we discover it ourselves, we are the first on the market.	We do not have to be the inventors in order to profit from R&D.
4	If we are the first to commercialize a new technology, we will win.	Building a superior business model is more important than being the first on the market.
5	If we produce the most and the best ideas in our sector, we will win.	If we can make the best use of internal and external ideas, we will win.
6	We must protect our intellectual property so that our rivals cannot profit from our ideas.	We must realize a profit on the use of intellectual property by third parties and we must purchase intellectual property from others if that strengthens our business model.

Source: adapted from Chesbrough (2011b)

Wrap-up

Firms constantly change their business models in order to compete effectively. They can use various levers: develop new or improved technology, create new management practices, adopt new organizational forms, and engage in co-creation. This leads to the improvement or replication of the existing business model or to the invention of an entirely new business model, that is, business model renewal.

To what extent do firms innovate their business models? How do they do that successfully? In the following chapter we deal with these and other questions and present new insights with the help of findings from our research.

3

How Firms Modify Their Business Model

Replication or Renewal

· ·

CLAYMOUNT TECHNOLOGIES GROUP EXPANDED ITS ACTIVITIES
FROM HIGH-VOLTAGE PLUGS AND CABLES TO SYSTEM COMPONENTS
SUCH AS THE SMARTBUCKY DM

Claymount Technologies Group, which is based in Dinxperlo in the Netherlands, is an example of a firm which has changed its business model fundamentally. Claymount designs and manufactures components for X-ray equipment in healthcare and industrial applications. While the firm at first limited itself to high-voltage plugs and cables, it now supplies a variety of system components for both ends of the cable, that is, generators on the one side and detection systems on the other. One such detection system is the SmartBucky DM. It can be used to upgrade analogue mammography equipment to a digital standard so that X-ray exposures can be digitized immediately, displayed on a monitor, and stored. Unlike its rivals, Claymount is not tied to specific brands, so the firm can offer universal and integrated solutions. Manufacturers of X-ray equipment such as Philips, GE, and Siemens are concentrating increasingly on the integration of systems. They subcontract the development of parts to firms like Claymount. Claymount has done well out of these developments. Since its establishment in 2002, the firm has grown from 38 employees to 240, and its turnover in 2012 grew by 26 per cent.

· ·

Introduction

In the preceding chapters, business model innovation was shown to be of vital importance to organizations which operate in markets with a high level of competitive pressure and environmental dynamism. We have seen how four levers (technology, management, organizational form, and co-creation) can be used to enable firms to replicate or renew their business model.

So much for the theory. Now for real life. How do firms 'innovate' their business models? What strategic choices are involved? To what degree are these choices affected by the level of competitive pressure and environmental dynamism the firm is facing? We questioned more than 590 firms on these points, and their answers form the basis of this chapter. We sketch a picture here of the situation in the various sectors. We also discuss how competitive pressure, environmental dynamism, and company performance are linked to the various options for business model innovation. When and why do firms choose replication or renewal? What do they gain by it? We have selected a number of case studies to illustrate our findings.

Business model innovation

The first thing which struck us in our research was that firms are more preoccupied with replication than with renewal. It should be noted, however, that there are few cases of 'pure' replication. Most commonly, firms will use a mix, though there is also a relatively large group of firms that do little in the way of renewal (see Figure 3.1). When we compare the two forms of business model innovation, certain things emerge quite clearly.

Cases of pure renewal or replication are rare

- There are almost no cases (0.3 per cent) of 'pure' business model renewal. This can be explained by the *renewal trap* (Levinthal and March, 1993). This means that organizations spend increasing amounts of time renewing their business model, but are not really capable of commercializing it. A new business model must start yielding a return at some point as the company exploits the competences and market positions it has acquired. If a firm fails to capitalize on the benefits to be gained from improving and expanding its business model, this will leave room for rivals to move in, and may also mean that the firm does not realize a sufficient return for its shareholders.

- Similarly, very few firms (2 per cent) focus exclusively on business model replication. This can be explained by the *competency trap* (Levinthal and March, 1993; Levitt and March, 1988). Here, because the first incremental improvements bring rapid success, organizations keep making further step-by-step refinements to their business model, leading to a vicious circle of replication. A firm which pushes the replication of its existing business model to the extreme discovers that the short-term success it achieves comes at the expense of the capacity to renew. At a certain point, rivals with radically different approaches will outrun these firms. When market demand declines, they will not have the necessary competences to renew radically (Volberda, 2003).

One in three firms has found a balance between replication and renewal

- About one in three firms (see Figure 3.1) has an average-to-high focus on both replication and renewal. Firms in this group are capable of both refining their existing model and developing new models. In some cases there is greater emphasis on replication, while in others the emphasis is on renewal. A select group (14 per cent) combines an above-average focus on replication with an above-average degree of renewal (*dual focus*). These firms have managed to find a balance between their new and existing business models in terms of where they gain their competitive advantage, and they jump from one product life cycle to the next, or switch to an entirely new sector.

One in three firms pays no attention to its business model

- The number of firms with extremely low scores on both dimensions is also limited (11 per cent). They suffer from what we term 'business model fixation'. They can apparently afford to hold on to their existing business models, which are regarded as cash cows. They do this by operating in a very rigid way, with stability and preservation of existing business as their key objective—and this will work so long as the market does not change.

- There is another group of firms which achieve no more than average scores on one axis and low scores on the other. They excel at neither replication nor renewal. Within this group we can see on the one hand highly entrepreneurial firms (8 per cent) that border on the chaotic and pay absolutely no attention to performance. On the other hand, we see organizations which focus on the short term (13 per cent). While they do change steadily in line with the environment, they produce virtually no fundamentally new knowledge or products.

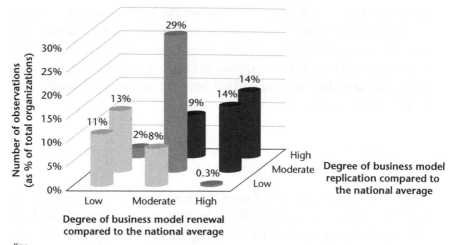

Figure 3.1 Distribution of organizations across renewal and replication

Key:
Low: 25% of the lowest scores of respondents on either business model replication or business model renewal
High: 25% of the highest scores of respondents on either business model replication or business model renewal
Moderate: remaining 50% of the respondents with average scores on either business model replication or business model renewal

One in three firms pays only moderate attention to business model innovation

- Finally, there is the largest group of firms, achieving average scores for both replication and renewal (29 per cent). The firms in this group pay similar amounts of attention to the two forms of business model innovation. Besides these 'average Joes', there are therefore two further categories which can be distinguished. The first is a group of firms with high to average scores on both replication and renewal (see dark grey bars in Figure 3.1). Around 37 per cent of the firms belong to this group. The second category of firms which differ from those in the average bracket are those which score average to low for both replication and renewal (see light grey bars in Figure 3.1). Around 32 per cent of the firms belong to this group.

Business model innovation according to sector

Do business model renewal and replication differ by sector? The level of replication and renewal in each industry reflects the clock speed of the sector— that is, the rate at which new business models evolve (Fine, 1998; Nadkarni and Narayanan, 2007). Environmental, economic, and technological shocks can increase the clock speed of an industry, forcing individual firms to renew or replicate new business models more frequently. The faster the clock speed of a sector, the shorter the life of a business model, and so the more frequently firms have to renew and replicate their business model. From our survey of Dutch firms, we can see several sectors that appear to have a high clock speed, with businesses scoring highly on replication and renewal: life sciences and information and communications (ICT), and to a lesser degree, the food sector (see Figure 3.2). One example of a life sciences firm is Roche Diagnostics (see case illustration). Firms in the government and the energy sectors score just below the Dutch national average for both replication and renewal. The same applies to a lesser extent for those in the construction sector. These sectors have a definitely lower clock speed.

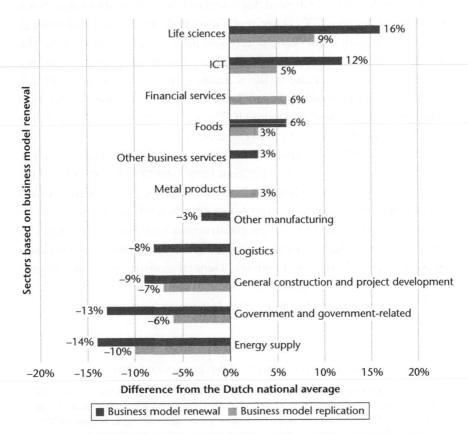

Figure 3.2 Degree of business model renewal and business model replication per sector

N.B.: Missing bars represent values that are not significantly lower or higher than the national average.

Table 3.1 Four categories of business model innovation and sector fit

Focus on fixation	Replicators	Radical renewers	Dual focus
Little renewal and replication	Average-to-high score on replication	Average-to-high score on renewal	Average-to-high score on renewal and replication
• government and government-related • construction • energy supply	• financial services • metal products • other manufacturing* • logistics*	• other business services	• life sciences • ICT • foods

* the other manufacturing and logistics sectors do not score above average on replication, but they do have significantly lower scores on renewal compared to the Dutch national average.

Of the sectors we investigated, life sciences (16 per cent above the Dutch national average) and ICT (12 per cent above) make the most use of renewal. Other sectors with above-average levels of business model renewal are the food sector (6 per cent above) and other business services (3 per cent above).

Replication is used most in life sciences (9 per cent above the Dutch national average), followed by financial services (6 per cent above). Replication is also used to a considerable extent in ICT (5 per cent above), foods (3 per cent above), and metal products (3 per cent above).

When we look at the combination of renewal and replication, the energy sector comes in last (renewal 14 per cent below the Dutch national average and replication 10 per cent below), closely followed by government (renewal 13 per cent below and replication 6 per cent below). Sectors with a low degree of renewal are the general construction and project development sector (9 per cent below), logistics (8 per cent below), and other manufacturing industry (3 per cent below). General construction and project development (7 per cent below) also score lowest on replication.

The main sectors represented within our research are grouped clearly in Table 3.1.

. . . .

BUSINESS MODEL RENEWAL AT ROCHE DIAGNOSTICS

Roche Diagnostics has set up a new arm, lab consultancy, designed to service hospital laboratories. The objective is to provide activities which hospitals used to carry out themselves. With this new arm Roche is anticipating specializing in healthcare. The biotechnological firm also organizes various events, such as 'the future starts today', which are intended to identify developments in the healthcare market. This is how Roche attempts to anticipate changes in the sector faster.

. . . .

The effects of business model innovation on company performance

It was shown in the previous section that a focus on renewal does not automatically have to be at the expense of a focus on replication, or vice versa. Firms with a dual focus perform considerably better than those which become fixated on one existing business model. If the performance of the latter group, which consists mainly of organizations in energy supply, government, and construction, is taken as the reference point, the first group performs on average 18 per cent better (see Figure 3.3). The firms with a dual focus also score highest on specific performance criteria (see Tables 3.3 and 3.4). From 2010 until 2012 this group achieved an annual growth in sales of 11 per cent and an annual increase in return on assets of 20 per cent. In terms of sector, the dual-focus firms are found mostly in life sciences, but also in ICT and the food sector.

Various management scholars (e.g. Benson–Rea et al., 2013; Markides and Oyon, 2010; Velu and Stiles, 2013) have indicated that using several

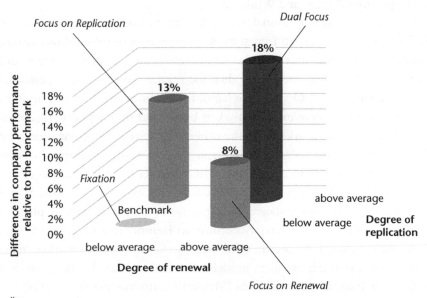

Key:
Below average: 50% lowest scores of respondents on either business model replication or business model renewal
Above average: 50% highest scores of respondents on either business model replication or business model renewal

Figure 3.3 Company performance at various levels of renewal and replication

business models which employ both replication and renewal is more effective for ensuring success than a single business model where the focus is on either replication or renewal. Firms that have multiple business models have been described as operating with dual (Markides and Charitou, 2004; Velu and Stiles, 2013), hybrid (e.g. Bonaccorsi et al., 2006), or parallel business models (e.g. Clausen and Rasmussen, 2013; Velu and Stiles, 2013), though there are some slight conceptual differences between these terms. These kinds of business models serve performance in the short and the longer term (e.g. Andries et al., 2013; Heij et al., 2014; Markides, 2013). Our results showed that firms with these dual business models not only had strong company performance, but also had a growth in sales of 11 per cent and in return on assets of 20 per cent (see Tables 3.3 and 3.4).

According to Velu and Stiles (2013: 445), business model renewal is 'inevitably disruptive of the existing business model—so the new business model conflicts with the old'. Notwithstanding the contradictory nature of these two business models, they are also interdependent, have the potential to be compatible, and can complement one another (Benson-Rea et al., 2013; Smith et al., 2010; Velu and Stiles, 2013). A new business model can to some extent have synergies with the existing model (e.g. Markides and Oyon, 2010), with shared elements such as branding or logistical activities serving a dual purpose (Helfat and Winter, 2011).

Combining business model renewal with business model replication enables a firm not only to capitalize even more on the value of its existing knowledge and activities but also to address unmet customer needs and preferences. Organizations with a dual focus raise their company performance in various ways. On the one hand, they refine their existing business model in order to serve existing markets better, and they replicate this business model in other markets. On the other, they seize new opportunities by developing fundamentally new business models. Using multiple business models enables a firm to address different customer needs and to target different markets or market segments (Benson-Rea et al., 2013; Clausen and Rasmussen, 2013)—for instance, by using e-commerce as well as physical outlets (Amit and Zott, 2001). According to Benson-Rea et al. (2013: 726), 'firms differentiate between their business models in terms of market channels.' Having multiple business models increases a firm's flexibility to deal with more dynamic environments (McGrath, 2010; Voelpel et al., 2005).

Firms which at least weigh up the pros and cons of both replication and renewal perform better than those that fail to consider either. The ones

Table 3.2 Performance of firms at various levels of replication and renewal

Focus on fixation	Replicators	Radical renewers	Dual focus
Little renewal, little replication	High score on replication	High score on renewal	High scores on renewal and replication
0% (reference point)	13% better performance	8% better performance	18% better performance

Table 3.3 Average annual growth in sales over a three-year period (2010–2012) at various levels of replication and renewal

	Business model renewal low	Business model renewal high
Business model replication low	1%	-1%
Business model replication high	7%	11%

Table 3.4 Average annual increase in return on assets over a three-year period (2010–2012) at various levels of replication and renewal

	Business model renewal low	Business model renewal high
Business model replication low	1%	3%
Business model replication high	7%	20%

that do weigh up are often found in financial services, other business services, and in other manufacturing industries. Here the scores for replication are slightly higher (13 per cent) than for renewal (8 per cent). The replicating group seems to be particularly good at creating and using opportunities in or close to existing territory. These opportunities involve relatively few risks and can be exploited relatively rapidly (Andries et al., 2013; Schneider and Spieth, 2013; Voelpel et al., 2005), so firms in this group deliver better performance—at least in the short run—than those in the group which focuses on renewal. Firms which replicate also perform better than those in the fixation group (see Tables 3.3 and 3.4). They demonstrate a higher growth in sales and a better return on assets (both 7 per cent). But the attractive returns offered by replication also entail risks, especially for the longer term. We explain this in more detail in Chapter 7.

Firms which mainly use a renewal approach experience an average 3 per cent increase in the return on assets, but also a slight decrease (a drop of 1 per cent) in turnover. They invest in the future, and they may also be active in a new and possibly smaller market (or market segment) and operate with more attractive margins than those firms that are in a permanent state of business model fixation.

Organizations which concern themselves very little with either renewal or replication perform the worst. For this group trapped in business model fixation, there had been scarcely any increase in turnover or return on assets over the past three years (both an increase of 1 per cent). Joseph Schumpeter's (1942) warning is especially applicable to this group: 'not investing in innovation may be riskier than investing in innovation because the risk of investing is limited to the investment while the risk of not investing may be complete erosion of the market' (Ahuja et al., 2008: 50).

Firms that focus on business model fixation stand by their existing principles; they are in denial mode. This seems to create certainty, but it actually causes uncertainty, because rivals rush ahead on all sides. The disclaimer often made in the world of finance—that past results are no guarantee of future performance—applies to these firms. Table 3.2 summarizes the findings.

The effects in more detail

Business model renewal and business model replication do not affect the company performance in identical ways. While replication yields immediate improvements in company performance, with renewal performance only starts to improve at a later stage (see Figure 3.4). In the first instance, there is more value to be gained from using replication.

Replication allows organizations to smooth out irregularities in their existing business models and take up existing opportunities, which results in further sharpening of the models (Demil and Lecocq, 2010; Schneider and Spieth, 2013). With replication, the organization's sphere of activity is gradually expanded. Japanese car manufacturers who constantly refine their models are a good example of this.

Organizations which undertake some degree of renewal run the risk of clashes with the existing business model. This can lead to the new business model not receiving the attention and resources it needs to become successful. Due to the threat of cannibalization of the old business model, the old

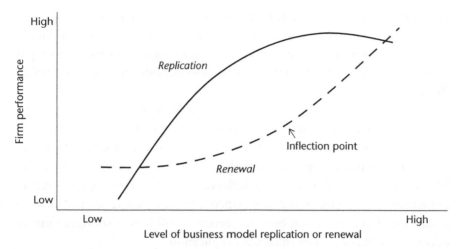

Figure 3.4 Renewal, replication, and company performance

model, with its more certain returns, is given priority in the short term (Srinivasan et al., 2004; Voelpel et al., 2005). Furthermore, a newish business model is often very close to existing markets (e.g. Casadesus-Masanell and Tarziján, 2012; Markides and Oyon, 2010), with the danger that rivals with aggressive short-term actions can undermine its value.

When business model renewal is more extensive, the effect on the company performance is positive. At that level, firms enter *blue oceans* (new markets) with more attractive returns or they create those new markets themselves (Kim and Mauborgne, 2005). Firms that renew more intensively have more experience, more courage, and more confidence to change their business fundamentally, which means they are also better able to identify new markets and develop new business models (Mitchell and Coles, 2003; McGrath, 2010). There is a virtuous circle at play here. Organizations with more expertise in renewal and a greater capacity to absorb knowledge can identify new opportunities faster and tend to take them earlier. This raises the level of aspiration within the organization. At the same time, the organization gains more expertise in renewal by seizing new opportunities (Cohen and Levinthal, 1990).

Organizations which develop new business models frequently have a more flexible structure (Bock et al., 2012; Wirtz et al., 2010). They are more willing to depart from current strategies in order to renew products fundamentally and to create new product/market combinations. Internally there are also fewer barriers to renewal, there is an environment in which new information is processed and used better, and there is a greater willingness to abandon existing investments in favour of investments in future developments. This means that organizational resources can be put to better use in order to seize opportunities outside the current domain (McGrath, 2010).

That is why, when the changes involve a high degree of renewal, the organization will do better to concentrate on this, rather than trying to focus also on replication. At a given point in time, the emphasis therefore has to shift from replication to renewal (see the turning point in Figure 3.4). This turning point, also called the 'inflection point' (Grove, 1997), is where the relative improvement in performance is higher with renewal than with replication. From this point onwards, renewal will have a stronger positive effect on company performance than replication.

An extreme shift, where an organization commits itself fully to using only radically new business models, entails a temporary reduction in company performance (McGrath, 2010; Volberda, 2003). In short, switching rapidly from replication to renewal comes at a price. Earlier in this chapter it was shown that organizations must combine renewal with replication in order to deliver better performance. That is how replication generates revenue which can be used to develop new business models and how renewal serves as a seedbed for further replication.

There are various ways for firms to shift from replication to greater renewal or to make a full switch to renewal. As research has shown (e.g. Anthony and Christensen, 2005; Casadesus-Masanell and Zhu, 2013; Christensen et al., 2002; Govindarajan and Trimble, 2011; Mullins and Komisar, 2009; Ofek and Wathieu, 2010), to develop a new business model an organization must take the following steps as a minimum:

• It needs to have processes in place that enable assumptions about the existing business model to be brought up for discussion.

• It must seek out non-traditional information (i.e. 'don't hear only what you want to hear').

• It must look at the deeper implications of certain trends (especially trends on the periphery of its core markets).

• It must have a vision of the areas in which it wants to operate. This can be achieved by bringing together people who have knowledge of technologies, who understand the deeper needs of the customer, or who have a long-term view of developments in a particular field.

- In view of the high risks associated with renewal, an organization must develop a portfolio of options (i.e. 'don't put all your eggs in one basket').

The new business model can then be activated in several ways (e.g. Baden-Fuller and Morgan, 2010; Dunford et al., 2010; Markides, 2013; Mullins and Komisar, 2009):

- It can be activated all in one go, across the entire group. The risk of failure in this case is high.
- It can be developed and tested in a particular organizational unit (possibly a new unit), and, if successful, then rolled out across other units or the entire organization. The risks at corporate group level are smaller than with the first option. Replication is needed to roll out the new concept internally.
- It can be inspired by elements from existing business models of other firms. This can vary from copying elements of those business models to copying the whole business model, or combining business models (or elements of models) from different organizations.

The three options are not mutually exclusive: they can also be combined. Chapter 7 deals in more depth with how organizations can develop new business models alongside existing models.

With the first option, the old business model is no longer replicated. Instead, once the new business model has been activated, any subsequent replication is of the new model. With the second option, replication of the old business model is replaced more gradually by replication of the new model. Depending on the degree to which the new model was inspired by business models from other organizations, the third option allows some replication of the old model to continue.

The degree of environmental competitiveness is particularly significant in determining when a firm needs to shift from replication to renewal or to switch fully to renewal. This point is dealt with in the next section. As discussed in the introduction to this book, trends such as globalization, deregulation, and *Walmartization* are clear signs that many environments are becoming more dynamic and more competitive (e.g. Prahalad and Ramaswamy, 2004; Volberda et al., 2011). A dynamic environment is not automatically a competitive environment, however, and vice versa. Thus ASML Lithography, the leading manufacturer of systems used to produce silicone chips, operates in a very dynamic environment where there is rapid technological change (the number of components on a chip doubles every twelve months) and extremely volatile market demands, but the firm does not have much to fear from rivals. It has a market share of 90 per cent, and its key customers (Intel, TSMC, and Samsung) co-finance the firm's R&D into next-generation lithography technologies. By contrast, logistics firms generally have to deal with an environment which is not very dynamic, but where the competitive pressures and number of similar competitors are very high.

Environmental dynamism

Environmental dynamism refers to the frequency and intensity of the changes taking place in a firm's environment (Dess and Beard, 1984; Volberda, 1998). Changes in technologies, variations in customer preferences, fluctuations in product demand and supply of raw materials, as well as regulatory changes (Volberda, 1998; Wirtz et al., 2010), make a firm's existing business model more short-lived (Demil and Lecocq, 2010). This increases the need to undertake business model renewal (Osiyevskyy and Dewald, 2015b; Voelpel et al., 2005).

Although our findings with various levels of environmental dynamism do not suggest that a high degree of business model renewal is significantly better for company performance than a high degree of replication, environmental dynamism does nevertheless have an impact on the relationship between renewal and company performance. Regardless of the environmental dynamism, the more firms replicate their business model, the more beneficial it will be in terms of company performance (a linear positive effect). By contrast, renewal flourishes especially in a moderately dynamic environment (see also Table 3.5).

While renewal has a positive effect on company performance in an extremely dynamic environment, in a moderately dynamic environment this effect becomes increasingly positive. One possible explanation is that organizations operating in reasonably dynamic environments have both the need and the time to develop a business model which is tailored to the characteristics of their particular environment (Mitchell and Coles, 2003; Mullins and Komisar, 2009). In rapidly changing environments, new business models can become outdated even before they have been developed and implemented. The poorer fit between the new business model and the

Table 3.5 Performance effects of business model renewal at various levels of environmental dynamism

Level of environmental dynamism	Effect of renewal on company performance
high	positive
moderate	increasingly positive
low	none

changing environment might decrease the financial rewards to be achieved from it (Heij et al., 2014; Posen and Levinthal, 2012; Schilke, 2014). Developing new business models takes more time and money than refining existing business models (Johnson et al., 2008; McGrath, 2010). And even if a new business model is a reasonably good fit for the firm's environment when introduced, rapid environmental changes such as changes in customer preferences might reduce the number of the opportunities to be addressed with that new model (Heij et al., 2014; Posen and Levinthal, 2012; Zook and Allen, 2011).

On the other hand, in stable environments firms have more time to develop a business model which is in line with environmental characteristics, but less need to do so (Heij et al., 2014; Posen and Levinthal, 2012; Schilke, 2014). In this kind of environment, business model renewal does not help to achieve better company performance.

Our data show that firms in more dynamic environments tend to go for renewal, rather than replication. When there is more environmental dynamism, options come and go more rapidly, giving firms less time to build on their existing business model. This forces them to search more for models that are radically different. As the environment becomes more dynamic, there must be sufficient investment in renewal as well as replication to prevent company performance from declining.

Environmental competitiveness

Environmental competitiveness refers to the degree of action and reaction between providers in a particular market (Matusik and Hill, 1998; Volberda, 1998). The number of rivals in a market can be used as a rough indication of this (Miller, 1987). High levels of environmental competitiveness are one reason why firms need to create new value for customers, and to find ways of wrong-footing their rivals (Markides and Oyon, 2010; Voelpel et al., 2005).

Many business models are unsuccessful because insufficient regard is paid to competition when they are being developed. The success or failure of a business model depends to a large extent on how it interacts with the business models of other players (Ansari et al., 2016; Casadesus-Masanell and Ricart, 2011). A business model does not always have to tackle rivals head-on: it can block or disrupt the development of rivals' business models, but it can also be positioned in such a way that it complements these other business models (Casadesus-Masanell and Ricart, 2011; Markides and Oyon, 2010).

. . . .

USE YOUR RIVAL TO HELP FORGE CLOSER RELATIONSHIPS WITH CUSTOMERS

A successful business model can be built on cooperation with rivals. When competitors are also a firm's collaborating partners, this is sometimes referred to as co-opetition (Brandenburger and Nalebuff, 2011). One example is Air France-KLM, which set up SkyTeam, together with various other airlines, in order to strengthen their relationships with existing clients and to attract new clients. This cooperative venture gives the airlines access to the regions and connections of their partners. The advantage for Air France-KLM is that code-sharing allows it to offer more destinations. This also increases the value of Air France-KLM's existing routes.

A more paradoxical example of how competition can help an organization is the carpet maker Desso, based in Waalwijk in the Netherlands. Desso is the leading supplier of floor coverings for cruise ships and aeroplanes. A large cruise line decided to switch to a cheaper Chinese supplier. However, the Chinese firm was unable to deliver the carpet to size, so it took more time to lay. The ship thus had to stay several days longer in dock. This costs millions, and the benefit for the cruise line was lost. As a result, Desso regained its customer.

The French firm Blablacar also benefited from mistakes by its rival, which allowed it to scale up its business model. Blablacar is a long-distance ride-sharing service which connects drivers with empty seats to people travelling in the same direction. To become members of Blablacar, individuals must register and create a personal online profile, which then subsequently features ratings and reviews by other members. Each user profile also includes a 'BlaBla' measurement, which indicates how much they are willing to chat during a trip. Blablacar wanted to expand into Germany. With earlier expansions, such as into Italy and Russia, they had acquired small local firms in order to grow rapidly. However, in Germany there was already a large local rival, Carpooling.com. With over six million members, this German company was too large to be taken over. The founders of Blablacar initially accepted this. They built their own German website, but only a few German drivers and hitchhikers joined their platform. Then their main competitor Carpooling.com made a huge mistake. 'From one day to the other, they started to charge the car drivers,' says Nicolas Brusson, one of the founders of Blablacar. In just eighteen months Blablacar had captured 15 per cent of the German market. German car drivers shifted in large numbers from Carpooling.com to Blablacar because on the

Blablacar platform it is only passengers who are required to pay a small fee. 'For a passenger this is normal. But for a driver this feels like paying tax,' says Brusson. Once Blablacar had gained a large share of the market, they were then able to take over Carpooling.com. The lesson that Brusson learned is that the first-mover is not always the winner. Sometimes mistakes by a first-mover rival allow you to scale up your business model (Financieele Dagblad, 2016).

The business model of Royal IHC, the global leader in dredging vessels and equipment, is based on cooperation with low-cost shipyards in emerging economies. The firm was criticized by its customers for being expensive. Some customers decided to find a cheaper alternative shipbuilder. 'They later told us that doing it themselves turned out to be a bit more difficult than they had anticipated,' relates Goof Hamers, former President of Royal IHC. The firm went some way towards satisfying the demands of these customers by starting to build ships in low-wage countries. As Hamers explains, 'We said that, in the existing market in particular, you have to develop a technology niche. But you then have to use your technology in combination with lower wages so that you can access the middle market segment as well.'

The examples of Desso, Blablacar, and Royal IHC illustrate how you can strengthen your customer ties by using your rivals, though this applies largely to specialized sectors.

. . . .

Our findings suggest that when organizations operate in an extremely competitive environment, extensive replication has a negative effect on company performance. In these kinds of environment, organizations have to invest in renewal earlier so that they can find the *blue ocean* where the competition is less intense and can establish better performance (Kim and Mauborgne, 2005). This is also known as 'escaping the competition' (Hecker and Ganter, 2013). Established firms have to develop a fundamentally new business model (new to the firm and the market) in order to enter new markets successfully.

Firms can also weaken or reverse attacks by rivals. This is known as 'disrupting the disruptor' (Markides and Oyon, 2010). Firms quite often tend to imitate the business model of the successful disruptor. This is a trap. Wanting to play the game better than the disruptor who invented the new rules of play is not only difficult but it also reduces the distinctiveness of the players, allowing the disruptor to play the game even better (Markides and Oyon, 2010).

A good example of this mechanism is what happened to the many clones of Ryanair and EasyJet, after these two low-cost carriers had dramatically shaken up the European market for aviation in the 1990s. Ryanair's strength comes from having an extremely short turnaround time for its aircraft, searching constantly for new sources of income, and continually keeping its prices low. It has even offered flights for one penny in order to attract new customers. There is a virtuous circle in Ryanair's business model which continually strengthens the firm's own competences. The low fares ensure more passengers, more passengers means the planes are better filled, and the fixed costs per passenger are therefore lower. This allows Ryanair to offer even lower fares (Casadesus-Masanell and Ricart, 2011). The established airlines tried to imitate the success of the low-cost carriers, but their attempts were a dismal failure. The new initiatives ended up strengthening the original disruptors themselves. The Go firm set up by British Airways was acquired by EasyJet in 2002 (Markides and Charitou, 2004), and KLM's Buzz planes went to Ryanair after Buzz was dismantled.

Although there is no 'one size fits all' solution, developing a radically new business model can be a good means of combating the effect of a disruptor and transforming it into an opportunity (Gilbert and Bower, 2002; Markides and Oyon, 2010). In brief, it is more worthwhile in a highly competitive environment to focus on renewal than on replication (see also Figure 3.5). Investing in replication is more worthwhile for organizations facing moderate competition than for those in extremely competitive markets (see also Table 3.6). There is then an incentive for firms to stay ahead of their rivals by sharpening and refining their existing business models.

However, a firm can also be inspired by a rival's business model and use it to sharpen its own business model without the rival responding immediately in ways which undermine the value of the refined model. This

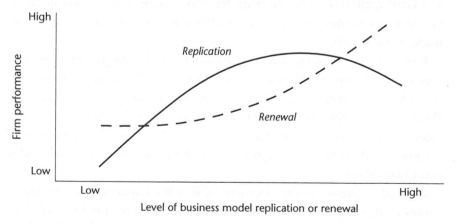

Figure 3.5 Effects of renewal and replication on company performance in a highly competitive environment

Table 3.6 Performance effects of business model replication and business model renewal at various levels of environmental competitiveness

Degree of competitiveness pressure	Better to renew or to replicate?
high	invest in a high degree of renewal
moderate	invest in a high degree of replication
low	use both approaches

provides scope for a firm to reduce the gap between it and leaders in the sector without those leaders responding with too much retaliatory action (Hecker and Ganter, 2013; Mol and Birkinshaw, 2009). The interplay of the business models of Airbus and Boeing provides a good example of this. Airbus's current business model is based on providing aviation services for large airports that use a hub-and-spoke system. Boeing's business model, on the other hand, has recently been oriented more to smaller airports that use a point-to-point system (Volberda et al., 2011). Airbus refined its model by introducing the Airbus 380 in order to compete with the Boeing 747. In response, Boeing refined its business model by bringing in a longer-range version of its 777-200 model line. It also developed the Boeing 787 Dreamliner, designed for comfort and efficiency, and Airbus then developed the A350 in response. The two companies are also sometimes triggered by each other's action in other areas, such as in fuel efficiency or in-flight entertainment. However, their duopoly market position gives each player enough room to partially replicate the opponent's model without the opponent taking immediate action to sabotage the replicated model.

Environmental dynamism and competitiveness

Environmental dynamism and competitiveness thus influence the relationship between business model renewal, replication, and company performance. Various sectors experience high levels of environmental dynamism (see Figure 3.6). This concerns ICT (20 per cent above the Dutch national average), foods (10 per cent above), life sciences (10 per cent above), financial services (7 per cent above), and construction (6 per cent above) in particular. It is not entirely coincidental that these sectors also score relatively highly on renewal and replication. In contrast to the high levels of environmental

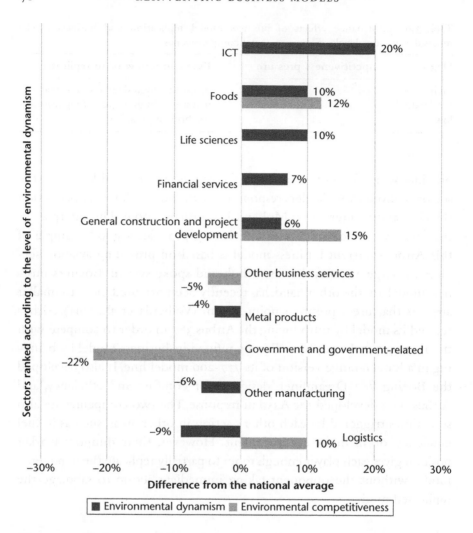

Figure 3.6 Environmental dynamism and competitiveness in different sectors in the Netherlands

N.B.: Missing bars represent values not significantly lower or higher than the national average. In particular, the levels of both environmental dynamism and competitiveness in energy supply are not significantly lower or higher than the Dutch national average.

dynamism firms in the ICT and life sciences sectors are facing, these sectors—the top two in renewal as well as replication—do not have significantly higher levels of environmental competitiveness than the 'average' industry. This means that firms in these very dynamic sectors are generally capable of finding *blue oceans* or even creating them themselves.

In this respect, the construction sector is the odd man out. Although there is an above-average level of environmental dynamism in this sector, and it also has the most competitive environment of any of the sectors we looked at, the firms in this sector nevertheless scored relatively low on both renewal and replication. One possible explanation for this is that extremely high levels of environmental competitiveness make the margins so low that there are scarcely any resources for renewal (Aghion et al., 2005), despite this being needed to keep up with or overtake the competition and adapt to the changing environment.

In an environment with little competition, renewal is less essential. The lack (22 per cent below the Dutch national average) of competitive pressure in government and government-related organizations thus explains why they pay relatively little attention to business model innovation.

In the metal industry and other manufacturing industries, the environment is not very dynamic. Firms in these sectors score 4 and 6 per cent below the national average, respectively. They do not score significantly higher on renewal either, although firms in the metal industry more frequently replicate their business model (3 per cent above).

The logistics sector is much more complicated. Our data show that firms in logistics definitely do not operate in a very dynamic environment (9 per cent below), but the degree of competition is, however, quite high (10 per cent above). This suggests that, to cope successfully with an environment which is relatively stable but highly competitive, firms in this sector should replicate their business model frequently in order to increase their efficiency and boost performance. Earlier in this chapter we highlighted that logistics firms do very little to renew their business model (8 per cent below), and this is in line with the low level of dynamism they face. However, they also do not excel at replication, and this leads to serious performance issues for firms in this sector.

Wrap-up

Firms prefer replication to renewal, although some firms may combine high levels of both renewal and replication. Most firms, however, have average scores for both renewal and replication. One in three firms pays no attention at all to its business model. Renewal works well in extremely dynamic and competitive environments, while replication is better suited to moderate levels of environmental dynamism and competitiveness. A dual focus—where a firm works on both renewal and replication—ensures high levels of company performance. However, what the 'optimal' balance between the two will be depends on the degree of environmental dynamism and competitiveness. The life sciences, ICT, and food sectors are front-runners when it comes to business model innovation. The government and government-related, construction, and energy sectors lag behind.

How do you go about changing a business model? What drives the change, and which element should you start with? In Chapter 4 we will deal with these questions in more detail by looking at levers of business model innovation.

4

Levers for Business
Model Innovation

· ·

POLAROID, A LARGE PLAYER IN THE INSTANT PHOTOGRAPHY
MARKET, INVESTED HEAVILY IN DIGITAL IMAGING

The American firm Polaroid dominated the instant photography market for a large part of the twentieth century. Like Kodak, it used a razor blade business model, the core of which was the large margin on rolls of film. This business model was overtaken by the rise of digital photography, which does not require rolls of film and makes it possible to share photographs on the internet.

How was it possible that Polaroid failed to switch successfully to the digital world? It was not due to the technological competences of the firm. Polaroid invested a great deal in the 1980s in developing state-of-the-art digital technology. The company's processes and capabilities were geared towards developing technological knowledge, which enabled them to develop good capabilities in digital imaging. But that strong focus on technological skills was not accompanied by exploration and targeting of new markets and distribution channels (Burgers et al., 2008). Top management remained so firmly wedded to their old formula for success that they ignored new rivals coming in from other sectors, such as computer electronics manufacturers (Tripsas and Gavetti, 2000). This resulted in Polaroid gradually losing its technological lead and not being able to capture a significant share of the digital photography market.

· ·

Introduction

Chapter 3 sketched a picture of successful and less successful business model innovation by firms. To gain more insight into how managers realize business model innovation, we also investigated the levers they use in this endeavour. In this chapter we examine the operation and the effects of the different levers.

The Polaroid case makes it clear that paying attention to one lever only—in this case new technology—will not necessarily make a firm able to cope with disruption. Other levers of business model innovation, including new organizational forms, new management practices, and co-creation, can be at least as important as technological innovation. As we argued in Chapter 2, mediocre technology combined with a superior business model can deliver more value than superior technology with a mediocre business model (e.g. Birkinshaw et al., 2008; Chesbrough, 2007; Teece, 2010; Volberda et al., 2014). For instance, why is Uber so successful with its online platform that connects passengers to taxi drivers, and why did the navigation system maker TomTom stop further investments in its taxi booking app?

Uber developed, markets, and operates the Uber mobile app, which allows consumers with smartphones to submit a trip request which is then routed to Uber drivers who use their own cars. As of May 2016 the service was available in over 66 countries and 449 cities worldwide. Around 2012, however, TomTom also introduced various apps, among them a taxi booking app which allowed people with iPhones to order a taxi (an Android version was not released). TomTom wanted to make the taxi market more reliable and transparent by providing all kinds of relevant information to taxi users, such as ratings and optimal routes. The app was free for users, but the taxi companies paid a fee (usually between €1 and €1.50 per ride) once they had taken more than 25 bookings. The app was rather similar to the one developed by Uber, but TomTom's management decided to retreat from that market in 2013. The two apps were very similar in functionality, suggesting that it was not a technological advantage that made Uber succeed where TomTom failed. In fact, TomTom is clearly superior to Uber in terms of technological capability, and is better able to facilitate mobility. However, its business model was not as advanced as that of Uber. Uber invested not only in technology, but even more in market development (attracting new taxi drivers and passengers) and in co-creation with new partners. Google Ventures invested $258 million in Uber in 2013. In December 2014 the Chinese search engine Baidu also made an investment in Uber in a deal that connected Uber to Baidu's mapping apps. In 2016 Toyota invested an undisclosed amount in Uber and looked into leasing options, which could potentially aid Uber drivers financially—a move made in response to other partnerships set up between Toyota's and Uber's rivals. And in 2015, two years after it had withdrawn its own taxi app, TomTom signed a multi-year agreement with Uber to provide maps and traffic information to Uber drivers in over 300 cities across the world.

Technology: limits of knowledge integration

In Chapter 2 we identified four levers of business model innovation: technology, management practices, organizational forms, and co-creation. First we will discuss the individual effects of these levers on replication and renewal. Later in this chapter we will discuss specific combinations which strengthen business model renewal in particular.

Not every lever contributes in the same way to business model innovation: the levers each have different effects on business model renewal and replication. Thus new technology (see Figure 4.1) makes a more significant contribution to renewal (27 per cent) than to replication (6 per cent).

Increases in new technology are not necessarily accompanied by correspondingly better performance in either replication or renewal (e.g. Acs and Audretsch, 1988; Zhou and Wu, 2010). Indeed, our data show that new technologies have a diminishing positive effect on both replication and renewal, and this applies especially to replication (see Figures 4.2a and 4.2b).

New knowledge and more diversity in the knowledge base give a firm more opportunities to commercialize that knowledge in ways that go beyond the logic of its existing business model. New technological knowledge is often the main source of business model renewal (Baden-Fuller

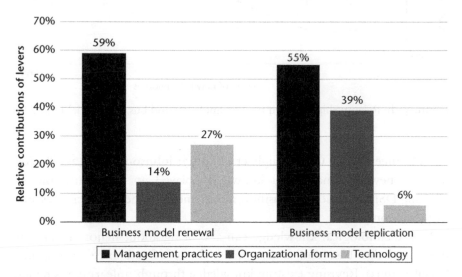

Figure 4.1 Relative contributions of levers to replication and renewal

N.B.: co-creation is not included in this figure. The effect of co-creation on renewal and replication will be explained later.

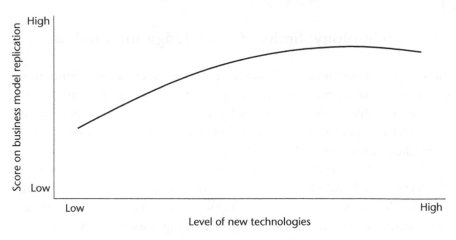

Figure 4.2a Relationship between new technologies and business model replication

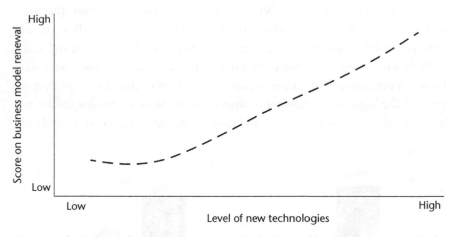

Figure 4.2b Relationship between new technologies and business model renewal

and Haefliger, 2013; Chesbrough et al., 2013; Johnson et al., 2008). For instance, new pharmaceutical knowledge played an important role in allowing DSM to renew its business model and become a life sciences and materials company.

New technological knowledge can also bring about major changes in the knowledge base and alter a firm's frame of reference (Zahra and Chaples, 1993). Revising existing knowledge through unlearning is beneficial for business model renewal (e.g. Forsman, 2009; Holmqvist, 2003).

New technological knowledge which challenges a firm's beliefs and core assumptions enables a firm to rethink and renew its operational processes and routines (e.g. Holmqvist, 2003; Wu and Shanley, 2009) and helps it to recognize new opportunities. These new opportunities often trigger the firm to renew its existing business model (Foss et al., 2013; Voelpel et al., 2005). For example, technological advancements enabled Amazon to renew its business model from online bookselling to an online retail, publishing, and media content organization.

However, the positive effect on business model renewal can diminish if there is an excessive amount of new knowledge (Acs and Audretsch, 1988; Graves and Langowitz, 1993). Integrating and utilizing a large quantity of new technological knowledge is more complicated and expensive, and requires more advanced and sometimes conflicting types of knowledge integration (e.g. Chesbrough et al., 2013; Erden et al., 2014; Grant, 1996). Business model renewal requires a firm to incorporate new technological knowledge into new processes, routines, and systems that deviate from or can even conflict with those already in place (Benner and Tushman, 2002, 2003; Zhou and Wu, 2010). In addition, the sheer volume of new knowledge can mean that the firm becomes less able to respond properly to the new knowledge (Katila and Ahuja, 2002) and can create confusion within the organization (Ahuja and Lampert, 2001). The additional cost of integrating new knowledge is ultimately greater than the advantages offered by the knowledge itself. The *information overload* reduces the capacity of organizations to react adequately to the new technological knowledge. Inertia and resistance within the organization can make organizations less able to incorporate new technologies (Ahuja and Lampert, 2001; Katila and Ahuja, 2002) and renew their business model. One of the results can be that these new technologies remain 'on the shelf'.

New technological knowledge not only broadens a firm's knowledge base but can also deepen it (Katila and Ahuja, 2002). Depth of knowledge is generally associated with increased experience and repeated usage (Levinthal and March, 1993). It often results in understanding of how to conduct operations more efficiently and smoothly (Szulanski and Jensen, 2008). When a firm has that deeper level of understanding of how its various activities are linked, its search for new ways of capturing or creating value will typically be based on either the same, or a very similar, logic to the one used in its current model (Benner and Tushman, 2003; Danneels, 2002).

The focus is thus on business model replication (Schneider and Spieth, 2013; Zhou and Li, 2012). For instance, knowledge refinement and improvement of their existing model in the domestic market, triggered companies such as ING Direct, Naturhouse, and Starbucks to replicate their business model by opening up branches in other countries (Dunford et al., 2010; Sosna et al., 2010). Nelson and Winter (1982) have drawn attention to powerful logics that apply when a technology is advanced in a certain direction. Knowing what the current and potential constraints of a given technology are can create what they call 'natural trajectories'. For example, advances in memory devices have gradually increased storage capacity from 1K to 4K, 64K to 256K and one megabyte, and so on (Nelson and Winter, 1982). A firm often needs to have used previous generations of a particular technology in order to use it for subsequent successful innovation (Ahuja et al., 2008; Levinthal and March, 1993).

On the other hand, the 'switching costs' or the costs of changing trajectories and acquiring knowledge that is unrelated to the firm's existing knowledge base can be quite high (Posen and Levinthal, 2012). In other words, the further you go in advancing a particular area of technology, the fewer benefits you are likely to gain from it (Katila and Ahuja, 2002). Extending the knowledge base beyond a certain point becomes increasingly complicated and expensive so the costs involved may eventually outweigh the benefits (Katila and Ahuja, 2002; Laursen, 2012). It thus becomes less likely that a firm will replicate its business model in order to commercialize that knowledge.

In addition, deepening a firm's knowledge base over time also reduces the value of new technological knowledge. If we think of a technology in terms of its life cycle, it will have three stages (introduction, growth, and maturity) and will follow an S-curve, with a definite flattening off as it moves into the third and final stage. In the maturity stage, moving towards the limits of a certain field of knowledge reduces the opportunities for more incremental steps, making it more likely that more radical steps will be needed to make progress (e.g. Sood and Tellis, 2005). Reduced potential for incremental steps implies that there will be fewer opportunities for business model replication. For example, as video technology reached its maturity stage, this restricted the potential for firms such as Blockbuster to replicate their movie rental model by opening further video stores (Volberda et al., 2011).

. . . .

HOW NETFLIX DISRUPTED BLOCKBUSTER BY ADOPTING NEW TECHNOLOGIES

Blockbuster opened as a small store in Dallas in October 1985. It became a dominant player in the video rental industry. The company operated over 7,400 video and game stores in the United States and in twenty other countries under the Blockbuster brand and under other brand names, including Xtra-Vision (in the Republic of Ireland and Northern Ireland) and Game Rush (Canada, Italy, Mexico, and Denmark). The business model was simple, as having the right titles in the right stores at the right times meant more rentals, so retailers could make even more money by making improvements to their distribution and inventory management. Figure 4.3 shows Blockbuster's impressive growth pattern up to around 2004. An important part of the firm's revenue model was the charging of substantial late fees. As such, a significant part of its profit came from penalizing its customers.

New technologies such as the DVD, and later streaming on the internet, seriously disrupted the firm's video delivery business model. The new entrant, Netflix, adopted these new technologies, and through a process of experimentation it evolved a superior business model based on prepaid subscription. Netflix first started a DVD-by-mail service in Scotts Valley, California, which allowed customers to have up to four movies at home at any one time, and to swap these for up to four new movies each month. The company initially had a hard time making its service commercially viable (as shown by the lowest part of Netflix's S-curve in Figure 4.3). At a point when it was close to folding, Netflix did simultaneous tests of three concepts that did work out: an unlimited rental programme, subscription billing, and a queue function for customers (a list of DVDs or streaming videos that they want to see). Co-founder Marc Randolph said, 'One of the most difficult things we ever did was to make the decision to stop selling, walk away from 95% of our revenue, and focus all our attention and resources on getting rental to work. What ultimately happened in sales—commoditization—turned out to be one of the smartest things we did as well.' Netflix's DVD-by-mail service, and later its personalized dynamic website, no longer required people to go to a video rental store. These technologies meant that firms like Netflix were able to offer greater variety to customers at lower cost, because they did not have to provide retail locations.

Blockbuster responded by trying to hang on and stretch the revenue S-curve of its existing business model (see Figure 4.3). Its board had a strong track record in retail, but not in e-commerce. Around the year 2000, Blockbuster even declined various opportunities to partner with Netflix or to acquire the company. Netflix subscriptions also diminished the value of Blockbuster's moneymaker: late fees. Netflix customers could keep a movie for as long as they wished, or return it and receive another one. In addition, Netflix invested in Cinematch technology, a software algorithm which gave customers recommendations on movies they might like, based both on the ratings they had given to other movies and on ratings provided by other people. This technology is aimed at maximizing the number of movies a customer rents. CEO Reed Hastings of Netflix commented that, 'It probably looks easy to imitate Netflix, but it's quite difficult to get all the details right that matter to a consumer. We've put four years' effort into building our service.'

While Blockbuster eventually started to offer internet-based subscription services in addition to its bricks-and-mortar stores (hybrid model), the threat of bankruptcy lingered on. Blockbuster's CEO James Keyes said in 2008, 'I have been frankly confused by this fascination that everybody has with Netflix. Netflix does not really have or do anything that we can't or don't already do ourselves.' By using cross-promotions, giving in-store rental coupons to online customers, and fulfilling online rental requests out of its store inventory, Blockbuster attempted to find ways of using its existing resources productively and improving its customer service. But Blockbuster's hybrid model resulted in a much higher cost structure. Blockbuster lost over $0.8 billion in revenues to Netflix and similar online competitors. In the end, Blockbuster's model could no longer compete, and the firm had little of value left in its business. In 2010 the company filed for bankruptcy in the United States.

Sources: Forbes (2014); USA Today (2015); Volberda et al. (2011)

Our data show that firms with a high degree of business model renewal invest on average 7.5 per cent of their sales in R&D. That is 1.4 times more than firms with a high degree of replication. Firms with a high degree of renewal which invest in ICT to support processes, products, and services devote an average of 5 per cent of their turnover to this. That is 1.3 times more than firms with a high degree of replication. By contrast, process innovation occurs more in firms which emphasize replication.

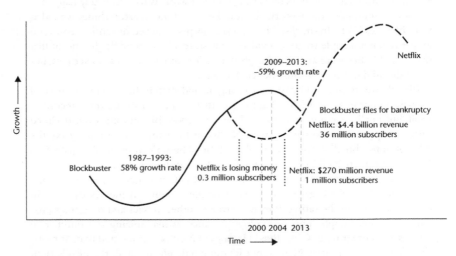

Figure 4.3 The Blockbuster and Netflix S-curves collide

Source: based on Samuel (2014); Volberda et al. (2011)

Management: adopting new management practices, processes, and techniques

Business model innovation requires a firm to reorchestrate its activities, resources, and relationships (e.g. Johnson et al., 2008). Management plays a fundamental role in taking care of this (e.g. Doz and Kosonen, 2010; Smith et al., 2010), but also in overcoming the associated barriers and challenges, such as organizational inertia, political forces, or fear of cannibalization (Cavalcante et al., 2011; Chesbrough, 2010). For example, incentive systems linked to sales of existing products encourage sales personnel to sell those products and make it less likely they will sell new products related to a new business model. Management practices such as providing appropriate sales training and the right incentive systems are required to ensure that business model innovation is easier to accomplish. It is quite surprising that the role of management practices in realizing and developing a business model (Mason and Spring, 2011) has received relatively limited attention (Baden-Fuller and Haefliger, 2013; Volberda et al., 2014).

A new management practice can be defined as 'the generation and implementation of a management practice, process, or technique that is new to the state of the art' (Birkinshaw et al., 2008: 829) and is intended to improve existing business models or develop fundamentally new ones. Basically, it involves changes in how managers perform their job (Hamel, 2006) and covers changes in the 'how' and 'what' of what managers do in setting directions, making decisions, coordinating activities, and motivating people (Birkinshaw, 2010; Hamel, 2006; Van den Bosch, 2012). New management practices are ambiguous and hard to copy, making them an important source of competitive advantage.

Management practices refer to what managers do as part of their job on a day-to-day basis, and include setting objectives and associated procedures, arranging tasks and functions, developing talent, and meeting various demands from stakeholders (Birkinshaw et al., 2008; Mol and Birkinshaw, 2009). For example, management can encourage employees to generate and develop ideas for business model innovation. Google's '20% time' philosophy is a renowned example. Google's employees are encouraged to spend 20 per cent of their time on initiatives they believe Google will benefit from. Typically, a project begins with around 5 to 10 per cent of the employee's work time. If it shows signs of success, then more time is devoted to the initiative by other colleagues—who volunteer for that project. The aim is to empower employees in order to boost their creativity and innovativeness. According to Google's HR manager Laszlo Bock (2015), the 20 per cent time 'operates somewhat outside the lines of formal management oversight, and always will, because the most talented and creative people can't be forced to work'. Business model innovations such as AdSense, Gmail, and Google News are all based on fun projects made possible by the 20 per cent time rule.

Management processes involve routines that govern the work of managers, which typically include performance assessment, strategic planning, and project management (Birkinshaw et al., 2008; Hamel, 2007). For instance, Whirlpool, one of the leading manufacturers of household appliances, introduced new management processes to improve its operations. The 'innovation from everyone, everywhere' idea of Whirlpool's CEO Dave Whitwam was brought in to increase the company's operational efficiency through major changes to management processes (Hamel, 2006). By combining a number of innovative internal management processes, such as putting innovation at the forefront of leadership development programmes, making it part of the top management's long-term bonus plan, and establishing innovation mentor programmes, the firm achieved an additional $500 million a year in operations. Modifying its managerial processes and routines in innovative ways allowed Whirlpool to differentiate its business model, enhance brand loyalty, and build a successful pipeline of new products (Genc et al., 2017).

Also firms such as HSBC in banking, Randstad in HR, and Aegon in insurance chose to compensate for their strict management processes focused on business model replication by adopting new incentive schemes and control systems in peripheral units. These new incentive schemes encouraged those units to experiment, to question existing assumptions, and to collaborate with outsiders, resulting in fundamentally new business models (Markides, 2015). For HSBC it led to the creation of an internet-based retail bank, First Direct, for Randstad to the provision of dedicated in-house services to large manufacturing firms, and for Aegon to the start-up of Kroodle, which uses an online insurance business model based on very widespread use of apps and social media.

There are also many different *management techniques* that can be used to support business model innovation, with common examples being the balanced scorecard and scenario planning (Waddell and Mallen, 2001). The balanced scorecard encourages managers to look at more than just financial metrics by putting a stronger emphasis on customer and innovation targets as well. It acts as a framework for translating strategic targets into coherent performance measures designed to stimulate improvement in, for instance, a firm's products, or its customer base and market position (Kaplan and Norton, 1995). For example, Procter & Gamble set a target of acquiring half of its innovation from outside of the company (Huston and Sakkab, 2006). This enabled the firm to develop new business models around Olay Regenerist (anti-ageing cosmetics), Swiffer Dusters, and Crest SpinBrush (Huston and Sakkab, 2006).

Scenario planning helps an organization to increase its ability to antici-pate and respond to relevant signals (Schoemaker et al., 2013). Such signals can play a vital role in driving business model innovation (e.g. Nunes and Breene, 2011), as we discuss in more detail in Chapter 7. Using scenario planning helped Shell to generate a long-term view of what the company might look like in the future. The value of this management technique for Shell lay principally in the fact that it has helped destroy the habit, rooted in most corporate planning, of imagining that 'the future will look much like the present' (Wilkinson and Kupers, 2013: 120). Because these scenarios were only hypothetical and therefore presented no direct threat, Shell executives were able to open their minds to developments they had never previously considered or countenanced. It facilitated a dialogue in which managers' assumptions could be brought into the open and challenged, which helped to reduce fragmented thinking and groupthink. This resulted in strategic conversations that went beyond the incremental, comfortable, and familiar progression (Wilkinson and Kupers, 2013). Challenging managerial assumptions and moving beyond incremental progression is precisely what is required for business model innovation, and business model renewal in particular. At Shell, scenario planning made managerial decisions more grounded in hypothetical futures, enabling the company to adapt faster. For example, Shell's takeover of BG Group in 2015 fits with its belief that natural gas will be vital to building a sustainable energy future. Shell proclaims itself to have been a pioneer in liquefied natural gas (LNG) for more than fifty years (Shell, 2016a), and this takeover should enable Shell to grow faster in the global LNG market, thereby replicating its business model. More recently, Shell's scenario of a lower-carbon future in which 'renewable energy sources like solar and wind could provide up to 40% of energy globally by 2060' (Shell, 2016b) encouraged the company to go beyond its dominant oil and gas activities by becoming active in new renewable energy, including offshore wind.

New management practices are fundamental for business model innovation (e.g. Foss and Saebi, 2015). They drive a firm's recognition of the need or opportunity for business model innovation and enable the firm to address that need accordingly (Doz and Kosonen, 2010; Gebauer, 2011). In addition, new management practices such as Toyota's lean production system are required to shape the organization of work and information flows both internally and externally in order to serve customers better (Itami and Nishino, 2010). For example, the shift by Hilti—a manufacturer of high-end power tools for the construction industry—from a product-based business model to a service-based model required it to bring in, among other things, new warehousing and inventory management systems (Johnson et al., 2008).

New management practices are also important in embedding a new business model in the organization. This involves the appointment of managers with responsibility for managing the new business model, and new management practices to build commitment to organization-wide goals and vision (e.g. Markides and Oyon, 2010; Smith et al., 2010). The new practices also provide a way of learning more about a firm's operations and customers (Itami and Nishino, 2010), which enables business model innovation (Dunford et al., 2010).

Our research shows that new management practices are found more in firms with high levels of renewal than in those with high levels of replication. Of all the four levers, new management practices contribute the most to both renewal and replication (see also Figure 4.1). The relative contribution in both cases is more than 50 per cent. Management is thus a crucial engine of business model innovation. The downside is that it can contribute to failure of an organization if deployed incorrectly, whether this is done deliberately or not. For instance, the system of management incentives at Lehman Brothers (the 'eat what you kill' compensation systems based on high individual bonuses) resulted in short-term vision, greed, internal competition, and an underestimation of the risks.

. . . .

NEW PROJECT MANAGEMENT PRACTICES: OTICON'S SPAGHETTI ORGANIZATION

In the 1980s Oticon, a Danish manufacturer of hearing aids, was a successful but traditional and hierarchical organization. In 1988, when Lars Kolind took up his position as CEO, he concluded that the firm needed more capability to renew itself and a stronger customer orientation. Kolind and his colleague Niels Jacobsen, who took over as CEO in 1991, brought in a new management practice based on self-managing project teams. All of the departments at Oticon were closed and replaced by projects. The resulting structure was a matrix, but a temporary and non-formalized one. Its uniqueness was defined by how projects were managed in the company. Kolind himself spoke of a spaghetti organization, because he himself saw connections in the apparent chaos. Employees could decide themselves to start projects or to sign up for one. There were project managers, but they did not have the power to force anyone to join a project group; they had to make the projects attractive to others through marketing activities. The system of voluntary subscription was implemented as Kolind believed that people are motivated if they choose their tasks themselves. The company did not use formal functions and even prohibited employees from focusing on one job. This measure was taken in order to promote diversity in the individual projects. The organization was left with just two levels: the CEO and his team of ten managers, and project teams. Physical changes were made to accommodate the new structure: in the new headquarters nobody had a permanent office and furniture could be freely moved around so that project teams could sit together. The offices were paperless and employees were given computers to use at home. Long before Google put one in, Oticon had a large transparent slide in the middle of its headquarters illustrating speed and openness. These new management practices were accompanied by slogans such as 'think the unthinkable'. By placing more emphasis on personal development, giving employees more responsibility for projects, and allowing them more autonomy, the firm was able to stimulate more intrinsic motivation among its workforce. This resulted in cost reductions on the one hand, as less control and coordination were required, and in significant growth in innovation and new business development on the other. New products were put on to the market twice as fast, leading to a tenfold increase in profit margins. This makes Oticon an example of business model renewal through new management practices.

Source: Volberda et al. (2011)

. . . .

The distance between a firm's current management and marketing practices and those needed to compete effectively can be bridged by introducing new management and marketing practices (cf. Capron and Mitchell, 2009). Our research clearly shows that this is particularly true of business model renewal, where we found that firms needed to bring in more new management practices and marketing practices (see also Table 4.1). In other words, a firm's existing marketing and management practices are more suited to business model replication than to business model renewal.

For renewal, it is important that management should be able to act rapidly and in different ways, because the organization cannot fall back on existing management practices. The same applies to marketing practices.

Table 4.1 Differences between firms showing high levels of renewal and replication

Category	Replication	Renewal
Degree to which current management practices are in line with required management practices	high	low
Degree to which current marketing practices are in line with required marketing practices	high	low
Attention to process innovation	high	low
Decision-making	decentralized	more centralized

Renewal also requires more resources to develop marketing methods and distribution channels and to approach new customers and markets.

Organizational forms: system–wide organizational change

Implementing new organizational forms within a firm is a third lever of business model innovation. Organizational forms specify how an organization aligns efforts of its members and how it arranges its communication (Birkinshaw et al., 2008; Hamel, 2007; Volberda, 1996). There has been much research on new hyperadaptive and agile organization forms that are able to quickly incorporate disruptive technologies and boost new business models: the ambidextrous organization (Tushman and O'Reilly, 1996; Gilbert, 2006), disposable organization (March, 1995), poised organization (Kauffman, 1995), at the edge of chaos (Brown and Eisenhardt, 1998; Kauffman, 1995), dissipative structures (Prigogine and Stengers, 1984), semi–structures (Brown and Eisenhardt, 1997), hypertext form (Nonaka and Takeuchi, 1995) or, more generally, flexible organizations (Volberda, 1997). Many firms, however, still operate with traditional hierarchical organizational forms that severely limit their capacity to develop new business models. To facilitate business model innovation and promote the development of new business models, these traditional organizational forms need to be either modified slightly or completely redesigned (Foss, 2002; Foss et al., 2009). One new type of organizational design is the holacracy, which is based on self-management rather than any hierarchical structure. Here the power of top management is embodied in a detailed 'written constitution' which sets out how the firm should be structured, governed, and run. This constitution evolves over time and serves as a key rulebook for organizational members. As such, power is distributed across every level of the organization, thereby reducing the burden of power for top management. Managers become more 'lead links' and employees have roles, rather than jobs. This allows for self-organization (Robertson, 2015).

The American online clothing retailer Zappos operates using a holacracy. Whatever position employees hold within the organization, they have the power to address tensions, problems, and opportunities by bringing about meaningful change. This increased the start-up mentality of employees who are continuously challenged to ask the question: 'If this was my company, what would I do?' (quote adapted from Robertson, 2015). In the case of Zappos, the holacracy works in such a way that if a particular business problem arises on a regular basis, a different team of employees is brought together each time to try to address it. The reasoning behind this is that recurrent problems indicate a market need which has not been addressed, and this creates a window of opportunity for the firm to come up with an innovative response (Robertson, 2015). If this approach is successful, Zappos can then capture opportunities beyond its existing business model which focuses on free shipping costs and relationship marketing (Vazquez Sampere, 2015).

A new organizational form can initially be introduced in a specific existing organizational unit, and then rolled out across the whole firm if it proves to be successful. This approach allows a firm to separate its emerging new business model from the core organization; because the change is made incrementally, the survival of the entire firm is not put at risk if the new business model is not successful. After piloting holacracy in a small unit, Zappos decided to extend this model to the whole company. After they had switched to the new holacracy and become more used to how it worked, Zappos employees ('Zapponians') became more comfortable with their new authority.

In a similar way, companies like Ericsson and Randstad have established new units dedicated to developing new business models based on cloud technology (Ericsson) and in-house HR services (Randstad). Such new units can also function as a business model accelerator to scale up a new business model. Kaplan (2012) refers to 'business model innovation factories' which carry out R&D on business model innovation and explore and test out new business models. In its search for new business models, Randstad, for instance, started an Innovation Fund which provides support for start-ups or acquires new firms. The company noticed that 85 per cent of its turnover in Europe still comes from supplying temporary agency workers, even though the margins in this traditional market are declining and there is more competition from individual flexiworkers and online firms. To develop new business models in HR technology, the Randstad Innovation Fund selects early- or expansion-stage companies in areas such as social sourcing and engagement, online platforms, and mobile solutions. It has invested in the chat-based platform Brazen, a web-based reference tool called Checkster for rapid gathering of references for job candidates, and an all-in-one collaborative recruiting platform, gr8people. They also acquired the German online freelance platform Twago, a global exchange for employers and freelance workers, and the Silicon Valley-based outplacement provider RiseSmart. These new acquisitions are market leaders in innovative, technology-led career services that complement Randstad's portfolio and drive technological disruption in the global HR services landscape. Besides promoting the Randstad Innovation Fund as a business model accelerator for moving HR services online, Randstad also promotes the internal development of new business models such as the Sales Navigator app, an online tool for finding out which companies need new employees.

Firms can also set up teams such as minimally structured teams or immersion teams to increase their awareness of what is happening on the periphery of their markets (Cunha and Chia, 2007), and this may speed up the process of business model innovation (Nunes and Breene, 2011). Minimally structured teams have inbuilt flexibility, allowing them to adjust to particular needs and circumstances. They operate with a minimum number of rules, and have a shared social objective but no immediate deliverables. The 'Goddess-team' used by Nike to generate a new women's sportswear market is one example of a minimally structured team. The researchers and designers involved were given a great deal of freedom and there were no formal rules. They spent many hours in fashionable fitness areas, picking up on new trends. One of the key things which this team did was to give Nike's retail stores a much more feminine feel. Many shops were given new decor designed to be much softer and more appealing to women, loud music was abandoned, and women no longer had to pass shelves laden with basketball, golf, and ice hockey gear. The company also hired designers to extend its range and make it more feminine, and this resulted in the first yoga shoe, Air Kyoto. Nike also altered its advertising campaign so that it was geared more towards female values and style (De Pelsmacker et al., 2007). In addition to minimally structured teams, other firms also use immersion teams, whose task is to focus on understanding what is happening at the periphery of a firm's market, and on how that can then be translated into new opportunities for the firm. Lego used teams of this kind, which it called 'mindstorm teams', as a way of rejuvenating its portfolio (Cunha and Chia, 2007).

New organizational forms contribute more strongly to business model replication than to renewal. For replication their effect is quite substantial compared to that of the other levers (39 per cent), but for renewal, their effect is much less significant (14 per cent)—as can be seen from Figure 4.1, which shows the results of our survey of firms. When a proven business model is extended to other markets (geographical replication), this is particularly likely to be accompanied by changes and improvements in organizational forms. In mature organizations, these changes in organizational form are more likely to target incremental improvement of the business model (longitudinal replication).

Our findings suggest that new organizational forms have an increasingly positive effect on replication. Making a slight modification to the existing organizational form thus gives less return for replication than a much more widespread change. Organizational forms must be modified in a coordinated, synchronized, and unique way. This demands a system-wide approach: modifications to the organizational form in a particular part of the organization must be accompanied by modifications elsewhere in the organization in order to effect a higher degree of replication. Compare it to a spider's web: if you pull on one corner, the whole web changes shape (Whittington and Pettigrew, 2003; Zhou and Wu, 2010).

. . . .

ZARA'S VERTICALLY INTEGRATED ORGANIZATIONAL FORM: CATWALK FASHION AT A LOW PRICE

Unlike its rivals Benetton, Gap, and H&M, fashion chain Zara took a radical step by adopting an organizational form which involves strong vertical integration. Zara controls the product process from design decision through to final sale, and has its own designers who monitor new trends in fashion. Thanks to just-in-time manufacturing, the firm is able to bring new fashion items to the market in just three weeks, while the standard for the sector is nine months. Zara can deliver new fashion items to shops in Europe within twenty-four hours and to retailers outside Europe within forty-eight hours, thanks to its efficient supply chain, which is based on a central distribution system in Spain. This vertically integrated organizational form ensures that Zara can limit the costs of stock, coordination, and marketing, and charge low prices. Zara has rolled out this business model successfully in more than seventy-two countries, including China and Russia. This makes it a good example of business model replication through system-wide implementation of a vertically integrated form.

. . . .

The place in the organization where decisions are made is also important for initiating business model innovation. Is the decision-making centralized or decentralized? In decentralized decision-making, more is delegated to 'lower' levels in the organization and to experts (Bloom et al., 2010). The decision-making in organizations with a high degree of replication is more decentralized (2 per cent above average) than in organizations with a high degree of renewal. This is an indication that renewal is more of a top-down process than replication (see Table 4.1).

For example, middle managers are often recruited in order to comply with entrenched views of top management, reinforcing the prevailing logic of the firm (Sheaffer et al., 1998). This works quite well for business model replication, but reinforcing an existing logic is less in line with business model renewal. Top management plays a crucial role in ensuring that the need or opportunities for business model renewal are recognized and understood: they need to take responsibility and use their authority to make sure that appropriate action is taken (Govindarajan and Trimble, 2011; Levitt and Snyder, 1997).

Co-creation: benefits and limitations

Co-creation can take place with a broad range of external partners, with varying degrees of intensity (e.g. Foss et al., 2013; Laursen and Salter, 2006), and at various stages of business model innovation (e.g. O'Hern and Rindfleisch, 2010). In order to cope with the increased pace of change, intense competition, and disruption created by new entrants in many of today's markets, many firms try to collectively create value by co-creating with external partners (e.g. Chesbrough, 2003; Vanhaverbeke et al., 2008). In this co-creation process, they put a stronger emphasis on the customer perspective (e.g. Prahalad and Ramaswamy, 2004; Teece, 2010; Vargo and Lusch, 2008). Prahalad and Ramaswamy (2004: 5) stress the importance of collaboration with customers as a means of ensuring competitiveness:

'The future of competition, however, lies in an altogether new approach to value creation, based on an individual-centered co-creation of value between customers and companies.' Co-creation with customers enables an organization to attract, develop, maintain, and protect its relationships with them (Harker and Egan, 2006; Jean et al., 2010), with the aim of increasing both sales (MacDonald, 1995) and profitability (Kalwani and Narayandas, 1995; Selnes and Sallis, 2003).

Such relationships also allow an organization to tap into external knowledge bases and increase the value of its own technological knowledge (e.g. Chesbrough, 2003; Prahalad and Ramaswamy, 2004). The organization and its customers have different, heterogeneous knowledge bases (Danneels, 2003; Vargo and Lusch, 2008; Von Hippel, 1998). The organization has more knowledge of how to realize a specific solution and focuses on specifications and features, while customers know more about their own context, needs, preferences, or what they consider to be important product characteristics (Chatterji and Fabrizio, 2014; Griffin et al., 2013; Von Hippel, 2009). When there is a strong overlap between the knowledge base of an organization and that of its customers, the organization is more able to identify, select, and integrate customer knowledge into its knowledge base (Cohen and Levinthal, 1990; Jean, Sinkovics, and Kim, 2012). However, when there is less overlap between the two knowledge bases, there are fewer benefits for the organization, because the knowledge acquired is less useful and provides fewer valuable new insights for the organization (Gilsing et al., 2008; Holmqvist, 2003).

Relational embeddedness with customers has been shown by various scholars to have both beneficial and detrimental effects (e.g. Andriopoulos and Lewis, 2009; Danneels, 2003; Uzzie, 1997). This has also been referred to as the 'paradox of embeddedness' (e.g. Meuleman et al., 2010; Uzzie, 1997). Stronger ties between an organization and its customers lead to more motivation, trust, and experience of exchanging more complex and richer knowledge, and to doing so in a more efficient way (Bonner and Walker, 2004; Meuleman et al., 2010). These stronger ties are needed to meet customer needs, so that the firm can 'foster client satisfaction and loyalty' (Andriopoulos and Lewis, 2009: 701), but they also narrow an organization's view of the market and inhibit experimentation (Andriopoulos and Lewis, 2009; Danneels, 2003; Uzzie, 1997).

Firms that undertake relatively little co-creation utilize a limited number of external relationships in which there is a low degree of knowledge exchange with external partners (e.g. Bonner and Walker, 2004; Venkatraman and Henderson, 2008). More co-creation, however, does not always result in a greater level of business model replication and renewal (see Figures 4.4a and 4.4b). It is important to note here that firms need to balance external growth, which involves collaboration with outside parties, against autonomous, organic growth. A high degree of external growth means little internal growth, and vice versa. With replication in particular, organizations should engage in relatively little co-creation with external parties—they should instead concentrate more on internal organic growth. Replication is about repeating the concept, and the firm itself knows that concept best. Internal growth often provides economies of scale, and this is beneficial for its existing competitive position. This does not mean that organizations pursuing replication should avoid working on co-creation. Collaboration with external parties can lead to additional economies of scale (for example, through sharing of resources) or—with geographical replication—can allow the firm to serve the new market better, for example, by working together with local distributors or sales agents. The participation of Air France-KLM in SkyTeam demonstrates this.

. . . .

CUSTOMERS HELP DESIGN AT MUJI

The Japanese firm Muji sells clothing and household goods with a simple, almost Spartan charm. This 'less is more' approach is successful not only in Japan: the group has now opened dozens of shops in Asia, Europe, and the United States. Buyers of Muji items are mainly people in their twenties and thirties. Muji is famed for its design department. But many of the successful products are the result of co-creation with customers. Customers can propose ideas via the internet and evaluate proposed products before they are launched on to the market. Around half a million people do this regularly. Muji works out the most popular ideas in more detail and estimates the anticipated sales on the basis of the reactions. It does this for clothing, but also for furniture, lamps, and similar items. In the final phase, customers are given the opportunity to place advance orders. Once a specified minimum level of orders is reached, Muji goes ahead with production and distribution. Impressive results have been achieved this way. Some items designed in collaboration with customers have sold better than similar items which came about the traditional way. This is a good example of co-creation with customers.

. . . .

More co-creation is required for renewal than for replication. A high degree of renewal flourishes when co-creation and internal growth are evenly balanced. Organizations can share knowledge, resources, and risks by

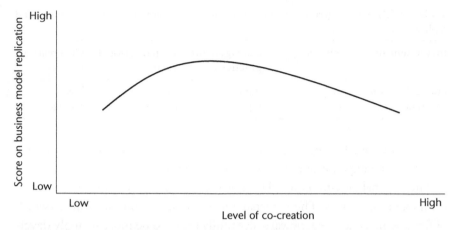

Figure 4.4a Relationship between co-creation and business model replication

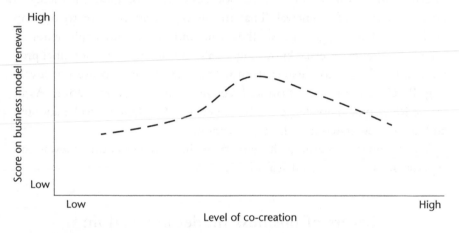

Figure 4.4b Relationship between co-creation and business model renewal

working together, but synergies can also come about between the knowledge bases of different organizations (e.g. Takeishi, 2001; Tsai, 2009). Tapping into different sources of knowledge enables firms to break with the status quo and arrive at radically new solutions (Chesbrough, 2007). In certain sectors, combining internal and external information can be a crucial source of competitive advantage (Harker and Egan, 2006). However, when a firm makes excessive use of external knowledge, it may be failing to capitalize on the unique knowledge which it has built up itself over time. It also increases the costs of finding, coordinating, and monitoring partnerships

Table 4.2 To what degree is investment in the levers required to realize renewal and replication?

Investment in	Technology	Management practices	Organizational forms	Co-creation
For replication	average	high	high	low
For renewal	average to high	high	average	average

(Hodgkinson et al., 2012; Laursen, 2012). Too much co-creation can therefore be at the expense of business model renewal.

The internal growth required for business model renewal can be fed partly from external sources. The external and internal communication networks of firms which exercise renewal successfully prove to be more strongly developed. This allows them to make better use of external knowledge. Combining internal basic research with external sources of technological knowledge is crucial for successful renewal. That means organizations have to develop an internal knowledge base so they can understand and apply external knowledge better. Internal knowledge is also needed to select potential projects and to know how external knowledge can be put to use effectively (e.g. Berchicci, 2013; Cassiman and Veugelers, 2006; Laursen, 2012). As in classic R&D, once knowledge has been generated, it then has to be adopted and further integrated into the organization.

The findings concerning the effects of the four levers on renewal and replication are summarized again in Table 4.2.

Levers of business model innovation: sector effects

We now know the effects the different levers have on renewal and replication. Which sectors score high on which levers?

Life sciences and ICT, which also lead the way in renewal and replication (the dual focus), score above average on three of the four levers (see Figure 4.5). New technologies, management practices, and organizational forms in particular help firms in these sectors to develop new and better business models.

The sectors with a low degree of renewal and replication (trapped in fixation)—government and the energy sector in particular—score relatively low on new management practices. They are 15 and 10 per cent lower

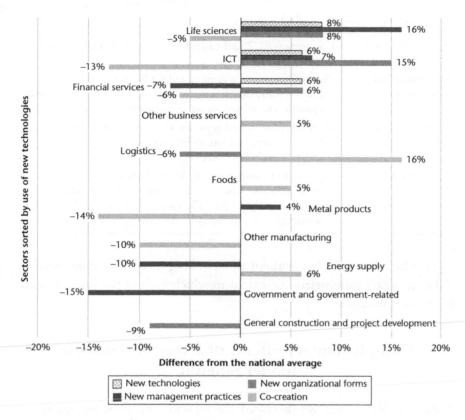

Figure 4.5 Levers of business model innovation per sector

N.B.: Missing bars represent values that are not significantly above or below the national average.

respectively than the national average. This low score can explain why this group lags behind in both forms of business model innovation.

We observed that firms in the financial services sector in particular paid a great deal of attention to replication. The levers used in this sector are new technologies (6 per cent above average) and new organizational forms (6 per cent above). New management practices (7 per cent below average) and co-creation (6 per cent below) are used much less. In financial services, business model innovation thus appears to take place mainly in familiar territory, using the reliable levers of ICT and technology, as well as restructuring operations.

There is one other striking finding in the logistics sector, which we had already noted for its relative stability. The logistics firms in the research showed high values in co-creation (16 per cent above average). The collaboration with customers and other links in the supply chain appears to be

Table 4.3 Use of levers in particular sectors

New technologies	Life sciences, ICT, and financial services show higher than average values.
New management practices	High values are once again noted for life sciences and ICT, but not for financial services. The energy, government, and government-related sectors score noticeably low values.
New organizational forms	High values are noted again for life sciences, ICT, and financial services. Here logistics and construction score conspicuously low values.
Co-creation	Logistics and energy score strikingly high values. There are noticeably low values for life sciences and ICT, which do use all the other levers. The financial services and industrial sectors also do not appear to use co-creation intensively.

present here naturally, but without this resulting in new business models. Table 4.3 again summarizes the extent to which each of the levers is used in the various sectors.

Complementary effects of levers on business model renewal

Earlier in this chapter we described the separate effects of the levers on renewal and replication. But the four levers do not operate in a vacuum, separate from each other: they can also be applied at the same time. This indeed often happens in practice. When different levers are active at the same time, it is evident that they strengthen each other (and, through that, the business model innovation). This is called a 'complementary effect'. Compare it to a puzzle, with the levers as the pieces. They can be laid in different ways in business model renewal, resulting in different effects each time.

In this section, we examine various complementary effects that our research revealed. When the right levers are combined, they have a mutually strengthening effect on the degree of business model renewal. We discuss what happens when you combine new technologies with new management practices, and what additional effects may be obtained if you then add new organizational forms. Next we look at the conditions needed to realize renewal using a combination of new technologies, new management practices, and co-creation in particular. Finally, we consider what happens when all four levers are used simultaneously.

Technologically oriented business model renewal

A new rival technology often results in the creation of a new business model. The Polaroid case shows that investing in a new rival technology is not sufficient in itself to create a new business model and gain competitive advantage. The success of new business models depends mainly on the way management puts new technologies, knowledge, and resources to use (Chesbrough, 2007; Teece, 2010). Thus Xerox researchers at the Palo Alto Research Center had developed many different types of hardware and software such as Ethernet and graphical user interfaces (GUI). The management at Xerox did not see much promise in these; the firm was oriented towards copiers and printers. The result? Other parties exploited or commercialized these inventions. The concept of GUI ended up being applied in Apple computers and in Windows (Chesbrough, 2011b).

It is extremely important not only to obtain knowledge and other organizational resources, but also to combine them, build upon them, recombine them, and put them to use effectively (Hansen et al., 2004; Eisenhardt and Martin, 2000; Sirmon et al., 2011; Teece, 2007). Distinctive and advanced management practices are crucial to this task (Bloom and Van Reenen, 2007). In comparison to new technologies, management practices (Bloom and Van Reenen, 2007) are more difficult to assess and quantify. Many of these practices derive from functional areas such as production, marketing, and HR management. But the more complex practices have a broader base, as they relate to the entire value chain. Consider product development practices, for example, or process innovation practices. Such management practices demand a broad and deep knowledge base (knowledge of technology, markets, products, and distribution) and varied management expertise (Volberda, 1996, 1998). These days, new business models often come from innovation which takes place at the interface between different specialities (e.g. De Boer et al., 1999; Hacklin, 2007). These advanced management practices which draw on different knowledge bases are often what distinguish business model renewal from business model replication.

Managers must be capable of identifying and supporting new ideas instead of continuing to follow the existing routines over and over again. If knowledge is being acquired simply by pursuing routine activities, this leaves managers only limited space for experimentation. Routines work like well-worn grooves to channel activities and focus managerial attention. In relying on these routines, management concentrates on its own specialized areas and does not have to form a notion of how the different areas of activity fit together—and how new activities might be integrated into that whole. Routines thus aggravate the separation of functional areas, hinder learning processes, and restrict the development of new business models by reinforcing established ways of thinking (Volberda, 1998; Sosna et al., 2010).

Experimenting and creating broad frameworks can contribute to an increase in new and advanced management practices for business model innovation. The experiences of NCR and General Motors are enlightening in this regard. Due to their reluctance to experiment and their continued focus on established lines of business (electromechanical cash registers and large cars), they were temporarily outstripped by other competitors. Likewise, the inexperienced Sharp was able to develop new management practices in the electronic calculator market, unlike the much larger Texas Instruments (TI), which originated from the semiconductor industry. This was due to the limited managerial mindsets of the managers at TI, who were narrowly focused on the semiconductor market. Also, Honda's success in the US motorcycle market was based in the first place on the firm's emphasis on experimentation and developing complementary managerial mindsets. Sochiro Honda, the inventive founder of the enterprise, had a huge ego and mercurial temperament and a strong bias towards motor technology, while his partner Takeo Fujisawa's primary focus was on the market, distribution, and financial knowledge (Volberda, 1998).

A firm cannot develop management practices such as lean production, flexible manufacturing, or fast product development overnight in order to develop a new business model. These management practices cannot be purchased off the shelf, but require a strategic vision, a long development period, and sustained investment. It takes a lot of time to identify, build up, and use them across the entire enterprise. Management practices are typically not capabilities that can be adopted and abandoned at will. Firms simply lack the capacity to develop new management practices rapidly. While routines also require learning and take time to develop, they can often be built on the basis of extrapolation of trends, imitation of others, or past experience (e.g. Teece, 2007; Teece et al., 1997). By contrast, new management practices require an ability to fundamentally challenge prevailing assumptions and given routines. In summary, we can assert that the development of new management practices for business model renewal requires:

- a broad and deep knowledge base and a management team with varied expertise (in order to respond appropriately)

- a passion for experimentation and broad managerial mindset (to enlarge the range of management practices)

- a strong capacity for learning (to develop and expand the range of management practices).

It is the combination of new technologies and new management practices which enables organizations to reap the benefits of business model renewal. Complementary management practices open up new technologies for the market. Small organizations often do this better than larger ones (e.g. Nooteboom, 1994). Established, successful firms are restricted by their age and tradition in the roll-out of fundamentally new business models (e.g. Chesbrough and Rosenbloom, 2002; Sosna et al., 2010). Even though technological breakthroughs often occur in the laboratories of large established enterprises, the successful marketing of those breakthroughs is usually done by small newcomers (Christensen, 1997). Examples include the replacement of microcomputers by PCs, fixed telephony by VoIP, large cars by smaller and cleaner cars, large, powerful motorbikes by smaller, more manoeuvrable ones, incandescent light bulbs by LEDs, and rolls of film by digital photography. Henri Peteri, while he was R&D manager at Unilever, developed the successful boiling-water tap Quooker, but in the end decided to put it on the market himself. Apparently, it was not possible to take forward this new technology within a large firm. Peteri's family firm, which is now managed by his two sons, holds global patents on the Quooker and has branches all over Europe. Its products are distributed through more than 2,500 dealers. Often it is the relatively small players whose adaptive management practices enable them to profit from breakthrough technologies. Another example is Claymount. This firm transformed itself from a supplier of plugs and cables into a provider of integrated solutions, occupying a different place in the value chain. The firm could only make that change thanks to its advanced management practices.

Combination of levers for technologically oriented renewal	new technologies new management practices
	technologically oriented renewal +

Internally oriented renewal

Larger organizations often forget that management must recognize new technologies and understand that they demand totally different methods of organizing. The combination of new technologies, new management practices, and new organizational forms has a strong complementary effect on renewal. Using new technologies effectively requires adjustments to and connection with complementary management practices and organizational forms (Bloom and Van Reenen, 2007; Taylor and Helfat, 2009).

Refreshing the management practices and the organizational form in minor ways is not sufficient to renew a business model fundamentally. The various management practices are closely interwoven at the corporate level. Renewing them partially can even be counterproductive (e.g. Siggelkow, 2001; Whittington et al., 1999).

New management practices such as total quality management (TQM), lean manufacturing, Six Sigma, activity-based costing, brand management, and scenario planning require the commitment of the whole organization and sometimes also of partners outside the organization. When there are outstanding management practices and new organizational forms which closely match with each other, it becomes possible for new knowledge to be linked to other complementary areas of knowledge and skills; this is essential for succeeding with new technologies (Damanpour and Evan, 1984; Damanpour et al., 2009).

Adopting outstanding management practices and redesigning the organization ensures that the potential of new technologies can be exploited more effectively. The organization's structure, its internal communication, and the degree to which knowledge is shared among employees determine whether the available knowledge can be accessed and used (Grant, 1996; Hitt et al., 2000). A new organizational structure influences the coordination and communication between people and, through that, their access to knowledge (Hamel, 2007). A decentralized organizational structure ensures that information is processed more efficiently (Tsai, 2002). The delegated decision-making found in this type of structure reduces the information overload for managers (Bloom et al., 2010), the overload being one reason why organizations are less able to cope well with new technologies (Katila and Ahuja, 2002).

One classic view is that a new technology—in conjunction with new management practices and new organizational forms—results in a new business model to commercialize that technology (e.g. Baden-Fuller and Haefliger, 2013; Chesbrough and Rosenbloom, 2002). This kind of journey involves few external parties compared to the combination we will discuss later in this chapter. The new business model is developed within the confines of the firm, without too much involvement from other potentially prying parties. New technologies can be an important trigger here, but so too can new management practices or new organizational forms. This is what we call internally oriented business model renewal.

Ericsson provides a good example of this. The Swedish firm contributed to upheaval in the telecom sector with its cloud computing. On the basis of this new technology, Ericsson created a new business model and also started to generate revenue from services as well as from hardware and software. This did not all happen automatically. The inert organizational structure and Ericsson's routine-minded management formed considerable obstacles. Cloud computing also demanded a different mindset. After all, it was to some extent cannibalizing the sales of traditional hardware and software with which Ericsson had until then earned its money. Ericsson was only able to break down internal barriers and roll out the new business model successfully by developing this new activity in a separate part of the firm and by introducing new management practices (Khanagha et al., 2014).

The technology can also come from outside the organization. External technological developments such as cloud computing require new skills. Introducing these within a firm often requires organizational changes (e.g. Hollen et al., 2013). New technologies also change a firm's external environment, the intensity of competition, customer preferences, and the barriers to entry within the sector. All these changes require, and result in, new management and marketing practices and different organizational forms (Foss and Saebi, 2015; Van den Bosch et al., 1999). For example, ICT made just-in-time management possible, while the internet allowed for the creation of virtual enterprises and stimulated the formation of network organizations (Currie, 1999). As noted earlier, it is mainly in renewal that technology functions as a trigger in this way.

New technology is not always the driver of renewal—new management practices and new organizational forms can also be drivers. New management practices have led to countless organizations becoming flatter and having a different structure (e.g. Camisón and Villar-López, 2014). The more organic structure of ABB is an example of this. Finext, a consulting firm which has virtually no hierarchy and offers its employees a huge

Combination of levers for internally oriented renewal	new technologies new management practices new organizational forms
	internally oriented renewal +

degree of autonomy, provides another illustration of the interplay between management practices and organizational form. With a management philosophy based on trust and a system of self-organizing teams, the firm operates as a collective of mini-enterprises in a network structure. The teams responsible for profit at Finext have greater scope for action and arrive at new business faster than large rivals with divisional structures. It would not be easy to create this kind of organization without modern information and communication systems, which emphasizes once again the complementarity of the levers.

Dell's revolutionary business model of *disintermediation* is based on a form of organization which was fundamentally new when introduced, as it cut out the traditional distributors of PCs. This business model also required superior technology, especially ICT, but the main lever for changing the business model was the organizational form of the chain. IKEA's business model of direct delivery and self-assembly in the furniture industry was also driven by distinctive management practices and a unique organizational form (Jonsson and Foss, 2011; Volberda, 1998). In sum, business model renewal can be boosted by complementarity between the levers of technology, management, and organization. The order in which this takes place is less important: the new technology, new management practice, or different organizational form can provide the first push. We look at these issues in more detail in Chapter 6.

Externally oriented renewal

External parties can be an important driver in business model renewal. Co-creation enables an organization to think up new concepts together with external parties such as customers and suppliers (e.g. Chesbrough, 2007; Prahalad and Ramaswamy, 2004). Earlier in this chapter we showed how renewal requires a balance between co-creation and internal growth. When

Combination of levers for externally oriented renewal	co-creation new management practices new organizational forms
	externally oriented renewal +

it is used in conjunction with new management practices and new organizational forms, co-creation has a strongly complementary effect on renewal.

Collaboration with external parties gives organizations opportunities for value creation which they would not be able to realize independently or only at a slower pace (e.g. Dyer and Singh, 1998; Lavie, 2006; Tsai, 2009). Organizations need to have the skill to select the right partners and be able to hold on to them (Capron and Mitchell, 2009; Cassiman and Veugelers, 2006). Making a success of external collaboration requires new management practices and the adoption of new organizational forms. Practices that can help in this respect include appointing dedicated alliance managers, providing alliance training, and using formal methods to evaluate the alliance in order to accumulate, store, integrate, and diffuse relevant organizational knowledge about alliance management. Also important are good internal communication and incentives for sharing knowledge and for creating value from the interaction with customers (Draulans et al., 2003; Foss et al., 2011). This combination of co-creation, new management practices, and new organizational forms is what we call externally oriented renewal.

. . . .

PROCTER & GAMBLE: FROM IN-HOUSE R&D TO OPEN INNOVATION

At the start of this century Procter & Gamble (P&G) was experiencing declining growth. The corporate group wanted to stimulate growth, but realized that its internally oriented business model was outdated. It had been developed in the 1980s and was based on using powerful in-house scientific capabilities to create leading brands. P&G had historically created most of its growth by building and leveraging global research facilities, hiring the best talent in the world, and generating innovations in labs. However, the firm saw that more and more often new products were coming from small entrepreneurial firms and start-ups or were the result of open innovation. Facing unprecedented levels of rivalry with stagnating R&D productivity and only a 35 per cent innovation success rate led to decreasing financial performance and a steep decline in market valuation. Newly appointed CEO, A. G. Lafley, challenged the management to look outwards and reinvent

P&G's business model. In what followed, the firm created a best-practice in open innovation that ties into strong internal resources. P&G changed its approach to innovation, extending its internal R&D to the outside world through the slogan 'connect & develop'. Since then, designers and developers at P&G have collaborated with almost two million external researchers active in areas relevant to P&G. The group appointed a manager of external innovation and set a goal: within five years, half of all innovations had to come from outside the firm. Previously, only one-fifth had done so. This goal was reached. One product that was developed in this way is the SpinBrush, now the bestselling electric toothbrush in the United States. The idea for this was submitted by four entrepreneurs from Cleveland. P&G later ruled that any idea from its own laboratories which was not used within three years should be made available to third parties—even to rivals, if need be. This rule is designed to speed up innovation and prevent promising products from becoming stuck in the pipeline.

Sources: Huston and Sakkab (2006); Chesbrough (2003)

. . . .

Integral business model renewal

In the previous sections we have looked at three possible routes a firm can take to renew its business model: a route with a strong technological orientation whereby management is able to open up new technologies through the use of new management practices, an internal route based on technological, management, and organizational changes, and an external route based on co-creation. The question is, are there particular benefits to be gained by using all four levers? Our research shows that the key to this is a high absorptive capacity.

Organizations with a high absorptive capacity are better at identifying technological developments and making use of opportunities in the environment (Cohen and Levinthal, 1997; Van den Bosch et al., 1999; Zahra and George, 2002). They can also use that capacity to pre-empt disruptions in their environment, and to predict more accurately the nature and commercial potential of technological disruptions. Firms who are prepared in this way have more industry foresight and are better at anticipating when there will be disruption. Their well-developed sensor function makes them better able to understand and react more quickly to weak signals of disruption.

Large organizations are often not sufficiently sensitive to these weak signals because they are listening too much to their current customers and are too busy protecting their existing products and markets (Christensen et al., 2015; Govindarajan et al., 2011). The capacity of managers to recognize the value of new information coming from outside, assimilate it, and apply it for commercial ends, is crucial for developing effective R&D and

Combination of levers for integral renewal	new technologies new management practices new organizational forms co-creation
	integral business model renewal

(+)

co-creation with external partners (Zahra and George, 2002). Using all four levers together has a stronger and more beneficial effect on renewal when the organization is skilled at identifying and using knowledge from within its own business environment.

The DSM example below shows clearly why a high capacity for knowledge absorption is important.

. . . .

KNOWLEDGE ABSORPTION AT DSM: INTEGRAL BUSINESS MODEL RENEWAL

DSM underwent a radical transformation at the end of the 1990s: it sold off its petrochemical business, its core activity at the time, and threw itself into life sciences. This put the group in a much more dynamic market. It had only limited internal expertise in life sciences. DSM expanded its expertise in that field by means of collaborative arrangements and acquisitions, including the acquisition of biotechnology company Gist-Brocades, which specialized in clinical medicine products including penicillin, yeasts, and enzymes. The change was brought about by transformational leadership. As managers needed to take on different roles, requiring a new and different set of competences, external awareness and knowledge absorption thus became more important. The firm adopted a more decentralized and exploratory form of innovation, following practices that had been used at Gist-Brocades. The knowledge absorption which had traditionally been mainly internally oriented turned more to the outside. Instead of wanting to develop everything itself through closed R&D paths, DSM embraced the 'proudly found elsewhere' philosophy.

. . . .

From our discussions of the effect of co-creation on renewal and replication it has already become clear that co-creation and internal growth need to be evenly balanced, especially for renewal. It is essential that firms should be good at picking up signals from outside the periphery of the enterprise. Absorptive capacity requires porous boundaries, scanning broadly for new soft information, and the ability to identify employees who serve as gatekeepers and boundary-spanners and to use them effectively (Volberda et al., 2010; Anthony and Christensen, 2005; Ofek and Wathieu, 2010). Successful new biotechnology firms, for instance, were able to develop new products because their management gave a high priority to absorptive capacity. They invested in social networks by organizing research seminars and workshops, and they expanded the boundaries of the firm by establishing joint ventures and alliances. This absorptive capacity helped these firms to source new knowledge quickly from universities and research institutes. This kind of knowledge could not be developed in-house or by drawing on these firms' existing knowledge base or experience. It required an openness to new ideas and values. Tolerance of ambiguity prevented employees from being blind to new developments.

A high absorptive capacity helps organizations to identify and process new internal *and* external knowledge, and to transform it into new business models. Taking on board both new management practices and new organizational forms makes it easier for new knowledge to be converted into new business models (Foss and Saebi, 2015; Van den Bosch et al., 1999; Volberda et al., 2010). The complementary effects that can be achieved by using different combinations of levers are shown in Table 4.4. Chapter 6 discusses the trajectories of transformation which firms go through when they use different levers either simultaneously or sequentially.

Table 4.4 Lever combinations that have complementary effects on business model renewal

Technologically oriented renewal	Internally oriented renewal	Externally oriented renewal	Integral renewal
new technologies + new management practices	new technologies + new management practices + new organizational forms	co-creation with customers + new management practices + new organizational forms	new technologies + co-creation with customers + new management practices + new organizational forms

Wrap-up

In this chapter we showed how the different levers affect business model innovation, how the different levers are interrelated, and how combinations of levers can provide an extra impulse to business model renewal (complementary effect). Sometimes the driver is technology, sometimes it is the adoption of a new management practice or organizational form, and sometimes it is co-creation.

In the next chapter we will examine what accelerates or slows down business model innovation. Which elements act as catalysts and which are obstacles?

5

Enablers and Inhibitors of Business Model Innovation

. . . .

IN 2008 AD SCHEEPBOUWER, FORMER CEO AT KPN, SAID THE IPHONE WAS A 'PRETTY USELESS PHONE'

In early February 2013 KPN shares experienced their worst fall in price since the former Dutch state-owned telecom provider was floated on the stock exchange. The CEO, Eelco Blok, pointed out the large investments the firm was making in the 4G network and optic fibre. Part of the problem for KPN was that many customers no longer communicate by phone calls or SMS, but use Skype or WhatsApp.

Even though the smartphone market has grown at an astonishing rate, few parties are actually doing well out of it. Samsung and Apple have a 60 per cent share of the market and pocket 90 per cent of the worldwide profits. Most of the traditional mobile manufacturers (LG, HTC, Motorola, Nokia) now have only a very small slice of the pie, faring little better than troubled European telecom providers such as KPN, Telefonica, and Vodafone.

None of these players believed it possible that an outsider like Apple could break down their power bloc this rapidly and radically. The mobile manufacturers matched the speed of phone development to the network capacity in each country so that firms like KPN would not be burdened suddenly with too much data traffic. The profit was thus shared reasonably: the mobile manufacturers were able to work on innovation at a manageable speed without cannibalizing their existing products, and the service providers could continue to milk their cash cows (calls and SMS) without having to invest immediately in superfast optic fibre.

Apple disrupted the party in 2007 when it introduced the iPhone. This was more than just a revolutionary device; the business model underlying it was also unique. The iPhone catered to people's wish for free communication and presented them with numerous functions (apps) of which they had never even dreamed, or which they knew at best from computers. Few new offers in history have created so much demand so fast.

By 2010 the iPhone was already beginning to cannibalize the profits of traditional network providers, and KPN in particular. In light of this, the firm may regret that in 2008, shortly before the iPhone was introduced in the Netherlands, former CEO Ad Scheepbouwer called the iPhone a 'pretty useless phone'. He complained loudly about its relatively short battery life and the touchscreen. Perhaps he was haunted by the idea that the phone would become an expensive proposition for KPN, if only because of the six hundred euros he would have to prefinance per phone.

Various factors prevented KPN from renewing its business model, while others helped it to replicate its existing business model. Scheepbouwer was 'shareholder-friendly' par excellence. His transactional leadership style, aimed at cost reduction and reorganization, resulted in rising share prices. During his tenure the firm sought to deliver short-term performance.

The conservative company culture also slowed down the development of a new business model. The firm was very cautious about approaching new markets as it did not want to jeopardize its established position. Only when customers started to leave did KPN decide to become more competitive and to consider developing new business.

KPN held on to the old business model for a long time under Scheepbouwer, but under the current CEO, Eelco Blok, it is now investing significantly to catch up. This has had an adverse effect on KPN's company performance in the short term. Shareholders did not like this, in particular the new major shareholder, Mexican Carlos Slim. As CEO of América Móvil he owned at that time 28 per cent of the shares in a failed attempt to take over KPN.

. . . .

Introduction

We have already seen how disruptive forces such as environmental dynamism and competition can force firms to reconsider their business model, and have looked at various levers which can be used in business model innovation. In this chapter we will put a few more pieces of the puzzle together by investigating the factors that can help or hinder renewal and/or replication. Table 5.1 shows a summary of the most important enablers and inhibitors. In this chapter we systematically review these enablers and inhibitors of business model innovation. We use the term 'transformation' here for the switch from business model replication to business model renewal or vice versa.

Even though some firms may have activated the right levers, the inhibitors described in this chapter can still make it quite difficult for them to revise their business model. Thus General Motors (GM) continued to build large, petrol-guzzling cars, while Japanese manufacturers were delivering smaller and more economical cars. Management was not willing to design and produce compact cars, because of the damage they feared this would do to their current market.

GM adhered to the outdated assumption that cars were status symbols and that styling was more important than quality. Finance also exerted a

Table 5.1 Enablers and inhibitors of business model innovation

Factor	Influence on replication	Influence on renewal
Transformational leadership	enabler	enabler
Organizational identity	enabler	–
Innovative culture	–	enabler
Length of CEO's tenure in organization	–	first enabler, then inhibitor
Knowledge-absorptive capacity	enabler	enabler
Listening to existing customers	enabler	inhibitor
Internal cooperation	enabler	inhibitor
Size of organization	enabler	–
Corporate governance	enabler (for shareholder-oriented firms)	enabler (for family businesses)
Laws and regulations	varies	varies

– = little to no effect

tremendous dominance over the entire organization. GM rewarded volume alone and simply ignored quality. The excessive bias towards existing customers, combined with a conservative company culture, led to complacency, myopia, and ultimately decline; proven successes led to a dogmatic approach and preserving the status quo became the norm (Tellis, 2012; Tushman and O'Reilly, 2013).

On the other hand, enablers clearly strengthen the effect of the levers discussed in the previous chapter. They can make it easier for firms to switch to a different business model. For instance, Honda's innovative culture and transformational leadership allowed the company to develop a new business model in the traditional motorbike market. Honda gave young employees responsibility and encouraged confrontation. In contrast with GM's 'Rank has its privileges', the Honda Way preached that 'to lead is to serve'. The firm asserted that the duty of the boss was to free up his subordinates. Employees were encouraged to think independently, experiment, and implement improvements themselves (Hutzschenreuter et al., 2007; Pascale, 1990). It was this capacity for reflection which enabled the firm to develop a new business model.

Honda dared to relinquish the idea that Americans are only interested in heavy motorbikes and that manufacturing light motorbikes would damage Honda's image in the macho motorbike market. Technical problems with the heavy 250 cc and 350 cc engines and limited cash reserves also played a part, but the innovative culture and transformational leadership were crucial to the introduction of light motorbikes on to the American market. Honda invested heavily in 50 cc motorbikes, opened up new distribution channels such as sports goods stores, and started an aggressive marketing campaign with the slogan 'You meet the nicest people on a Honda' (Pascale, 1996).

Transformational leadership: a catalyst of renewal and replication

Our research shows that transformational leaders are major enablers of both business model renewal and business model replication. Through their vision, commitment, and conviction, they can facilitate small or much larger changes to the business model. Transformational leaders motivate employees to achieve organizational goals by identifying with those goals (Bass, 1985). In terms of replication, they encourage employees to be fully committed to the company's current activities, and in terms of renewal they help them to envision a future in which they may take on different responsibilities (Dvir et al., 2002). Their leadership is made up of four elements (Avolio et al., 1999):

• idealized influence
• inspirational motivation
• intellectual stimulation
• individualized consideration.

Idealized influence refers to the degree to which the leader is admired, respected, and trusted. Included within this is charismatic behaviour that causes followers to identify with the leader and increases their intrinsic motivation to achieve goals. Leaders can operate as a champion in order to bring about change (Crawford et al., 2003) which increases followers' commitment to specific goals and to an overarching vision. This is fundamental for realizing business model innovation (Smith et al., 2010). *Inspirational motivation,* however, strengthens team spirit among followers and encourages them to envision attractive future states (Vaccaro et al., 2012a). In this way, it gives meaning to the business model but also challenges it. *Intellectual stimulation* encourages employees to think beyond traditional ways, bring assumptions up for discussion, and become more creative (Avolio et al., 1999). Business model innovation can only take place if there is a vision and if existing assumptions can be questioned (Cliffe and McGrath, 2011;

Mullins and Komisar, 2009). *Individualized consideration* is about the degree to which the potential of employees is developed by attending to their individual needs, and by creating learning opportunities and a supportive environment for growth. A transformational leader brings out this potential so that existing problems can be examined in new ways and creative solutions can be found (Avolio et al., 2009; Bass et al., 2003). Transformational leadership thus helps firms to find new ways of creating and appropriating value (Vaccaro et al., 2012a).

Strong leadership and perseverance are required to overcome organizational resistance to business model innovation. Transformational leaders stimulate renewal not only through their challenging vision, but also by creating a context which enables renewal, for example, by bringing existing assumptions up for discussion and dispelling organizational inertia (Chesbrough, 2010; Roberts, 2004).

Transformational leaders strengthen the capacity of individuals to absorb knowledge beyond the boundaries of the firm, thereby increasing the knowledge absorption of the organization as a whole. This increased capacity to recognize the value of new, external information in turn makes it possible for the firm to adjust better to changes in the environment (Aragón-Correa et al., 2008). In addition, transformational leadership helps build the organization's capacity for change (Yukl, 1999).

Our research revealed that transformational leadership is beneficial for both renewal and replication (see Table 5.1). For instance, it facilitates the adoption of new management practices and organizational forms (Vaccaro et al., 2012a). In Chapter 4, we showed how these two levers contribute very significantly to renewal and replication. In the example that follows, we can see how transformational leadership was the most important enabler of renewal at DSM Anti-Infectives. The transformational leadership programme for DSM top managers led to the creation of self-managing teams and the adoption of a flat organizational form.

. . . .

DSM ANTI-INFECTIVES, DELFT: HOW TRANSFORMATIONAL LEADERSHIP FACILITATED A NEW BUSINESS MODEL

A transformational leadership initiative by top management enabled the introduction of a new business model at DSM Anti-Infectives in Delft. In order to compete with Chinese competitors, many European and North American companies are increasingly moving production to Asia where the costs of production are lower. The global industrial production of penicillin is characterized by excess supply, most of which is produced in China, where DSM itself produces, through a joint venture with a local partner. Royal DSM, however, continues to produce parts of its volume in Europe. One of the reasons for this is the new business model of DSM Anti-Infectives based on the production of a type of anti-infective through a revolutionary process involving biotechnology instead of chemistry. The new technology, however, could only operate in a more efficient way if changes to management practice were introduced as well: the elimination of certain supervisory positions and the implementation of self-managing teams. Top management gave operator teams the freedom to gain experience in roles that were not part of their job description. By scrapping the position of team supervisor, senior management gave teams the power to decide for themselves how they would carry out their tasks. Through this kind of leadership behaviour, leaders inspired operators to identify with the plant's goals, stimulating them to take charge of their jobs and be creative. Teams responded to this intellectual challenge by organizing their work differently. They matched their actions to the goals of the firm, elaborating on the vision of top management. Meanwhile, the top managers adapted the firm's structure to the new way of working, flattening the organization. This resulted in a cost-effective business model (annual increase in productivity of 12%) through which DSM has been able to cope with Chinese rivals. Although the labour costs are much higher in the Netherlands, the increased productivity more than compensates for the higher labour costs.

Source: Vaccaro et al. (2012b)

. . . .

Identity of the organization: an enabler of replication

A firm's identity is about what it stands for and how it should operate (Berg, 1986). That identity is expressed through values and cultural practices (Hofstede et al., 1990) and creates a much stronger connection between employees than the structure or technology of the organization do. It determines how a firm differs from other firms, and how interaction with customers, competitors, and other stakeholders takes place (Albert et al., 2000). Organizational identity affects how people within the organization—including leaders—interpret threats and opportunities, resolve problems, and set specific goals, and how customer target groups are defined (Foreman and Whetten, 2002).

At the very deepest level of identity formation, there are values. Cultural practices are the more superficial expressions of those values, and involve symbols, heroes, and rituals. They are visible to the outsider although their meaning lies in the way they are perceived by insiders. At the surface level, symbols are words, gestures, pictures, or objects with a particular meaning. Symbols must be unique to the organization in order for a sustainable and powerful identity to be created (Hofstede, 1990).

Heroes or champions—whether dead or alive, real or imaginary—are shining examples of desirable behaviours. The characteristics of the heroes are highly prized in the culture of the organization and serve as role models for behaviour. At an even deeper level, we find rituals and ceremonial behaviour, collective activities that have no particular practical or functional value to the firm, but which are vitally important for its identity in a social sense. In contrast to these cultural practices, the core values of a firm's identity are feelings that are often unconscious and rarely discussed; they cannot be observed as such but are ultimately manifested in behaviour (Hofstede et al., 1990). These core values are largely shaped by the history of the firm and its mission.

An organization with a strong identity has a coherent collection of convictions and values shared by everyone, a common language, and full agreement on appropriate behaviour. All employees try to fulfil the company's current mission in the best possible way. In such organizations, identity is an integrating mechanism which leaves very little space for differing interpretations. In this way, a strong identity works as a kind of filter. It encourages the perpetuation of established ways of doing things, and ideas which might call into question existing assumptions are brushed aside because of the prevailing logic (Perra et al., 2017).

Our research shows that a strong identity is beneficial for replication but has no significant effect on renewal (see also Table 5.1). Unlike renewal, replication is particularly common in organizations with a strong organizational identity. The homogeneity around the organization's identity is essential for deepening and improving an existing business model, but not for the ability to fundamentally change the model. At the semiconductor company NXP, the company's strong identity is expressed in its mission statement: 'customer-focused passion to win', and even in its name (NXP stands for Next eXPerience). This new identity has further strengthened the replication of the firm's customer-driven business model.

Large firms with self-confidence, such as GM, IBM, and Philips, realized much too late that their identity was so strong that it had blinded them to drastic changes in their environment. The downside of an exceptionally strong identity is xenophobia, or intolerance of everything which is foreign (Ouchi, 1981). Such organizations do not tolerate any ideas which deviate from the norm, and are resistant to change. They often display a lack of creativity and discourage independent thinking. In principle, a strong identity is inconsistent with renewal, because change and creativity are embraced only by those at the top of the organization, not by those lower down (Burgelman, 2002).

Innovative culture: an enabler of renewal

The identity of an organization is partly hidden in its culture. That culture is a series of beliefs and assumptions which people in the organization generally accept and take for granted. These beliefs and assumptions are implicit in the minds of employees and to some extent shared. The organizational culture plays a role in how core values are interpreted (Schein, 1985). Shared values are important determinants of which kinds of initiative can be expected from employees and which are less likely (Anthony and Christensen, 2005; Zook and Allen, 2011).

In an organization with a conservative culture, there will be a strong and homogeneous identity and a very narrow focus. In this type of culture there are many unwritten rules, dominance by one particular discipline, strong peer pressure on individuals to conform, and little tolerance of ambiguity. There is also a strong internal orientation, which is mainly short term and reactive (Leonard-Barton et al., 1994; Volberda, 1998). Indeed, in service companies such as McDonalds, Southwest Airlines, and Walt Disney, the strong culture puts significant pressure on employees to conform, and they do so collectively, without being aware of it.

While the dominance and coherence of culture can prove to be an essential quality in these excellent organizations, strong cultures can also easily become dysfunctional. For instance, the strong occupational culture at Kodak obstructed the development of a new business model (Leonard-Barton, 1992). Chemical engineering was the dominant discipline. Because chemical engineers were regarded as high-status, there were few opportunities for lower-status mechanical and production engineers to contribute. This restricted Kodak's product development and limited the cross-integration of diverse knowledge bases so necessary for renewal.

Similarly, the dominance of design engineers at Digital Equipment Corporation and HP enabled these firms to become very strong in design but they lagged behind in marketing and manufacturing skills. There was a deep-rooted perception that production and marketing specialists and their interests were irrelevant. This became an irreconcilable problem in both firms (Leonard-Barton et al., 1994).

An innovative culture is accompanied by a weak and less focused identity (Volberda, 1998). The leaders in this kind of organization lean towards improvization. There is usually no single dominant profession or discipline, and there are typically very few rules. The formal rules that do exist can also be broken. This helps to ensure that talented employees are retained (Hamel, 1998), which is very important for driving business model renewal (Nunes and Breene, 2011). Knowledge and information are exchanged freely between people from different disciplines and there is a great tolerance of ambiguity (Bock et al., 2012; Perra et al., 2017). This horizontal exchange of knowledge between experts or functional disciplines brings professionals out of their comfort zone and increases their level of creativity, risk-taking, and experimentation (Dombrowski et al., 2007; Menguc and Auh, 2010). The organization has a strong external orientation and focuses mainly on the long term.

An innovative culture is flexible and adapts more easily to changing market circumstances (Bock et al., 2012). There is no taboo on taking risks and making mistakes. This is expressed in mantras such as 'thou shalt not kill ideas' (3M) and 'ask forgiveness, not permission' (Royal DSM). This kind of attitude is necessary in order to change the path of the organization radically (Volberda and Baden-Fuller, 2003). Our research shows that a more innovative culture results in a significantly higher degree of renewal, but does not have any significant effect on replication.

Length of CEO tenure: neither too long, nor too short

Many CEOs are under great pressure to perform in the short term. Various factors contribute to this: unwillingness to cannibalize the firm's existing business, risk aversion, orientation towards quarterly results, desire to build further on existing competences, attachment to existing customers, and a strong focus on existing rivals (Chesbrough, 2010; Voelpel et al., 2005). This leads to the retention of existing business, replication, or possibly even fixation. And that does not help the long-term viability of the organization. One of the most important tasks for the CEO is to find a balance between retaining present activities, discarding certain previous activities, and initiating future activities (Govindarajan and Trimble, 2011).

Our research reveals that the number of years a CEO spends at an organization affects renewal in particular. CEOs who spend too long in the same organization are more inclined to spend less time on business model renewal. Instead, they keep building on the models that have brought them success.

On the other hand, if CEOs stay with the firm only relatively briefly, there is not enough time to pay attention to the longer term. By the time investments in a radically new business model might have been recouped, many CEOs have already left (Govindarajan and Trimble, 2011; Wu, Levitas, and Priem, 2005). The optimal length of time for a CEO to remain with a firm is around thirteen years. This means that if a CEO works at an organization for a shorter or longer period than this, there is then often a lower degree of renewal. In particular, our research findings show that CEOs who spend less than three years in a firm typically focus mainly on replicating the business model in order to boost short-term results. CEOs who stay between three and thirteen years create fertile pockets within the company where business model renewal can be achieved. Those with tenures of more than thirteen years no longer want to change the existing business model and are clearly in business model fixation mode.

· ·

RENEWAL AT VNU AND THE CEO'S TENURE

In 2000 VNU was a Dutch publisher of newspapers and general interest magazines and well on its way to becoming one of Europe's largest publishers in this area. When a new CEO, Rob van den Bergh, was appointed in April 2000, he set about reorienting the firm's core activities. The company began to renew its business model, with the aim of moving the firm into marketing and media information. In 2000 VNU acquired AC Nielsen, which provides consumer data primarily to large wholesalers throughout the world, and Nielsen Media Research. After a failed takeover bid for IMS Health—a US company providing information, services, and technology for the healthcare industry—in 2005, van den Bergh left the company. VNU was acquired by American investment firms in 2006, and is now called The Nielsen Company. The last Dutch CFO, Rob Ruijter, was replaced in 2007. These days the group deals in business information, earning 80 per cent of its turnover in the United States, and has not published any newspapers for several years. It sold its general interest magazines to the Finnish group Sanoma. The Nielsen Company is now the market leader in business information, a market with considerable potential because firms always need market data. Magazine publishing has become a peripheral activity for the firm, and in consequence it is no longer so sensitive to the changing economic climate, specifically in terms of dependence on the advertising market.

An excessively short term in general makes it less attractive for a CEO to take risks and invest in the longer term. Former CEO Rob van den Bergh was clearly an exception. Although he was appointed for a specific short term, he may well not have foreseen his departure and was therefore unable to reap the rewards. On the other hand, CEOs who have been in post for a long time can restrict themselves to business models which have brought them success (Wu et al., 2005). This can reduce their adaptability, making renewal less likely or less possible.

· ·

Absorptive capacity: a catalyst for renewal and replication

In Chapter 4, we saw how organizations with a high capacity for absorbing knowledge are able to realize synergies between the four levers. Absorptive capacity is the ability to identify, take up, process, and use knowledge from the environment (Cohen and Levinthal, 1990). It has a significant strengthening effect on both renewal and replication. However, the effect is stronger with replication than with renewal, possibly because organizations which have this capacity use their knowledge of existing customers and markets as a seedbed for new knowledge. That allows those who are replicating business models to be much faster at identifying, processing, and using knowledge which follows on naturally from the firm's existing knowledge base (Volberda et al., 2010).

With renewal, there is a larger gap between existing and new knowledge (Capron and Mitchell, 2009). It is more difficult for a firm to identify new external knowledge properly and make effective use of it, yet absorptive capacity still has a positive effect on renewal. Firms with more expertise and greater absorptive capacity are better at identifying new opportunities. This then increases their ambition to exploit these opportunities (Ben-Menahem et al., 2013). That is why publishers with a high absorptive capacity were better able to make the change from offline to online publishing (De Boer et al., 1999; Van den Bosch et al., 1999). Porous boundaries, scanning broadly for new information, and identifying and using those employees who serve as gatekeepers and boundary-spanners helped these first-movers to make the transition to a new business model.

The Dutch financial paper FD (*Financieele Dagblad*) was one of the first newspapers in the Netherlands to make this change successfully. Although the organization had already moved away from the traditional publishing mindset, it entered into an active partnership with a software firm and set up multifunctional teams with the aim of internalizing new knowledge of how the multimedia market was developing. The newspaper also developed other sources of revenue by cooperating with a radio station (Business News Radio), organizing business debates and congresses, and moving to a building with a restaurant and a fitness centre.

A high capacity to absorb external information and identify incipient changes in the market at a very early stage (weak signals) helps the firm's own employees to be the first to pick up new trends, ahead of rivals. Firms often overlook trends which managers consider to be peripheral to the core market. As a result, they may miss new opportunities for profit, or the sector could even be transformed by rivals, thereby endangering the organization as a whole (Ofek and Wathieu, 2010). Organizations which can absorb a lot of knowledge fast can change the rules of the game for a sector (Anthony and Christensen, 2005; Christensen et al., 2002).

. . . .

HOW THE EXTREME ABSORPTIVE CAPACITY OF TOMTOM FACILITATED RENEWAL AND REPLICATION

TomTom, a global leader in mapping and navigation products, is a firm with a high absorptive capacity. Employees are selected for their innovativeness. There is an open and creative atmosphere at the firm, where people come up with ideas and dare to contradict the leaders. There is considerable freedom and trust. There is a relaxed attitude towards whether people are in the office or how long they work: for many people, working at home is fairly normal.

When asked what kind of person his firm would be, Carlo van de Weijer, vice-president of Traffic Solutions at TomTom, replied, 'A colourful person at any rate; a skater, an artist, a dressmaker. If you step into our lift, you hear all kinds of languages and you see all kinds of races. More than half of the people do not speak Dutch. Nationality is not an issue, no more than religion, sex, or orientation. The typical TomTom employee starts talking with you and you have a good conversation straight away.'

That explorative atmosphere, created partly by the huge diversity, is now throttled back rather than stimulated. With the shift to built-in navigation equipment in cars, TomTom has entered a less dynamic environment. The changes in this business-to-business market are by definition slower, and cycles take longer than in the business-to-consumer market in which the firm first operated. There is now more emphasis on exploitation. TomTom has therefore started to separate development and sales within the organization.

. . . .

Listening to the customer: enabler of replication, inhibitor of renewal

Although customers, and end-users in particular, can be a major source of new ideas (Von Hippel, 1977), it is dangerous to listen to them too much (Atuahene-Gima et al., 2005). This tension between the focus on existing customers and the desire to acquire new customers is described by Christensen (1997) as the innovator's dilemma. It has even been said that having fully satisfied customers can lead to bankruptcy in the long term

(MacDonald, 1995). A firm's largest customers (often the *laggards*, those who do not want renewal) often resist new technologies and products, and demand incremental improvements to existing products and services. Firms not infrequently give in to this (Bower and Christensen, 1995; Chandy and Tellis, 2000; Govindarajan et al., 2011).

In the first instance, the effect is positive. But in the long run, the firm runs the big risk of being pulled into a competence trap. It refines its existing skills more and more to serve the existing customers better, and therefore fails to build up new skills. This is how core rigidities arise. As a result, new opportunities do not get noticed, or the firm fails to respond in time to changes in the market (Hamel and Välikangas, 2003; Slater and Mohr, 2006). Paying too much attention to one's largest customer thus usually helps replication, but hinders renewal.

The strategic behaviour of most daily newspapers provides a good example of this. They are now having to deal with an ageing readership which has less affinity with 'digital' reading than young people. For this reason, and because they fear that making the content available online (or digitally) will cannibalize their existing business model, many newspaper publishers are finding it difficult to move to different (particularly digitally oriented) business models. For years they have also gone back and forth between diverse revenue models as far as digital content is concerned. Thus initially they tended to hide content behind payment walls, then it was all free again, and now the payment walls are reappearing. The success of *NRC Next* (a Dutch print-based paper, read mainly by young people) and *The Huffington Post* (a high-profile digital newspaper which is also flourishing commercially) proves that business model innovation in the newspaper world can bring the anticipated returns (Smith et al., 2010; Teece, 2010).

Internal cooperation: an enabler of replication

Knowledge is in general asymmetrically distributed across an organization (Tsai, 2002), and therefore internal cooperation is often necessary to share knowledge. Internal cooperation refers to the extent of direct personal contact among members within an organization (Jaworksi and Kohli, 1993). It helps employees with different knowledge and experience to exchange ideas and learn from one another, and enables that knowledge to be used better (Hansen, 2002; Tsai, 2002). Cooperation with other employees also acts as a bridge, giving people access to external sources of knowledge to which they would otherwise not have direct access (Ritter et al., 2004). Greater internal cooperation also increases internal alignment and reduces the number of overlapping activities (De Luca et al., 2010).

Our research shows that connectedness between employees strengthens replication. Having more internal cooperation helps the organization to focus more on its mainstream activities, because it helps to establish a set of norms and expectations across the organization (Hill and Rothaermel, 2003). In settings with a high level of internal cooperation, it is however more difficult to protect the development of new business models (Benner and Tushman, 2003; Burgers et al., 2009). More internal cooperation may also reduce a firm's focus on acquiring external knowledge (Jansen et al., 2005; Laursen and Salter, 2006).

There can be various reasons to boost internal ties and cooperation. For instance, an island mentality may have developed (as regards organizational units, disciplines, or expertise), or the organization may have become fragmented due to growth, internationalization, or acquisitions. Many traditional newspaper firms were characterized by multiple 'functional silos', where there was limited knowledge exchange between them. However, the online new business with its fast-changing nature required more integration and communication across those functions (Smith et al., 2010).

A number of large organizations have tried to increase internal cooperation and create synergies between the various functions. It is striking how often the projects they set up for this purpose had the word *one* in their names: *One ABB, One Siemens, One Philips, One DSM, One IHC* (see case illustration). The construction firm Heijmans chose to set up a separate unit, Heijmans Infra Integrated Projects, which is responsible for obtaining, preparing, and coordinating projects in which several internal and external parties are involved. The unit also has a coordinating role between the different specialities. Heijmans has also set up Spark, a centre for open innovation in the built environment. This is the firm's first crossover with knowledge institutes, cities, government, and new start-ups that bring in new technology, knowledge, and innovation.

. . . .

ONE IHC

Royal IHC has identified internal cooperation as one of the firm's strategic pillars. Goof Hamers, the former president of the company, underlined its importance as follows: 'Nothing is more important than the people and arranging the way they work together: the organization.' He realized that it is a challenge to accomplish this kind of cooperation. In an interview in 2010, he said that 'a large holding company can degenerate into a snake pit where everyone would rather fight each other than the market. That's not the case here at all. We fight our battles outside' (Management Scope, 2010). At IHC Merwede, the goal of the One IHC project is to create uniformity in the company's systems and methods of working. This project contributes to the facilitation of internal cooperation and the firm's replication strategy.

It is also possible to achieve more internal cooperation by standardizing processes. This increases the reliability and facilitates the exchange of experience between individuals (Levinthal and March, 1993). It stimulates the use of existing knowledge, reduces the range of actions employees can take, and increases expertise in particular areas. This helps to ensure more efficient knowledge exchange, and more interaction and mutual dependencies within a firm. As a result, incremental improvements can be realized relatively rapidly (e.g. Benner and Tushman, 2002; Galunic and Rodan, 1998). Standardizing processes thus makes it easier to achieve replication.

At the same time, standardization reduces variation and flexibility, making a firm less able to adapt and thus less capable of radical renewal (Benner and Tushman, 2002, 2003). This means that a high degree of standardization is counterproductive for renewal, for which flexibility, variation, and experimentation are necessary. In Chapter 7 we examine how firms that want to renew their business models can avoid processes of standardization.

Organizational growth: promotes replication, hinders renewal

Large organizations have various advantages over small organizations. They often have a better reputation, higher customer confidence, more control over their external environment, and more resources. The downside is that large organizations are usually inert and oriented towards strengthening their existing competences (Chandy and Tellis, 2000). This is also known as the 'liability of age and tradition' (Tushman and Anderson, 1986; Hensmans et al., 2001). Smaller organizations are able to adapt faster, and have shorter communication lines and more space for creativity (Ebben and Johnson, 2005). Larger firms also run the risk of cannibalization, where bringing in new products can have a damaging effect on revenue from existing products

(Srinivasan et al., 2004). Cannibalization can lead to conflicts which frustrate the development of a new business model (Markides and Oyon, 2010).

Our research showed that the larger firms become, the sooner they are inclined to replicate their business model. Here they use distribution advantages that allow them to reach their existing customers faster and serve them better (Chandy and Tellis, 2000). Larger firms also have more resources, such as a sales force, to help increase take-up of products, which is essential for remaining active in the market (Rubera and Kirca, 2012). But because larger firms are also more predictable, small rivals can react more effectively over time (Volberda et al., 2011).

Those rivals are not only existing players but also newcomers who can change the rules of the game in a market fundamentally. The business model of a newcomer with an initially inferior solution which over time attracts customers from a mainstream market is called a 'disruptive business model' (Christensen et al., 2015; Gans, 2016; Govindarajan and Kopalle, 2006; Govindarajan et al., 2011). Larger firms therefore cannot simply build on their existing model, they also have to work on renewal. In our next case, we see how Randstad, the largest temporary employment agency in the Netherlands, felt obliged to react to the arrival of many small temporary employment agencies in the Westland region of the country.

· ·

RANDSTAD VERSUS SMALL TEMPORARY EMPLOYMENT AGENCIES IN THE WESTLAND

The horticultural area of the Westland in the Netherlands employs many Polish people. Most of these workers have typically been taken on through so-called 'papa and mama' employment agencies, often run by fellow Poles. Individually, these agencies were not serious rivals for Randstad, but together they did make it difficult for the market leader to gain a foothold in this segment. Instead of following the model of the small agencies, Randstad decided to penetrate the large Westland market in a different way, by developing a low-cost self-service concept specifically for this market. The group launched Randstad Direct, an innovative online planning system which enabled it to deploy temporary workers more quickly, simply, and cheaply. Or, as it said on the website: 'Suppose you need 100 packers in the coming months to process your harvest. Wouldn't it be great if you could organize the best temporary workers with a single press on the button? You can do that now. With Randstad Direct.' This new method of approaching the market (digital recruitment business model) turned out to be successful and is currently being replicated in other sectors.

· ·

Small firms, particularly start-ups, often have more radical ideas than larger players. But they usually do not have the means of commercializing them. The 'liability of newness' makes it difficult for young, small organizations to break into established markets (Hensmans et al., 2001). It is easier for larger firms to improve and scale-up breakthrough ideas. To commercialize an idea, a firm needs not only money, but also particular expertise or access to distribution channels. By working together, smaller and larger firms can make use of one another's strengths. This kind of cooperation can result sooner or later in a takeover. Larger firms can thus achieve a more effective balance between renewal and replication by cooperating with or taking over smaller firms. This is what happened to the firm in our next case, Roche Diagnostics Netherlands.

· ·

ROCHE DIAGNOSTICS NETHERLANDS: COOPERATING WITH SMALL FIRMS FOR BUSINESS MODEL RENEWAL

'We are extremely large, and that is always a disadvantage, since start-ups can think up much cleverer things than we can,' says Josefien van der Meer, communications manager at Roche Diagnostics Netherlands. 'At some point we have to buy them if we are to remain innovative. We admit that in a firm of eighty thousand employees innovation sometimes simply has to come from outside, from people who can still think freely. But anyhow, eventually we do get that innovation in our firm.'

· ·

Creating a new ecosystem in order to reap the profits from start-ups is a practice that is well understood by the three largest financial players in the Netherlands: ABN-Amro, ING, and Rabobank. ABN-Amro is investing €10 million in innovative start-ups specializing in the digitization of financial products and services. They are actively approaching promising fintech start-ups. A growing number of these are developing financial products and business models that enhance user friendliness and can provide ABN-Amro's private and business clients with more financial insight. Moreover, they opened an innovation centre, a place where they explore problems, collect insights, and validate new business models. ING chose a more radical approach. In order to make the bank more agile and responsive, they are in the process of transforming a large hierarchical bank with 52,000 employees into a flat horizontal network. Inspired by the online heavyweights Spotify and Google, the bank has organized into 'tribes' and 'squads', the latest jargon for working groups. People from different backgrounds ('chapters') work on the development of a single new service. If successful, the new horizontal approach will be rolled out more widely within the bank to boost innovation. In addition, they also invested heavily in start-ups and created innovation studios (a corporate accelerator programme), a safe environment where start-ups (so-called Ninjas) and ING teams can quickly experiment with new business models. Rabobank also formed alliances with several small players in the fintech industry, and at the same time encouraged intrapreneurship within the firm by starting boot camp programmes such as 'Destroy your own bank'.

Corporate governance: short term versus long term

If a firm intends to change its business model radically, its shareholders are not always eager for this to happen. They do not like their firm dispensing with its assets in exchange for the less certain radical new business model (McGrath, 2012). The governance model which seeks to create value for the shareholders is referred to as the 'Anglo-Saxon corporate governance model' (Bezemer et al., 2015).

To investigate how far the Anglo-Saxon model has spread in the Netherlands over the past few decades, we analysed the contents of more than two thousand annual reports of top 100 listed Dutch firms between 1992 and 2012 (Bezemer et al., 2012, 2015), and our findings revealed a clear increase in the use of this model. While 13 per cent of the top 100 listed firms mentioned shareholder value (or an equivalent term) in their 1992 annual report, by 2012 this figure had increased to 83 per cent (see Figure 5.1). It is noticeable that in the last years of the analysis, the number of top 100 firms endorsing a shareholder-value orientation had dropped, from 86 per cent in 2007 to 83 per cent in 2012. This seems to suggest that the financial crisis caused a change in the way firms regard shareholder value. Time will tell whether this represents a permanent change in emphasis. The Anglo-Saxon model is still the dominant governance model for the time being, and adoption of this model has even slightly increased again since 2010 (Bezemer et al., 2012, 2015).

The top 100 listed firms which refer to shareholder value in their annual reports also implement practices associated with shareholder-value orientation more often (Fiss and Zajac, 2004). These practices include value-based management tools, stock option compensation schemes, share buy-back programmes,

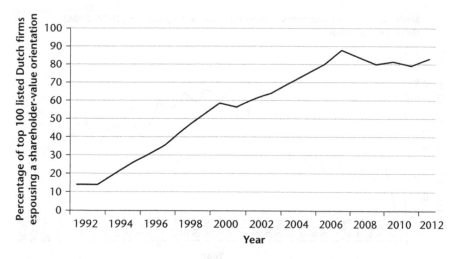

Figure 5.1 The diffusion of shareholder–value orientation among Dutch firms (1992–2012)

Source: adapted from Bezemer et al. (2015)

and presentation of annual figures in accordance with internationally accepted accountancy standards. This seems to show that there is actually a change in the company philosophy of the top 100 listed firms in the Netherlands.

The same research (Bezemer et al., 2015) shows that there are two groups of influential shareholders which have played a significant role in this development. First, the firms are more likely to emphasize shareholder value in their annual reports if they have large shareholders with a financial background (banks, venture capital companies, hedge funds, and pension funds). Second, shareholder value is also mentioned more frequently in the reports if the companies have large shareholders with an Anglo-Saxon background. This makes the growing orientation towards shareholder value in the Netherlands more than just a financial phenomenon (Christensen et al., 2008); the expectations of Anglo-Saxon investors also play a major part. Their attention is focused mainly on short–term results. The shareholders demand a reliable growth in profits and pay handsome rewards to CEOs who achieve this growth (Govindarajan and Trimble, 2011).

This kind of short-term approach promotes replication and even fixation, and can come at the expense of renewal. A recent study by Kwee et al. (2011) confirms this. When Shell was run by Anglo-Saxon managers, the group generated fewer radical innovations than when Rhineland-oriented managers were in command. Shell previously had a number of ideas in

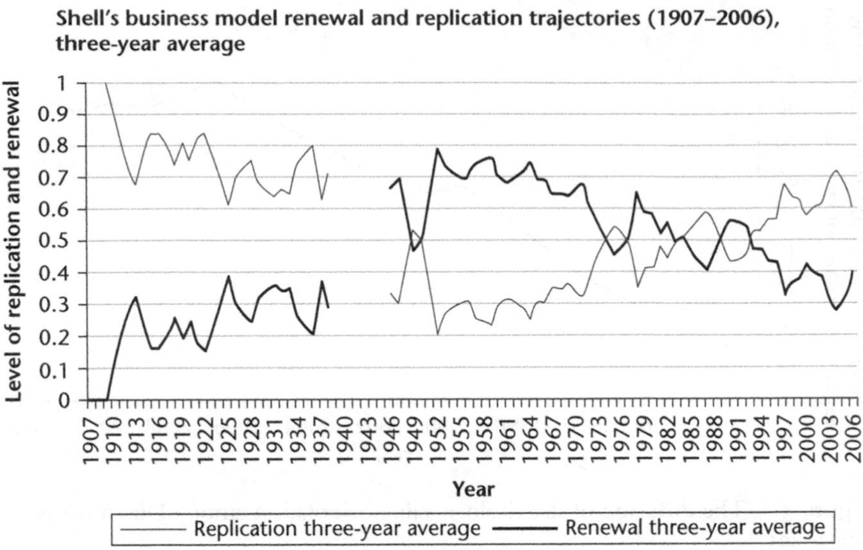

Shell's business model renewal and replication trajectories (1907–2006), three-year average

Figure 5.2 graph with y-axis "Level of replication and renewal" (0 to 1) and x-axis "Year" (1907–2006). Legend: ——— Replication three-year average ——— Renewal three-year average

Figure 5.2 Replication and renewal at Shell
Source: Content analyses of Shell annual reports, 1907–2006 (Kwee, 2009; Kwee et al., 2011). Adapted with the permission of the authors

reserve which might be used as the basis for new business models. These ideas were given considerable investment. Ultimately, however, the group chose to disinvest in solar and wind energy and other renewable sources of energy. The existing business model, based on the extraction of fossil fuels such as oil and gas, was replicated to the maximum extent (Kwee et al., 2011).

Figure 5.2 shows the degree of replication and renewal during the more than one hundred years of Shell, based on an analysis of all Shell's strategic activities over that period. The pattern confirms that the closer we get to peak oil, the more inclined established players are to replicate and hold on to their existing business model. If Shell continues this pattern of replication, it might run into a business model trap. The question is therefore will Shell become the next Kodak or Nokia?

But it does not always have to be the case that value creation for shareholders leads only to a focus on the short-term results and therefore to replication. When a firm signals its desire to become a technological leader, the reaction from shareholders is often positive. This can also help to make shareholders more willing to accept a firm overturning its business model. Sometimes renewal is necessary to preserve the shares' value. If the business model does not undergo fundamental renewal, it can be taken as a sign that the firm is not capable of transforming technological changes into value.

Some firms look for investors with sufficient patience to wait for the returns. Family businesses generally accept that it takes longer before investments pay (McGrath, 2012). For instance, Freddy Heineken once said that the then board members of Heineken thought in terms of years, while he thought in terms of generations. Another good example of a genuine family company is Bose, which spent five years developing a business model around the home theatre concept (Cliffe and McGrath, 2011). Germany has a relatively large number of family companies and banks which operate regionally and cooperatively. Thanks to this, German firms are not so subject to short-term focus, but tend to look to the longer term. Large firms have relatively little dominance in German markets, so it is not entirely coincidental that the German business sector is highly advanced and innovative (Schwab, 2017). All in all, family companies can offer a better context for renewal than organizations which aim predominantly at creating value for the shareholder.

Privatization or spin-offs also contribute to business model innovation. Thus the former Rotterdam Municipal Port was transformed in 2004 into a public limited company with the municipality of Rotterdam and later the State as public shareholders. The transformation was driven by external developments such as an increase in world trade, the shift in the economic centre of gravity to Asia, containerization, and growing competition. Those developments demanded a high degree of efficiency and related infrastructure. Vision, leadership, innovation, and business model renewal were also required. The privatization of the Rotterdam Municipal Port made it possible for the new entity, the Port of Rotterdam Authority, to operate independently on the capital market, be more flexible, and take action more *within* the business sector instead of *alongside* it. This meant that it was easier to realize co-creation, which led to new business and revenue, as we will see in Chapter 6.

Compliance with laws and regulations: enabler and inhibitor of business model innovation

In Chapter 3 we discussed how environmental changes influence business model innovation. However, environmental change can also come about through changes to laws and external regulations, often referred to as regulatory uncertainty. This may force organizations to adjust or replace their business model in order to comply. Organizations grappling with a high level of external regulation are 8 per cent more active in renewing their business model than those which are relatively unaffected by external regulation.

But in any given sector, the regulations in force apply equally to all players, so complying in full with external regulation does not confer any competitive advantage. Several disruptors such as Uber and Airbnb have demonstrated that a failure to comply with industry rules and regulations can actually be very lucrative (Klitsie et al., 2016). For instance, Uber continues to roll out its quite radical UberPop business model (an online platform in which it works with non-professional drivers) in various countries, despite strong opposition from governments, cities, taxi drivers, and unions. Uber is not complying with taxi regulations and laws, but as an active agent is trying to change these regulations and laws. The company has worked hard to present a more grown-up image and brought in a board of heavyweight policy advisors including Neelie Kroes (former European competition commissioner) and Ray LaHood (former US secretary of transportation). By using 'give and take' (for instance, Uber's non-professional drivers have to do some extra tests) it is attempting to please the regulator, and to bend or soften the rules and regulations in such a way that its business model becomes legitimate. Yet the company has clashed with city after city. In Austin, Uber pulled out after a voter referendum that demanded fingerprint checks for its drivers, a measure with which Uber refused to comply. In San Francisco, the company pushed ahead with testing self-driving cars even though it lacked a permit to do so. However, the long-term threat to Uber's business model is the question whether its drivers are independent contractors or employees. The firms considers all its drivers to be independent contractors, which mean they do not receive benefits such as healthcare and are not guaranteed a minimum wage. However, it could see its business model upended if courts determine that their workers should be treated as employees. In 2016 Uber agreed to a payout of up to $100 million for drivers in California and Massachusetts, who argued that they should be classified as employees. Moreover, a ruling in London found that Uber drivers should be considered workers entitled to a minimum wage and holiday pay. Uber is appealing the ruling, but at the same time it is trying to replace its more than one million drivers with robots (driverless car service).

Similarly, Airbnb, the home-sharing platform, has been challenged by legislators in cities such as Amsterdam and New York. It makes its money by charging both hosts and guests transaction commissions, and in exchange provides services such as payment handling, insurance, a private messaging system, and collecting reviews from previous users. While founded in 2008, it became profitable for the first time in the second half of 2016. In 2017 it had already hosted more than 60 million guests in 34,000 cities around the world. Along with this tremendous growth in the hospitality industry, Airbnb has prompted discussion of regulatory issues, because traditional hotels reacted strongly to Airbnb's arrival in their industry (Mikhalkina, 2016). These traditional players tried to enlist the help of regulators by arguing that Airbnb's business model was illegal. New York State's attorney-general demanded that Airbnb hand over records of its hosts in New York City so that it can be verified whether they were paying taxes levied on hotels. In order to increase its legitimacy and satisfy regulators, Airbnb has had to respond to complaints from New York State and Amsterdam City Council. In New York, the company has banned new hosts from having more than one listing, in an effort to limit commercial operators. In Amsterdam, Airbnb users now pay standard city tax, and only the owners of apartments and houses (and not the tenants) are allowed to put their property on the platform. Moreover, Airbnb will block its hosts from letting homes for more than sixty nights, which will curb its revenue growth in Amsterdam. Such concessions are a stark reversal by a company that long resisted policing its hosts on the ground that it is the hosts, not Airbnb, who are responsible for complying with local laws. Some analysts see Airbnb's new, conciliatory approach as a sign that it is eager to resolve regulatory conflicts ahead of its initial public offering, which could come as soon as 2018. To sum up, the two icons of disruptive tech, Uber and Airbnb, struggle to shed their rule-breaking habits and take a more mature, conciliatory tone. They have tried working more closely with regulators to craft policy, although with mixed results. They have clashed again and again with courts and lawmakers, and found in the end their business constrained by increasing regulation.

Besides failing to comply, firms can also choose to go beyond the statutory requirements (Klitsie et al., 2016). They can voluntarily adopt standards along with a select group of other industry players in order to influence regulators and actively shape the business environment. Firms that over-comply in this way are ahead of industry regulations but also of customer requirements. When industry regulations are made more rigorous, these firms will not have to incur the extra costs of adapting to the new standards. For instance, some first-movers in the Dutch financial industry have voluntarily abandoned their commission-based business model based on bonuses from insurance companies and commissions on products delivered (Volberda and Heij, 2014). Now that the Dutch regulator has forbidden commission payments for certain financial products, these companies that have adopted a more transparent business model (based on a fixed fee per hour) well in advance are definitely outperforming the firms which did not over-comply.

According to Atzo Nicolaï, former director of DSM Netherlands, clever, international legislation in food, safety, the environment, and sustainable energy supply can help business model innovation and the competitive position of firms. New or tightened rules on the job market, social policy, or targets for sustainability can challenge the business models of established players and also encourage new entrants to develop new models in line with those regulations. With environmental legislation, this has also been called the 'California effect', in reference to the strict legislation introduced in that US state for vehicle CO_2 emissions. This legislation gave a boost to the development of electric cars, among other things.

DSM also profited from different rules. The stricter Californian legislation on evaporative emissions from the fuel tanks of agricultural and horticultural equipment inspired the group to develop and patent a new device, the Akulon Fuel Lock, which releases almost no evaporative emissions. 'Thus legislation was the motor behind innovations which firms could use to conquer new markets and which delivered a clear safety advantage to customers. Everybody wins,' says Nicolaï. 'Being entrepreneurs they grumble a bit about it at first, but then they can make the most of their leading position for years' (FD Outlook, 2012).

New laws and changes to regulation can not only force firms to adjust their existing business models, but also give them opportunities to develop entirely new models. For example, when the Global Positioning System (GPS) developed by the US Army was released for non-military applications as well, TomTom profited from this. Changes of regulation, including deregulation of the European aviation industry—with Britain and Ireland as pioneers—enabled the rise and growth of the low-cost, low-fare concepts of companies such as Ryanair and EasyJet. These changes influenced not only the business model of established commercial airlines, but also those of airports (Barrett, 2000).

Laws can also obstruct and inhibit renewal. Medicines have to go through lengthy and expensive procedures before they can be put on the market. On the other hand, technologies and concepts are protected through intellectual property rights in the form of patents. This kind of protection makes it easier to replicate a successful new business model. Thus media company Talpa was able to sell its concept of *The Voice* to around 45 countries, including China and Brazil.

Protection through intellectual property rights is not always a guarantee of success, because alternatives can be developed around a technology or concept with the same or a similar function (Ettlie and Reza, 1992). Buck Star Coffee and Wumart are suspiciously close in concept to Starbucks Coffee and Walmart, for instance. Protection through intellectual property often gives a company a false sense of security, which can in turn encourage replication that continues for a long time or even fixation. Thus former state-run enterprises in the telecom sector found it very difficult to renew their business model after privatization. In a free market, they no longer had the advantages of their previous monopolistic position but had to compete with other players, although they had little experience of renewal.

Laws and regulations can therefore affect business model innovation in different ways. New rules can (indirectly) force organizations to change their business models or develop new ones. They can also offer various opportunities, although these may sometimes be limited in some way.

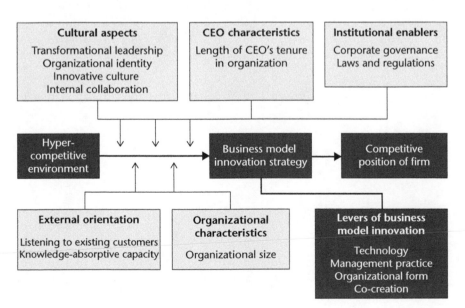

Figure 5.3 Enablers of business model innovation

Finally, regulations can offer security, because they establish and protect the ownership of new inventions. However, as there is considerable scope for imitating new concepts, this often offers a false sense of security.

Wrap-up

As shown in Table 5.1, various internal and external factors can inhibit or facilitate replication and renewal. The list of factors in this table is not exhaustive, but from our research and the case studies we can conclude that they are the most important enablers and inhibitors. In Figure 5.3, these enablers are clustered into cultural and leadership factors, CEO character-istics, degree of external orientation, organizational characteristics, and institutional factors.

To what extent are organizations tied to either replication or renewal? In Chapter 6 we use four extensive case studies to illustrate how firms have different business model transformation trajectories. These include firms which first used replication and then made the change to renewal, or vice versa, but also firms which were fixated upon particular business models and have since had to replicate at an accelerated pace in order to remain successful.

6

Business Model Transformation

Driven by Strategy or Customer?

. . . .

THE MINIDISC, ONCE A MODEL OF STATE-OF-
THE-ART TECHNOLOGY

Do you still remember the minidisc? Not so long ago—back in the 1990s—it was state of the art. Music lovers were delighted when Sony launched it. The minidisc combined the best of its predecessors (the cassette tape and the CD): good sound quality and the ability to make your own recordings. In addition, the minidisc recorder was cheaper and more practical than the DAT recorder. Sony seemed to be extending the dominance in the personal audio market which the group had established in the 1970s when it brought in the Walkman.

But things turned out differently. Apple, a brand until then associated mainly with graphic designers, launched the MP3 player at the start of this century. Its arrival indicated that the Americans were laying down a new standard. The physical sound carrier disappeared. Files could also be copied much faster and storage capacity was expanded.

Instead of entering the MP3 market, Sony stuck to its minidisc. It was not only that the group had a great belief in its own concept, it was also because the group had acquired a vast music catalogue with the recording company CBS. The ease of copying which the MP3 offered was a serious threat to this. And how did Sony react? With a minidisc recorder and inbuilt security which could convert files at high speed—and a security device which prevented the user from copying more than three times. It was a case of 'too little, too late'. Apple also had an answer to illegal copying and downloading: iTunes. The rest is history. Apple developed from a niche player into a trendsetter. The last minidisc recorder rolled off the production line in March 2013.

A future version of this book might ask, do you still remember the iPad? The fact is, investors and shareholders are currently grumbling about Apple simply relying on updating existing products—in other words, practising replication. There have been no new technological breakthroughs since the death of the company's leader Steve Jobs in 2011. Apple is now mainly launching new versions of the iPad, and doing this with increasing frequency. Just a bit longer, and will Apple be the Sony of this decade?

. . . .

The business model innovation matrix

The moral of the story above is that once you have reached the stage of business model renewal, you do not get to stay there automatically. More than that, it seems to be almost unavoidable that a period of renewal will be followed by a period of replication. Incorrect estimations, defensive strategies, the loss of key figures, complacency—various causes can quickly undo the benefits of a head start. Nokia, the firm which was in at the birth of the mobile phone, is all too familiar with that. And the cases later in this chapter provide other examples of this phenomenon.

The two dominant types of business model innovation, renewal and replication, were introduced in Chapter 2. In Chapter 4 we saw how business model innovation can be boosted by different combinations of levers which can be either more internal or more external in nature. Internal business model innovation is strategy-driven, while external business model innovation is driven by the customer. Combining types of business model innovation with differing business model orientations gives us four possible variations (see the business model innovation matrix in Figure 6.1):

- *strategy-driven renewal.* This is characterized by transformational leadership, a committed top and middle management, an innovative culture, a focus on internal knowledge absorption, a dynamic environment, and an internal organizational identity subject to frequent change. We call this variation 'explore and dominate'. This proactive renewal of the business model entails an organization-wide transformation which involves all levels of management.

- *customer-driven renewal.* This is characterized by transformational leadership, a committed top and frontline management, an innovative, customer-driven culture, a focus on external knowledge absorption, a dynamic environment, and an external organizational identity in flux. We call this variation 'explore and connect'. Renewal here occurs by upgrading the business model in response to completely new customers.

- *strategy-driven replication.* This is characterized by transactional leadership, a committed top management, a less innovative culture, a focus on internal knowledge absorption, a competitive environment, and a strong internal organizational identity. We call this variation 'exploit and improve'. In this case, a directive management improves and perfects the existing business model.

	Strategy-driven	Customer-driven
Business model renewal	**Explore and dominate:** *organization-wide transformation* 1. Transformational leadership 2. Commitment of top and middle management 3. Innovative culture 4. Internal knowledge absorption 5. Dynamic environment 6. New internal identity	**Explore and connect:** *upgrading to new customers* 1. Transformational leadership 2. Commitment of top and frontline management 3. Innovative, customer-driven culture 4. External knowledge absorption 5. Dynamic environment 6. New external identity
Business model replication	**Exploit and improve:** *directive improvement* 1. Transactional leadership 2. Commitment of top managers 3. Less innovative culture 4. Internal knowledge absorption 5. Competitive pressure 6. Strong internal identity	**Exploit and connect:** *linking with existing customers* 1. Transactional leadership 2. Commitment of top management 3. Customer-driven culture 4. External knowledge absorption 5. High competitive pressure 6. Strong external identity

Figure 6.1 The business model innovation matrix

- *customer-driven replication.* This is characterized by transactional leadership, a committed top management, a customer-driven culture, a focus on external knowledge absorption, a high level of competitive pressure, and a strong external organizational identity. We call this variation 'exploit and connect'. In this variation, the business model is improved significantly by being linked more strongly to existing customers. Knowledge combination and exchange are particularly important in this variation.

Firms can be positioned in one of the four quadrants of the business model innovation matrix. DSM, for instance, fits into the 'explore and dominate' quadrant (see Figure 6.2). The firm has fundamentally transformed its business model several times: having started with coal, it moved to bulk chemicals, then to fine chemicals, and more recently to life sciences and materials. Firms like Apple and Google can also be placed in this quadrant. Apple has changed its initial business model radically within a short period of time. The firm switched from providing personal computers to supplying entirely new devices for new markets, including the iPod (music market),

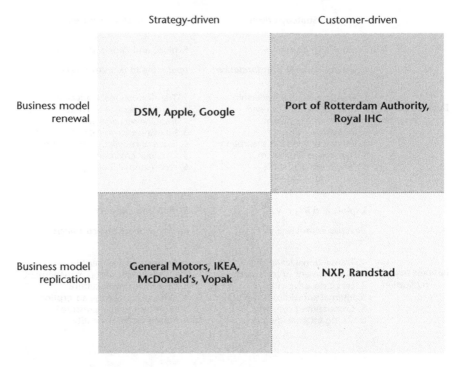

Figure 6.2 Four types of business model innovation: firms in each quadrant

iPad (tablet market), and iPhone (telephony), and services linked to those devices. Google, too, diversified, and stacked up a series of business models. Instead of being purely a search engine, the firm began offering 'business intelligence' to firms, for instance, and developed automated control for cars and activities in the optical industry (Google Glass). At DSM, Apple, and Google, renewal of the business model was driven more from the inside out. The firms saw that there were more attractive returns to be gained by going into unfamiliar territory. In these cases, it was not direct customer needs in the market which led to business model renewal (market response), but a pro-active strategy of management to create new markets (market creation).

The Port of Rotterdam Authority and Royal IHC fit in the 'explore and connect' quadrant (see also Figure 6.2). The Port of Rotterdam Authority transformed its business model from that of *landlord* to *port developer* by working closely together with customers and attracting new customers. The business model of Royal IHC, which supplies vessels and services for the offshore, dredging, and wet mining markets, changed abruptly from 'if the slipways are full, then it's OK' to a more customer-oriented model. The firm created value by offering integrated technological solutions.

NXP and Randstad belong in the 'exploit and connect' quadrant. NXP's current business model is considerably more strongly customer-driven, and large customers such as Apple and Samsung are involved early on in the development of customized semiconductors. Randstad Netherlands scaled up its business model of providing temporary agency workers to offer 'integrated HR solutions' in which it takes over HR activities from customers such as rostering, planning, outplacement, and recruitment and selection.

The 'exploit and improve' quadrant includes General Motors (GM), IKEA, McDonald's, and Vopak. GM lost ground in the long run by continuing to refine existing models. Being in this quadrant does not necessarily have to be negative, though. IKEA and McDonald's are highly successful at replicating their existing business models in many different countries. Using their experience, they have been able to refine their business models repeatedly over time. Vopak, the world's leading independent tank storage company, has also learned by trial and error that strategy-driven replication of its business model for tank storage (liquid gas, biofuels, and oil) was more likely to provide long-term success.

In this chapter, we focus in detail on the levers used in the particular approaches mentioned above. Some levers figure more prominently in some approaches than in others. We also illustrate the most important enablers and inhibitors of business model innovation. Some of these factors can also be found in the four types of business model innovation shown in Figure 6.1. Here, too, different factors are present to a greater or lesser extent, varying according to the quadrant.

In Chapter 3 we saw how the level of disruption in the business environment (dynamism, competitiveness) affects the degree to which renewal and replication result in better company performance. Environmental dynamism also influences the sequence of business model innovation. Acquiring knowledge from the market in an environment which is not very dynamic—for instance, through market research—can result in refined technologies and business models which form the basis of better company performance (the 'exploit and improve' variation). When replication follows the market in this way, the emphasis is on discovering the causes of customer satisfaction or dissatisfaction, correcting errors, increasing positive experiences, and giving customers what they want (Berthon et al., 2004).

In a dynamic environment, the sequence is very different: renewal leads to new markets. This sequence is to be found mainly in firms with a strong technological orientation (the 'explore and dominate' variations). Sony's release of the Walkman was a case in point. Market research had indicated that the consumer did not want to walk around with this kind of device, but when introduced by the obstinate Sony the Walkman proved to be a resounding success nevertheless. Customers are not always conscious of their need for new technology, new products, or new services (Berthon et al., 2004). Sometimes new technologies, products, and services even create their own demand (market creation). The iPhone is a good example.

Of course, this is only a model, and in reality organizations may not always fit neatly into any one of these quadrants. How good the fit is will also depend on the point at which one measures it. Over time, most firms move between different quadrants of the business model innovation matrix. An organization which has initially worked on renewal can be actively replicating just a few years later, as the case of Sony shows.

Likewise, firms can also move relatively swiftly from replication to renewal. In business model innovation it is also possible to be strategy-driven one moment and customer-driven the next. We call this migration from one stage to another 'business model transformation'. In the current dynamic context, firms can go extremely rapidly from one stage to the next. In theory, an organization can go through all quadrants of the business model innovation matrix in a single decade, although what happens more often is that it moves between two or three quadrants.

Our field research has provided a number of cases which show how firms make different transformation trajectories between the various quadrants of the business model innovation matrix. These firms include DSM, the Port of Rotterdam Authority, NXP, and Royal IHC. The cases below provide more insight into the practicalities of reinventing business models, with all the successes, difficulties, and ups and downs which that involves.

DSM: explore and dominate

The Dutch firm DSM has undergone various radical transformations in terms of the activities, strategy, and ownership of the group. Within the group, they talk about 'reinventing yourself'.

Based in Limburg, DSM began life as a mining company in 1902, and was a fully state-controlled enterprise. When the mines in the Netherlands were closing down in the 1960s and 1970s, the firm chose to specialize in bulk chemicals. It later shifted to petrochemicals and fine chemicals.

The firm was privatized in two tranches: two thirds of the firm's operations were privatized in 1989, and the remaining third in 1996. The most recent strategic reorientation, which is also the starting point for this case, began in 1997. From that time onwards DSM positioned itself as a life sciences firm and managed to build up a world-leading position in this field. This transition arose from one of the Corporate Strategic Dialogues which the group holds every three to five years. In these dialogues, key figures develop scenarios and future visions, and the group's strategic priorities are established.

In the period leading up to 1997, DSM was a petrochemical firm which changed itself through replication. Subsequently, the greater potential for growth and profit offered by life sciences and the declining attraction of petrochemicals inspired the top managers at DSM to undertake a radical form of renewal. The renewal was more strategy-driven than customer-driven. The petrochemical division, which had been the core unit of the group for decades, was sold off in its entirety. Top management announced this decision long before a buyer had even been found.

. . . .

THE TIMELINE TO DSM'S MOST RECENT STRATEGIC CHANGE

1997	Analysis of societal trends and of the group's current activities convinced the top management that DSM should concentrate on biotechnology.
1998	After a period of collaboration with Gist-Brocades, DSM took over this food and biotechnology firm which had a great capacity for innovation, but insufficient capital. Feike Sijbesma, director of Gist-Brocades, became director of DSM in 2000 and CEO in 2007. The takeover had a huge effect on the R&D approach at DSM.
2000	DSM strengthened its position in the life sciences sector by acquiring the American firm Catalytica Pharmaceuticals. The larger profits in this sector led to discussion of whether DSM should stay in petrochemicals. The decision was taken to leave it.
2002	DSM's petrochemical division was sold to the Saudi Arabian firm SABIC.
2003	The firm acquired the vitamin and fine chemicals division of the Swiss company Roche.
2005–2010	DSM divested businesses from the Industrial Chemicals cluster, and strengthened its position in life sciences and material sciences.
2011	The firm took over the American Martek Biosciences Corporation and established a joint venture with the Sinochem Group (anti-infectives).
2012	DSM took over the American biomedical firm Kensey Nash, the Canadian firm Ocean Nutrition (food and diet products), and a number of other biotechnological and food firms.

. . . .

The transition at DSM was completely strategy-driven. At the start of the twenty-first century when the proactive DSM management initiated renewal, the group fitted perfectly in the top-left box in Figure 6.1. In subsequent years, the total group moved from extreme renewal to relatively more replication. DSM reinforced its position in life sciences, partly through takeovers, but was no longer following entirely new paths, with the exception of biomedical materials and biofuels. In addition, the remaining renewal in some parts of the group became more customer-driven. Innovation now takes place together with the customer, rather than in protected R&D centres. In order to stimulate this more external orientation, DSM introduced the slogan 'proudly found elsewhere'.

The strategic reorientation which started in 1997 resulted ultimately in an almost totally new group. Hein Schreuder, former Executive Vice-President Corporate Strategy & Acquisition at DSM (also called 'the architect of the new DSM'), notes in a statement made in 2012 that, 'In the past fifteen years, 83 per cent of DSM has changed.'

The most important lever in DSM's transition was technology. Petrochemicals and life sciences are two very different branches of industry. Yet it is too simplistic to assert that DSM got rid of old technology and embraced new technology. Although a lot of knowledge disappeared when the petrochemical branch was sold off, the firm's existing technological expertise and competences definitely helped in the transition. For instance, there was already a *special products* business unit at DSM. It produced components needed for penicillin, among other things. 'But we saw that we did not earn the money in the penicillin value chain,' says Robert Kirschbaum, former Vice-President Innovation at DSM. This stimulated the firm's interest in life sciences, with its higher margins. What had at first been a peripheral technology became the core technology. In that sense, technology was not only an outcome of the transition of DSM, but also an essential for the transition to take place.

The method of innovating changed significantly after the change in policy. The life sciences sector is much more dynamic than the petrochemical sector. The old way of working, with central R&D laboratories, did not suit this. The group therefore made innovation more central to the organization and used a wider range of approaches. Usually the acquired party has to adjust to the ways of the acquirer, but it is striking in this case that Gist-Brocades in fact served as the model for DSM. A worldwide network of R&D centres was set up to concentrate on innovation. The company also has a separate Innovation Centre (IC), which explores technologies and other areas that might be of interest in the future.

The IC operates according to the *open innovation funnel*, a concept developed by Henry Chesbrough, the open innovation guru. The principle here is that ideas and concepts flow into the funnel, either from internal research or joint ventures, or from other external parties. Contact with the external parties is maintained during all stages.

The IC tries to accelerate the process of technological innovation by exploring entirely new activities. The culture in the IC is very different from that in the other units of the organization. Informal statements often heard in the IC include 'Ask forgiveness, not permission' and 'Open innovation is no longer a competitive advantage. It has become a competitive necessity.' Robert Kirschbaum clarifies this: 'You don't say that kind of thing in a large firm. Perhaps you do them, but you don't say them. There are implicit rules, and they are sacred.' DSM attempts to spread the radical thinking on innovation rapidly by moving IC employees to other organizational units and vice versa.

DSM's new business model combines the explorative approach of the IC with the more exploitative activities of the various business groups. Now that DSM has been active for almost a decade in life sciences and has achieved much renewal through takeovers, the group is shifting towards replication. Customers and other external parties play an increasingly important part in innovation through co-creation and open innovation. The mergers, takeovers, and joint ventures provide a way of obtaining expertise and competences which the firm does not yet have, or not in sufficient quantity. The group's philosophy here is that expertise and competences should not come solely from outside: an internal basis should already exist. The new must take root in the old.

Top management plays an important part in driving the innovation. In 2005 the company expressed the ambition that €1 billion of its revenue should come from new products by 2010. 'Usually that would be 500 to 600 million in five years,' says Rob van Leen, Chief Innovation Officer (CIO) at DSM. 'That meant that we had to double the speed of innovation. It was translated into everyone's targets. Many people needed assistance with this. It helps a lot that the Managing Board and the CEO are seeking to make the firm much more innovative.' In fact, the group exceeded its target, achieving €1.3 billion in revenue.

Technology has been an important lever for transforming the business model at DSM. The firm invests a total of 5 per cent of its annual revenue in research and innovation. This amounts to around €450 million, and about 20 per cent of that goes to the IC. It is striking that the Chief Technology Officer (CTO) is accountable to the CIO, who in turn reports to the CEO.

Management forms the second lever at DSM. The transition from petrochemicals to life sciences demanded a great deal from management. To ensure that the changes were supported across the organization, top management invested heavily in new management practices such as inspiring leadership, exemplary behaviour, transparent communication, and several activities to promote a new identity. A fundamental change in mindset was required. The focus on security that is so dominant in the petrochemical sector was replaced by an emphasis on sustainability. Thinking in terms of rules gave way to thinking in terms of trust. Managers were assigned different roles and had to acquire new competences, partly because of the many joint ventures. More emphasis was placed on the capacity to integrate and connect. External awareness and (externally oriented) knowledge absorption became more important. Job rotation was used to help ensure that the focus on innovation extended to those parts of the group less inclined to renewal.

The organizational form lever was used to effect drastic changes to the way the organization was structured. In three phases, over the course of nearly fifteen years, DSM changed from being a firm with strongly centralized management to one which was decentralized. This was later adjusted again, when ICT and Purchasing were grouped together, for example. New operating companies and positions were created. The firm began to recruit people from outside more than it had done previously, and the provincial Limburg profile became blurred. The management control systems within the firm were also adjusted. In the petrochemical sector it is crucial that the fixed expenses are covered. In life sciences, the aim is to realize the largest possible margin. That requires different control systems.

The drastic changes have meant that over the past decade DSM has needed to pay a great deal of attention to its corporate identity and to its internal culture. 'We are a collection of tribes, with different genes coming from either the old DSM, or the acquired companies such as Gist-Brocades and Roche,' says Robert Kirschbaum. At Gist-Brocades the mindset was more entrepreneurial than at DSM, for instance, while at Roche people had been used to a more directive style of management. The *One-DSM* programme was set up with the aim of creating a common culture. However, the programme also allowed plenty of room for manoeuvre at the local level.

A recurring element in the renewals at DSM was the presence of leaders with strong personalities who combined inspiration and charisma with a vision for the future. They were often very alert in their reactions. Hein Schreuder gives an example: 'The former board chairman, Wim Bogers, had realized that the region of South Limburg lacked an economic basis for mining. The mining industry in Germany and Belgium kept going for much longer, buoyed up by considerable subsidies. DSM was very future-oriented. Even while it was still a state-run enterprise, it made the change to being a chemicals firm.'

For Schreuder, the shared understanding that you have to fundamentally reinvent yourself is 'part of the history of the firm. It is in our genes. We know that what is sufficient today can be insufficient tomorrow. It is part of the culture at DSM that we are in a continual state of renewal.' Board chairpersons sometimes stepped out of their own shadow and were willing to explore new and unfamiliar territory. For instance, the reorientation to life sciences was initiated by CEO Simon de Bree, who came from petrochemicals.

The DSM leaders used transformational and transactional leadership to bring about the intended change. Transformational leadership helped to create enthusiasm, belief, and support for the huge shift. Transactional leadership, traditionally very much part of DSM, was used to ensure the new behaviour, roles, and methods of working became firmly anchored within the organization. This sometimes entailed using assertive communication: if people could not or did not want to cope with the changes, they were asked to look elsewhere. The observation that more than a century of transitions had only made DSM more successful was vitally important in convincing employees of the need to change.

DSM has remained a firm on the Rhineland model. This implies that to ensure successful business model transformation, top management focused on long-term continuity so that they could satisfy multiple stakeholders simultaneously: shareholders, NGOs, and customers, but also DSM employees. In this connection, the leadership was not only results-oriented, but also process-oriented. As Schreuder notes: 'you cannot achieve a result with behaviour that we find unacceptable. That aspect weighs as heavily as the result for us. That's what we understand inspiring leadership to be.

Results have to be achieved from an inspired attitude. We want people to work with all their heart on projects, not just because their boss says they have to do it.'

The balance sheet

- In the late 1990s, DSM started switching its business model from strategy-driven replication to strategy-driven renewal. In the first decade of this century, the group shifted to a model of customer-driven replication.

- The transition at DSM shows that a change in business model has an impact on all departments and activities. Using one lever (technology) also has direct consequences for the other levers (management, organization, and co-creation).

- Technology was the most important lever at DSM. The group turned a peripheral technology (life sciences) into its core technology, especially through takeovers, and divested itself of the old core technology (petrochemicals).

- Transformational and visionary leadership played an important part in the transition. Transactional leadership was used to anchor the changes. Changes were initiated top-down.

- Top and middle management were the architects of the changes. They used practices such as exemplary behaviour and intensive (transparent) communication to move the organization in the desired direction. A lot of attention was paid to changing the identity and culture of the organization.

- The nature of innovation at DSM has changed significantly. Takeovers brought in new expertise and competences, but also different cultures and mentalities. More is now being done on open innovation and co-creation.

- Knowledge absorption was traditionally a mainly internal matter, but since the transition there has been more of a focus on external knowledge absorption (from a 'not invented here' attitude to a 'proudly found elsewhere' philosophy).

- In moving to life sciences, DSM entered a much more dynamic market.

Figure 6.3 shows the business model transformation trajectory of DSM. Table 6.1 outlines the essential areas of focus for top and middle managers.

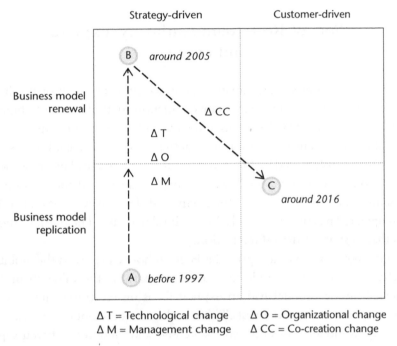

Figure 6.3 Business model transformation at DSM

Table 6.1 Management roles in business model transformation: DSM

	Trajectory A > B	Trajectory B > C
Top management	• from transactional to transformational leadership	• more focus on transactional leadership
	• initiating changes in levers: new technology, new organizational forms, and new management practices	• focus on co-creation and open innovation
	• creating an innovative organizational culture	
Middle management	• more decentralization, more emphasis on trust	• adjustment of coordination systems
	• strengthening internal cooperation	• strengthening internal and external cooperation

Port of Rotterdam Authority: explore and connect

The Port of Rotterdam Authority, established in 1932, traditionally had a largely administrative and exploitative function. It took care of shipping transactions, leased quay locations and sites, and collected port dues. It also earned most of its revenue from those activities. The term 'landlord' is very fitting for the role played by the Port Authority. The landlord business model focuses on land exploitation (lease and maintenance) and the handling of shipping traffic in the Port of Rotterdam and the nearby coastal area. The firm operated reactively and had a hierarchical structure. The business model was that of strategy-driven replication.

In its 1997–2000 business plan, the Port Authority expressed the ambition to change from being a landlord to an orchestrator in the value chain. This renewed business model had an explicit focus on creating strategic value based on customer requirements. This was done by developing strategic connectivity in the form of knowledge-intensive and innovation-driven supply chains, networks, clusters, and customer relationships. The firm did indeed gradually take on a different role after 2000, a development which was boosted by its privatization in 2004. The best description of its new role is 'port developer'. The port developer business model focuses on entrepreneurship (often in cooperation with the private sector) and on innovation-driven port development in a broad sense. The Port Authority now controls developments in the port industrial area in and around Rotterdam. It operates more proactively and more innovatively, and the organization has a more decentralized structure. There is more collaboration with customers. The business model has become one of customer-driven renewal.

The Port Authority, which had a turnover of around €615 million in 2012 and employed 1,160 people, operates in an international and highly dynamic environment. There is stiff competition between the West European ports, especially in the area between Hamburg and Le Havre. The (petro)chemical clusters are also increasingly competing with one another internationally and also face disruption from renewable forms of energy such as biomass.

The international environment in which the Port Authority operates has changed significantly in the past ten years:

- world trade has grown
- the economic centre of gravity has shifted to Asia, and with it the transport flows

- transport has grown in scale
- more freight is now being transported by container
- raw materials have become scarcer
- logistics chains have been integrated.

The Authority's domestic environment has also become increasingly complex. New projects, such as Maasvlakte 2 (a man-made port area which has been reclaimed from the sea), bring with them many new laws and regulations. More and more stakeholders have to be taken into consideration in the planning and execution of projects. Safety requirements are becoming increasingly stringent, and there are also greater demands for sustainability. Hans Smits, former CEO of the Port Authority, said: 'We conduct many more debates, including different types of debates. The process in itself has become more complex, not only in the number and kind of stakeholders but also in the issues we have to consider. We are right in the middle of this debate with various stakeholders and it determines the decision-making process and outcomes. That is new for us.'

The Port Authority became an independent governmental public limited company (NV) in 2004, with the municipality of Rotterdam and later the State as public shareholders. This privatization gave the Port Authority greater independence in the capital market, more flexibility, and more scope to engage directly with business. As a result, more options opened up for the Authority, particularly for co-creation.

An important lever in the transformation of the Port Authority was the organizational form. Successive changes in the internal organizational structure of the Port Authority, both before and after privatization, led to a flatter organizational structure with more horizontal relationships. This brought the organization closer to the market and into closer contact with the customer than before. Operations also were more project-based, and project coordination was professionalized. Financial and operational audits were introduced as standard. Employees were deliberately given more opportunities to switch functions within the organization. All in all, this resulted in greater internal flexibility.

Various new business units were set up between 2000 and 2015, aimed at generating new business and income streams. These include the Innovation Board, the Port of Rotterdam International department (PORint), designed to help ports worldwide achieve their maximum potential, and PortXL, the first 'world port accelerator programme' that supports start-ups in the Rotterdam Port area on their entrepreneurial journey. The Innovation

Board was established in 2012 to bring together innovation-related issues and give them more prominence. The new PORint department covers all the international activities of the Port Authority, and is designed to establish a stronger portfolio of foreign participation. The accelerator PortXL was launched in 2015 in order to boost the number of successful harbour-related start-ups in the Rotterdam Port area. PortXL focuses on building a viable ecosystem, consisting of founders, investors, and corporate partners, aimed at growing and disrupting the maritime, logistics, energy, and chemical/ refinery markets.

The second lever was a different way of managing. In the new organ-ization, the number of management layers was reduced substantially. New managers were also appointed. In 2005 Hans Smits became the new CEO. Many of the original top twenty managers were replaced in the subse-quent period, and in their place came managers who each had their own defined area of responsibility, such as corporate strategy or treasury. These days managers report directly to a member of the board which consists of three members: the CEO, the Chief Financial Officer (CFO), and the Chief Operating Officer (COO). This direct reporting approach is a break with the past.

Another management innovation at the Port Authority is that external stakeholders such as firms, non-government organizations, and employer and employee organizations are more involved in projects. The goal is to make final decision-making run more smoothly and to create a wider support base for projects. Hans Smits explains: 'I can only see one way of avoiding paralysis and remaining flexible and decisive. And that is to seek dialogue: to really listen to each other properly.' This stakeholder manage-ment can also be seen in the implementation agenda for the Port Vision 2030 future plan.

Today, the Port Authority is positioned by its senior management as more of an 'entrepreneurial developer'. Co-creation, especially with customers, is used expressly to increase the port's competitive capacity.

A slightly less important lever in this case is technology. The nature of the Port Authority means that technological changes affect the business model only to a limited extent. However, the Authority has brought in new ICT systems that enable it to provide more efficient and safer ship-ping handling. The Port Management Information System HaMIS, the first phase of which was delivered in 2011, makes the Port Authority better able to coordinate the nautical chain. And the innovative communication system Portbase (set up in 2009 through co-creation with the Port of Amsterdam) optimizes the cross-port logistics of firms. Nonetheless, new technology has played a supporting role in the Port Authority's transformation, rather than a leading role.

. . . .

THE ROLE OF THE LEADERSHIP IN BUSINESS MODEL INNOVATION

The Port Authority had two leaders between 2000 and 2012. Willem Scholten was CEO from 1992 to 2004. He was considered to be a transformational leader, a strategic thinker, and a visionary. Under his leadership, the operations of the Port Authority became far more commercial and businesslike. However, the financial irregularities in what became known as the 'RDM affair' led to Scholten's enforced departure in 2004. He was blamed for the illegal issuing of €183.5 million in bank guarantees by the Port of Rotterdam on behalf of an embattled Dutch company, RDM, run by Joep van den Nieuwenhuyzen. The guarantees were given to ensure that the port gained several production contracts, including submarine construction orders, and were also needed to ensure a line of credit from the banks to four RDM subsidiaries. When the guarantees were later turned into loans for RDM subsidiaries, the German Commerzbank and the British bank Barclays demanded that the money be repaid.

Hans Smits was CEO between 2005 and 2014. His appointment heralded a period in which there was a greater emphasis on transparency and a more focused participation portfolio. Smits can also be typified as a transformational leader, with a businesslike and pioneering way of operating. With his arrival, the process of making the Port Authority more businesslike continued. The firm also operated more transparently, both internally and externally. For instance, a great deal of information was put on the intranet. Steps were taken to improve the Port Authority's financial position so that dividend agreements could be fulfilled and customers could be offered a good price to quality ratio.

The Port Vision 2030 and the business plans (2006–2010 and 2011–2015) drawn up under Hans Smits emphasize the role of the Port Authority as a port developer. Smits advocated simplifying procedures, so that action could be taken more efficiently. He emphasized the importance of innovation, because it enables an organization to remain competitive in continually changing market situations: 'The fact that we are a world market leader increases the pressure on the organization to always be at the front and to renew ourselves again and again, which will enable us to reinforce that position in the increasingly competitive environment.'

Smits believes that continued attention to business model innovation is a condition of good leadership. In his eyes, changing human behaviour through social innovation is the crux. This would only be made possible by changing the organizational form and adopting new ways of managing. To realize the new business model, he believed that stakeholder management—and especially achieving a good balance between the interests of the various stakeholders—was also essential.

. . . .

Once the conditions were in place (a flatter organization, project-based management, and stakeholder management) the Port Authority created different forms of new business together with external parties such as customers from the petrochemical, energy, transport, and logistics sectors, and other port authorities. The advantage of partnerships for the Port Authority is that it can continue to concentrate on its own core business, while at the same time benefitting from the expertise of the joint venture partner. This cooperation with other firms also aids in integrating logistics chains and making them more efficient. In the words of Smits: 'The Port can play a role in this as an intermediary: getting parties around the table to bundle transport activities, or as an investor: becoming the owner of large inland terminals for inland shipping or the railway.' Co-creation has ultimately proved to be the most important lever for the Port Authority. It has resulted in strategic renewal, knowledge development, innovation, and an international strategic positioning which is more difficult for others to copy. Four examples of co-creation at the Port Authority are discussed next.

Joint venture with the Port of Sohar in Oman

The port of Rotterdam is becoming an increasingly important link in global transport chains. This makes it important for it to have a presence on the growth markets as well. By participating in the activities of other ports, the Port Authority makes its own competences more visible to others within the market and boosts its role as chain director. Being active in growth markets also increases its knowledge of those markets.

All these considerations formed the background to the decision to take a 50 per cent participating interest in the Sohar International Development Company and the Sohar Industrial Port Company, the landlord of the Port of Sohar in Oman. The joint venture with the government of Oman involves both managing and developing this port industrial complex. It is the Port Authority's first participative venture internationally. Besides direct revenue, the Port Authority's involvement in the Port of Sohar also creates a demand for the expertise of Dutch firms such as Arcadis, BAM Groep, C. Steinweg-Handelsveem, Royal Haskoning, Tebodin, and Van Oord.

Multicore: an underground distribution system

The Port Authority set up the Multicore joint venture together with Vopak Chemicals Logistics in 2003. Multicore operates a system of underground pipelines in the port area for the (petro)chemical and gas industries. The system is used to transport chemical products more efficiently and it strengthens the petrochemical cluster in the port. Investing in Multicore was a high-risk enterprise, intended to increase the vitality of the port industrial complex. The investment was necessary because the pipeline system would not have got off the ground (or at least, not cost-effectively) if it had been left to the firms themselves. The cross-firm character of the project makes the Port Authority the right party to play an active role in building and providing this infrastructure. In initiating Multicore, the Port Authority developed from being a landlord and operator to a chain director and facilitator. Firms such as Abengoa, Air Products, ExxonMobil, Koch, Linde Gas, Shell Chemicals Europe, and Shin-Etsu all now make use of Multicore.

Alpherium: a logistics hub in the hinterland

The Port Authority wants to increase the percentage of cargo transported by rail and inland shipping. This is necessary in order to cope with the considerable growth anticipated in container transport and to avoid congestion on the Dutch highway. The Port Authority therefore invested in establishing a trans-shipment terminal called the Alpherium in the town of Alphen aan den Rijn. The terminal opened in 2010, and at six hectares is the largest inland port for container handling in the Netherlands. The Alpherium expands and improves the 'back door' to the port, ensuring a more efficient transport flow to and from the hinterland.

The Alpherium was established through co-creation with the business sector. The Port Authority purchased the land and is therefore the owner of the site. The main initiators were the logistics service provider Van Uden Groep and the brewer Heineken. The Van Uden Groep invested in the construction and is the shipper and operator of the inland port. Heineken, which had been looking for an alternative to truck transport from its brewery in Zoeterwoude to the ports of Rotterdam and Amsterdam, took the role of *launching customer*. The retail companies Blokker, Intertoys, and Zeeman followed as customers. Although the Port Authority is the landlord of the Alpherium, it can be said that this initiative represents a new area of business for the Port Authority because it invested in this terminal together with customers (and customers' customers) from outside the Rotterdam port area.

Portbase: an extensive logistics communication system

The Port Authority continued to develop into a chain director through its investment with the Port of Amsterdam in a joint port communication system, Portbase, which came into existence in 2009. It is a communal ICT platform which provides more than forty intelligent services for information exchange both between firms and between firms and the government. It is suitable for all sectors of the port. Because the entire information exchange runs via a central point, firms no longer have to develop and maintain a multitude of bilateral connections themselves. By establishing Portbase, the Port Authority has thus created strategic value for shippers and carriers.

Portbase, which now has wide support from the port business sector, arose from the Rotterdam Port Infolink and the Amsterdam PortNET. One of its main objectives is to make the logistics chains of both ports more attractive by providing a central point of access. In addition, the ambition of Portbase is to play a key role in inland and foreign port logistics networks. With its investment in Portbase, the Port Authority is driving innovation in the port industrial complex at Rotterdam and strengthening the strategic connectivity with the Port of Amsterdam.

The balance sheet

- From 2000 onwards, the Port of Rotterdam Authority changed from being a *landlord* to being a *port developer*. It switched its business model from strategy-driven replication to customer-driven renewal.

- The increasing complexity and dynamism of the market and the growing competition were important triggers for the transformation. Privatization in 2004 boosted the renewal.

- The initial levers were decentralization of the organization, fewer management layers, and a different management style. Together these paved the way for co-creation, which provides a great deal of new business.

- Transformational leadership played an important part in the changes. An inspired CEO, with a long-term vision, acted as the driver. New managers, a flatter organization, and direct reporting helped in implementing the renewal.

- The focus of the knowledge absorption shifted from internal to external. A great deal of new expertise was opened up by working together with customers and other external parties.

- Entering new geographical areas (the Dutch hinterland, emerging markets) and the adoption of new roles (chain director, and provider of infrastructure) were important elements of the co-creation.

Figure 6.4 illustrates the business model transformation trajectory of the Port of Rotterdam Authority. Table 6.2 outlines the essential areas of focus for top and middle managers.

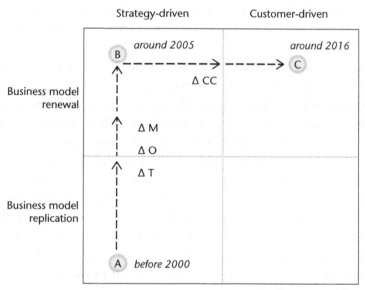

Δ T = Technological change   Δ O = Organizational change
Δ M = Management change   Δ CC = Co-creation change

Figure 6.4 Business model transformation at the Port of Rotterdam Authority

Table 6.2 Management roles in business model transformation: Port of Rotterdam Authority

	Trajectory A > B	Trajectory B > C
Top management	• from transactional to transformational leadership	• transformational leadership
	• responding to environmental changes	
	• initiating changes in levers: organizational forms, management practices, and technology	• more customer focus and co-creation
Middle management	• implementing changes in levers	• implementing co-creation
		• strengthening internal and external knowledge-sharing

NXP: exploit and connect

In 1975 Philips acquired Signetics, the forerunner of NXP. This firm, established in 1961, was the first to concentrate fully on the production of integrated circuits (silicon chips). Under the wing of Philips it expanded to become the largest silicon chip manufacturer in Europe. Philips was still operating on many different fronts, so the former Signetics did not specialize. 'You made what the Philips divisions needed. That meant we didn't target the products with the best market opportunities. It's great to have an internal customer, but it also holds you back,' reflects Guido Dierick, CEO Netherlands of NXP and board member of NXP worldwide.

Philips focused increasingly on health and lifestyle products. In the meantime, the market for silicon chips was declining. Considerable investment would have been needed for NXP to keep its competitive edge. Philips and its chip manufacturer thus grew apart. The parent company originally sought a merger with or a takeover by another chip manufacturer. When that failed, the silicon chip arm was sold in 2006 to a mainly American private equity consortium, consisting of Kohlberg Kravis Roberts & Co, Bain Capital Partners, Silver Lake, Apax Partners, and AlpInvest Partners. The consortium acquired 80 per cent of the shares, while Philips retained the remaining 20 per cent. The new name of the firm was NXP (as in *Next eXPerience*) Semiconductors.

NXP was left with a debt of $6 billion from its privatization. In addition, shortly after the takeover the firm was confronted by the banking crisis, which also affected the silicon chip market adversely. As the firm had not acquired any experience of doing business independently in the more than thirty years it had spent under Philips—many departments and positions were located at the corporate level at Philips—NXP initially did not even realize how serious the problems were. According to all the parties involved, the firm was on the brink of collapse during that period, between 2006 and 2008. At one point there was an acute lack of cash, without people even being aware of it.

In order to save the firm, all the parts which were not expected to yield any profit in the long term were sold. Under Philips, NXP had concentrated on the complicated chips which form the heart of devices such as televisions or smartphones. Hundreds of millions of euros were often involved in developing these chips. It is a risky business, because often there are only a small number of buyers—and if they pull out, the investment comes to nought.

The sale of several businesses in 2008 (mainly the Mobile & Personal division), headed by the current Philips CEO Frans van Houten, delivered more than one billion euros. 'Looking back, you could say that is what saved us,' says Dierick. 'If those sales hadn't taken place, we would certainly have been bankrupt six months later. But the debt also helped us to get back on our feet again. It created a crisis atmosphere, since without the debt there would have been no question of bankruptcy. This created discipline.' Besides dropping its television and telephony arm, the firm also divested itself of many support staff. The number of employees dropped from around 37,000 to 25,000.

Under the tight supervision of the consortium, which appointed external managers, or 'hired guns', to strategic positions, NXP mastered the art of running a business. Drastic cuts were implemented. People who could not cope with the changes were urged to leave. The character of NXP changed swiftly: decisions were made more quickly, and the mentality became more results-oriented.

The last step towards independence was taken in 2010 when NXP was turned into a public limited company and listed on the NASDAQ. Fifty-four per cent of the shares remained in the hands of the consortium. Managers also obtained shares and options, a deliberate strategy on the part of the consortium to push shareholder value higher up the agenda. Partly due to this, NXP shifted increasingly from the Rhineland model to the Anglo-Saxon model.

In 2015 NXP completed a merger with its US competitor Freescale in a stock and cash transaction. The merger created a high-performance mixed-signal semiconductor industry leader, with a combined revenue of more than $10 billion. The corporate headquarters of the new NXP are still in Eindhoven and the firm has become the market leader in automotive semiconductor solutions and in general-purpose microcontroller (MCU) products. NXP is currently the fifth-largest non-memory semiconductor supplier globally, and the leading supplier of semiconductors to the secure identification, automotive, and digital networking industries. In 2016 NXP decided to divest its Standard Products business to a consortium of Chinese investors (JAC Capital and Wise Road Capital). The NXP Standard Products business is now branded Nexperia, and the new firm has its headquarters in Nijmegen in the Netherlands.

On 27 October 2016 it was announced that the San Diego firm Qualcomm, a world leader in 3G, 4G, and next-generation wireless technologies, would buy fellow chip maker NXP, the world's leading supplier of automotive chips, for $47 billion. The acquisition by Qualcomm was approved by NXP shareholders on 27 January 2017. This acquisition represents a huge gamble by Qualcomm on cars becoming the next smartphone—and, like smartphones, offering a way of rolling together communications and services once handled by dozens of other devices. This can be regarded as a potentially game-changing deal that could add both scale and completely new markets to Qualcomm's portfolio. According to Qualcomm's CEO Steve Mollenkopf, 'The NXP acquisition accelerates our strategy to extend our leading mobile technology into robust new opportunities, where we will be well positioned to lead by delivering integrated semiconductor solutions at scale [. . .] we will be even better positioned to empower customers and consumers to realize all the benefits of the intelligently connected world' (Qualcomm press release, 27 October 2016).

While Qualcomm has bought into the future with the NXP merger, its journey towards automotive growth may not be smooth. Qualcomm operates in the smartphone market, where it deals with a few very large mobile OEMs (original equipment manufacturers) and coming up with winning designs is easy and fast. On the other hand, NXP operates in the IoT (Internet of Things) market, which is fragmented and made up of a large number of small customers. Qualcomm uses a fabless model, in which the fabrication or manufacturing is outsourced to a third party, in this case the Samsung foundry. NXP is an integrated device manufacturer with seven fabrication facilities (or fabs) and seven packaging and testing facilities. These differences in business model could have a negative impact on Qualcomm's gross margin, which could fall when factory overhead costs are added to the cost of goods sold. Qualcomm also specializes in R&D and lacks experience in running fabs. However, there is also scope for synergies between the two business models: for example, Qualcomm could initially use NXP's expertise in running fabs to manufacture its existing products, and NXP could use Qualcomm's R&D expertise to speed up its technological innovation in the automotive industry.

. . . .

TWO KINDS OF CHIPS

NXP had two arms: one for 'standard' chips and one for special chips, or 'high-performance mixed signals' (HPMS). Standard chips accounted for around 12 per cent of its revenue, and HPMS for the remainder. As is common in this sector, the standard chips are usually made in low-wage countries and are less R&D-intensive,

requiring approximately 4 per cent of annual sales revenue. The factories put out large volumes at low margins and compete on price. Eighty per cent of these chips go to large distributors. NXP recently decided to divest its standard chips to a consortium of Chinese investors. The consortium agreed to pay approximately $2.75 billion for the business.

HPMS are made in Nijmegen, in the Netherlands, among other places. They require more R&D (around 16 per cent of annual sales) and have higher margins. The competition comes mainly from the United States. The HPMS arm frequently works together with customers. Sometimes the chips are made specially for one or more customers and are delivered directly to the customer. For this type of chip, the centre of gravity of development, production, and sales is shifting to Asia. One third of NXP's revenue already comes from China. The chip industry has always been strongly cyclical: buoyant one moment, and struggling the next. The market is very fragmented, with many players and a very high level of competition. Asian firms in particular receive additional support in the form of government subsidies.

. . . .

NXP's new market strategy comes down to specializing in niches where there is a good chance of success. It focuses on the HPMS segment, dividing this into four business lines: automotive, secure identification solutions, secure connected devices, and secure interfaces and infrastructure. In short, NXP's strategy is to detect sweet spots in the market. NXP has now developed into the unrivalled market leader in the field of chips for car keys, for instance. Dierick estimates that NXP chips can be found worldwide in 95 per cent of all car keys. The head start that it has in this segment, and the high profits it derives from it, make it possible for the firm to put a lot into research so that it can retain that lead. The firm is also market leader in chips for passports, with an estimated share of 60 per cent. 'Green' chips (which help limit energy loss in devices, for example) are becoming an increasingly important part of NXP's business, as are chips for identification systems.

The criterion for entering and remaining in a particular segment is that NXP must be the market leader in that segment, and should either be, or be capable of becoming, one and a half to two times larger than the number two. Growth should also be faster than that of the market. If the firm does not manage to achieve this, after a period of time it will stop that activity. Objectives are monitored frequently to see whether they are being reached.

Chips—or the HPMS variant at least—are products which require intensive R&D. Dierick estimates that when the firm was previously part of Philips, the R&D undertaken by the chips division constituted 40 to 50 per cent of all research at Philips. In spite of the popular view that private equity firms often squeeze their takeover partners dry, according to Dierick

R&D expenses have actually grown in relative terms since the restructuring at NXP, even though many R&D people disappeared with the sell-off of the Mobile & Personal division.

NXP now has about 3,500 people worldwide working on R&D, spread across twenty locations. Most R&D is decentralized and takes place in the business units. The innovation generally does not involve any fundamental research, but is based on what they term 'applied engineering' at NXP. Fundamental research only takes place at Leuven in Belgium, at Eindhoven in the Netherlands, and in Singapore. The group involved in this activity is smaller than when the firm was part of Philips.

NXP initially engaged in more cooperation with research institutes and other parties, sometimes subsidized by the European Union, for instance. 'We stopped doing that, because the returns are not high enough, and before you know it you have become addicted to those subsidies,' says Dierick. 'In addition, there are all kinds of conditions: you have to work in a particular direction which you don't like, or continue with projects you would rather stop, or keep factories open which you want to close. In short, it holds you back and ties your hands.' There are still collaborative ventures with the Technical University of Delft, Eindhoven University of Technology, Radboud University in Nijmegen, the Swiss Chalmers University, and the German research institute Fraunhofer.

Explorative innovation, meant to lead to totally new directions, occurs less frequently. Theo Kedzierski, Director of Technology Licensing and former works council member at NXP, believes that NXP should not fall into the same trap as Nokia, which missed new developments (the smartphone) partly because it failed to devote sufficient time to explorative innovation.

Choosing to go for niche markets is a strong determining factor for the direction of innovation. If the laboratory comes up with an invention for controlling car windows, management is quick to say no. In the Philips period, when there was more money, there was also more space for experimentation. 'We had the luxury then of being able to develop things that might never be used,' says Kedzierski. But that could get out of hand, too. He remembers an earlier era in which there were programmes for 'TriMedia' chips which had hundreds of millions of euros poured into them, even though the end-products failed to capture a sufficient share of the market. He believes that this kind of experimental development is no longer possible.

Another internal criticism is that knowledge is not shared enough, especially since R&D has been concentrated more in the business units. Those within the company feel that there are inadequate mechanisms for sharing knowledge, or that the mechanisms that do exist are not used sufficiently. Although *technology frameworks* have been established around certain competences, it is estimated that only 15 per cent of the R&D people at NXP participate in them actively. That is why the firm wants to encourage greater knowledge-sharing.

In the niches in which it is already active NXP tries to anticipate what will happen a couple of years ahead. The board frequently organizes what are called 'deep-dive sessions' for those in charge of business lines, designed to help them to analyse how their particular market might develop in the future and to visualize what implications that might have for NXP's competitive position. 'By the time you start by scanning the market, then you are actually already too late,' says Dierick. For example, NXP is already anticipating that consumers will be making all their payments by smartphone within two years. It is therefore working intensively on the technology which this will require. It is also assuming that improvements to cars in the coming years will have a particularly significant effect on the electronics, so it is putting a lot of its research energy into that area. As Dierick says, 'The only way to stay competitive is to be more innovative than your rivals.'

But at the same time, the time horizon for NXP has actually become shorter in many respects. This is partly due to shorter product life cycles, sometimes now only months, rather than years. There is no longer a lengthy process of deliberation—new versions are now brought out frequently. The firm's entry on to the stock market has also had an effect: various managers observe that since its NASDAQ listing in 2010, NXP has been more focused on the short term.

But Dierick does not believe that the flotation has resulted in less investment in R&D: 'Investors in chips want to see growth, and standard products are too stable. We want to grow at least twice as fast as the market with our products, so we pay a lot of attention to them. That is what investors want. And if they want it, they pay for it.'

There has been more development undertaken with customers over the past few years, but not in the same way as previously. As Dierick explains, 'Instead of joint development agreements, we now have contracts of confidence, which contain few restrictions. Because we also want to sell to customer B those things we develop for customer A. For instance, we go to

Samsung and say we want to develop something and want to invest a certain amount in it. Then what we expect of them is that they contribute with money or researchers. Afterwards we keep the patent and the customer has a three- to six-month head start on the market. Then we sell the same chip to other customers, otherwise it's not economically viable. It doesn't pay to develop products for just one customer.'

Although the product focus is different these days, NXP has not adopted a business model very different to the one it used in the Philips period. The firm continues to work on replication. It is more customer-driven than was previously the case. NXP also looks further ahead within the niches it has chosen, and works more proactively on R&D. This approach sees NXP starting to move cautiously in the direction of strategy-driven renewal.

The change in ownership structure, which in this case differs from most of the other cases featured in this book, has been the greatest driver of the transformation at NXP. The economic crisis and the debt burden have also played an important part, paving the way for a different management style. That might well have come anyway, given the background of the new owners. Technology and co-creation, important levers for other groups, were of far less importance for NXP.

Dierick confirms that changes in management have been a major factor in the transformation. Eleven of the twelve members of the management team have been replaced. At the end of 2008 CEO Frans van Houten also had to leave. The consortium replaced him with the American Richard Clemmer, who had a great deal of experience in reorganizing American chip manufacturers. The hired guns placed everywhere in the firm by the consortium made high demands and exercised a top-down mentality. This led to an acceleration in decision-making at the traditionally rather sluggish NXP. These days employees are also working a lot harder than previously. John Schmitz, Senior Vice-President of Intellectual Property and Licensing, estimates that 30 per cent fewer people are doing just as much work as before.

There was a more bureaucratic culture in the Philips time. According to Maarten Dirkzwager, manager of NXP's Strategy Office, people were more introvert. Under the new owners there are now more openness, directness, and speed within the firm. Schmitz compares NXP to a footballer—in the Philips period, he says, he was a little slow and fat and kept shooting just to the side of the goal, but now he is *mean* and *lean* and shoots straight into the goal. The will to win and be the biggest has become stronger.

The top management rolled out across the firm a programme called 'the culture project', designed to give shape to the new mentality and values and to anchor them within the firm. The management team left for the Sinai for a five-day primitive camping experience, long walks, and mountain climbing. While walking, the groups of managers discussed issues concerning culture, standards, and values. Later another 150 managers went to Croatia with the same objective. Similar activities were organized in some of the business units. Role models were used, slogans created, and five NXP values were introduced. A mission statement was also created: 'Customer-focused passion to win.'

The new NXP took shape with the use of a strongly transactional management style, but there were also reactions to this. Many NXP workers, including managers, feel that the changes have come at a price: in their eyes, NXP has become too American and too short-sighted. Frans van Heesbeen, former Vice-President of Human Resources, also sees danger in this: 'We focus too much on the short term now, highly driven by how the investors regard the value of the NXP shares. One of the dangers is that this will obstruct the explorative innovation in the long term.' He notes that cynicism has crept into the firm and that the sell-offs and frequent reorganizations have caused uncertainty and even distrust, because people no longer know for sure whether they will still have a job in a year or two. Schmitz finds that people take little pride in their work; he notes that at social events they will not even say they work for NXP. According to him, this is not down to the fact that they work for a supplier, because there is a sense of pride at Intel and ASML. Dirkzwager would like to see more passion in the organization. He does not believe that this can be created by means of programmes—in his opinion, it can only come through by giving people role models.

The balance sheet

- NXP was sold by Philips in 2006 to a private equity consortium. The change of owner was the most important lever in the changes the firm subsequently went through. In 2015 NXP acquired its US competitor, Freescale, and in 2016 it divested its Standard Products business and was subsequently taken over by Qualcomm.

- The burden of debt from the privatization, together with the economic crisis shortly afterwards, led to an acceleration of business model replication, and it also threatened the very existence of NXP.

- NXP changed from being a largely strategy–driven replicator into a more customer–driven replicator. The firm has started to move towards strategy–driven renewal, focusing on disruptive technologies in the automotive industry. The takeover by Qualcomm might speed up this process, although Qualcomm and NXP have very different business models.

- Since privatization, NXP has approached the market in a much more focused way. Units with less favourable long-term expectations have been hived off, and promising niches have been sought out. Ambitious performance objectives are formulated for those niches; market shares for NXP business have to be at least one and a half times higher than those of its largest competitor.

- There is more intensive cooperation with the customer within the niches and there is more proactive innovation than before.

- A new and much more transactional management style has brought with it faster decision-making, greater internal flexibility, and a stronger orientation towards results.

- The new owners have also introduced a more American mentality and culture to the firm.

- Innovation has been decentralized to the business units, and thus linked more directly to the business. In contrast to the Philips era, there is now very little explorative innovation.

- The many changes have also provoked resistance. The strong orientation to the short term, which became evident after the firm's listing on the stock exchange in 2010, has been particularly controversial.

Figure 6.5 illustrates the business model transformation trajectory that NXP has gone through. Table 6.3 outlines the essential areas of focus for top and middle managers.

Royal IHC: explore and connect

Royal IHC is a traditional Dutch shipbuilding and dredging firm with a long history going back to 1642. IHC Holland was founded in 1965 after twenty years of close cooperation between five shipyards. As a result of the global recession in 1970, IHC was restructured into two separate firms: IHC Holland, which focused on dredging, and IHC Caland, which concentrated

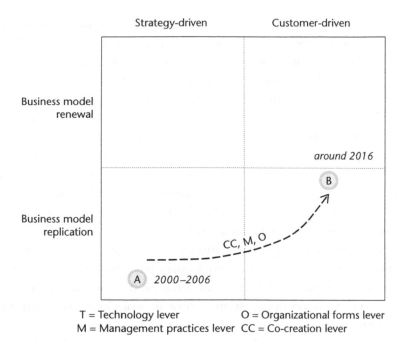

Figure 6.5 Business model transformation at NXP

Table 6.3 Management roles in business model transformation: NXP

	Trajectory A > B
Top management	• transactional leadership • responding to new ownership structure and downsizing • creation of customer focus (number 1 or 2 in the market) • transparent culture
Middle management	• top-down implementation • acceleration of decision-making • increasing efficiency • focus on key customers

on the offshore industry. In 1989 IHC Caland regained control of IHC Holland and in 1992 it also acquired the De Merwede shipyard. In 2005 IHC Caland sold both IHC Holland and De Merwede, but these two companies subsequently merged and in 2007 the merged company adopted the name IHC Merwede. In 2014 his Majesty the King of the Netherlands awarded IHC Merwede an honorary title and the company was renamed Royal IHC.

The merged company of IHC Holland and De Merwede was not in a good way at the point when it became independent from IHC Caland. Goof Hamers, who was appointed president of the firm in 2005, describes it as 'quite an old-fashioned shipbuilding firm, which I think was doomed to die'. What he found most remarkable was the firm's defensive approach to the business. 'IHC has always been good at combining ships and equipment. That is something most shipyards have divested. The most famous Dutch shipbuilding model, which started to be used in the 1980s, was based mainly on outsourcing and working with suppliers. When you look at it properly, that was a model about avoiding risks. Its basic principle is that you need to have very few people and activities on your own payroll, so that you also have fewer problems with them when things aren't going so well. I find it a very strange model. What you're doing is working on avoiding trouble, not on creating business. I think that that was the most important change. We started focusing on the issue of how to create business instead of on the question of how to avoid losing our shirt when times were harder.'

Hamers tried to depart from the traditional mentality that things are going well if the slipways are full, and that therefore nothing else is required. Customers used to be referred elsewhere if the slipways were full, or were told that they had to wait a few years. Hamers believed that there should always be capacity. That is why he reactivated the shipyard in Krimpen aan den IJssel, near Rotterdam, which had been closed a few years earlier. Slipways and other facilities were rented elsewhere in the Netherlands. When no facilities were available in the Netherlands, Royal IHC looked abroad. New production facilities were opened in China, among other places.

· ·

ROYAL IHC, ITS PRODUCTS AND MARKETS

Royal IHC employs around three thousand people. The firm has twelve business locations in the Netherlands, and it also has branches in various other countries, including China, Dubai, Singapore, and the United States. The particular expertise of the firm is in providing highly advanced technological solutions, or—as expressed in one of its annual reports—'deliver cost-effective, complex, customized and reliable equipment with a high degree of added value in technology and system integration'. Many of those custom-built solutions are one-off orders. It is a risky business: the investments are high, and rivals quickly do the same more cheaply. Royal IHC's answer is to tap into other markets and also to provide products for the mid-price range, which often involves ships and equipment that are just a little too difficult for shipyards from low-wage countries to build. Increasingly, the firm either manufactures parts and components abroad, or outsources them from foreign firms. Only the knowledge-intensive and strategic work, which is closely tied up with the design element, is still done in the Netherlands, as is the assembly.

The firm's core business has traditionally been dredgers, such as trailing suction dredgers and cutter dredgers. In 2005 it expanded its areas of operation to also include offshore, marine, and deep-sea dredging, maritime mineral extraction, and renewable energy. Until 2010 the firm claimed it wanted to be market leader in all the segments in which it operated. After 2010 it shifted its focus to being the market leader in efficient dredgers and mining ships and machines. It also wants to secure a position in the market for oil, gas, and renewables, and in June 2016 it announced that it was expanding its activities by providing equipment for off-shore wind farms. Royal IHC also now offers more consultancy and provides financing solutions.

The markets in which Royal IHC operates are subject to much fluctuation, and the prospects are different in each segment. The demand for offshore activities, for example, goes up and down with the oil price. While demand for trailing suction and cutter dredgers was booming between 2005 and 2008, in 2009 there was a big drop in demand for such large custom-built ships. Other shipbuilders moved into this segment, increasing the competitive pressure. Royal IHC managed to retain its market share, and the firm's financial results remained stable. China, India, and the Middle East were relatively unaffected by the crisis, which meant that demand for dredging continued to exist there. The outlook for deep-sea dredging and maritime mineral extraction is favourable, and demand is growing, especially from emerging economies like India, Brazil, and China.

. . . .

When increasing its shipyard capacity, Royal IHC usually chose to rent additional locations or engage in joint ventures that would give them access to partners' shipyards. The aim was to avoid structural overcapacity, which would be a millstone around the neck of the firm in bad times. This meant that the firm could also choose the best possible locations for production. Producing elsewhere also allowed it to tap into other larger and cheaper labour markets (Royal IHC has a notorious shortage of trained technical staff in the Netherlands) and gain access to new markets. Unfortunately, the more recent drop in demand in dredging, partly due to low oil prices around 2015, forced the firm to take action, just like many other offshore companies. It decided to close a shipyard, lay off part of its personnel, and move a larger share of its production activities abroad.

The new goal of Royal IHC is value creation. The firm wants to do this by four means: growth, internationalization, innovation, and cooperation. The growth is to be realized by promising new markets such as deep-sea dredging and maritime mineral extraction. Pressure from shareholders is one reason why this is happening because these shareholders want to reduce the dependency on dredging.

In part, the firm is building on its existing knowledge and experience. On the other hand, it is also acquiring new knowledge and competences through takeovers and collaboration with external parties or by setting up its own start-ups, to which it recruits new people. Thus Royal IHC is now collaborating with the Belgian firm DEME in a joint venture named OceanflORE, which offers solutions in mining at sea. Royal IHC designs and builds the equipment, while DEME contributes its experience in complex maritime operations. The firm has moved more towards integrated machines by acquiring shares in Hytech (design and construction of diving equipment), Vremac Hydraulics (hydraulic cylinders), Vuyk Engineering Rotterdam (maritime engineering), and The Engineering Business (design, engineering, and construction firm). Through these kinds of joint ventures and takeovers Royal IHC also attempts to offset its own shortage of trained technical staff. The firm also collaborates intensively with its customers, and it is not unusual for customers to modify specifications during an order.

When Royal IHC enters a new market, it puts a lot of time and money into it. Or, as Hamers puts it: 'You create an organization. Not two men and a dog, but bang, ten, twenty people straight off. When you do something, you have to do it properly, otherwise you might just as well not start at all.'

Regarding the organizational structure, Royal IHC has carried out several organizational changes. When he was appointed Hamers encountered, in his own words, 'a bundle of a few shipyards scraped together. It was extremely unorganized, a real mess.' People thought from the viewpoint of the shipyards—namely, filling the slipways—much too much for his taste. 'We redefined the firm from a shipyard into a firm which makes large-scale maritime systems, tools, and equipment. Thinking in shipyard terms was too much of a straitjacket.' The way of working also changed. Building a ship at Royal IHC used to be approached as a project, but Hamers wanted to see it more as a logistical process. That is why he kept emphasizing the need for better internal cooperation.

In order to enable different parts of the organization to work more closely together, in 2007 the business units were clustered into three divisions: *dredging and mining* (for the supply of dredging equipment), *offshore and marine* (for the supply of offshore equipment), and *technology and services* (for the supply of products, systems, and services for dredging and offshore). Product–market combinations (PMCs) were introduced in 2010, with the aim of increasing market awareness and customer orientation. According to Hamers, it was the first organizational development since the big lay-offs and restructuring of the 1980s. The PMCs are responsible for a particular product in a particular market, from cradle to grave. They can make use of division-wide functions such as engineering, project management, production, and supply chain management in order to develop and manage projects. A separate division for deep-sea mining was established in 2012 because of the favourable market developments in that segment.

Internationalization was emphasized by opening offices on different continents. In 2009 Royal IHC opened new offices in the United Kingdom (Aberdeen), the United States (Houston), India (Bombay), Nigeria (Lagos), and Brazil (Rio de Janeiro). The regional headquarters for Southeast Asia was opened in Singapore in 2012.

All in all, the organizational lever has played an important part in the firm's business model innovation. But it is not right to highlight just one lever at Royal IHC: it was the combination of organizational and technological renewal and new management practices which made the business model transformation possible.

Royal IHC calls itself a 'technology innovator'. This gives the employees direction and motivation. The creed is given substance by spending around 3 per cent of the turnover on R&D. Much of that money goes to MTI Holland, a knowledge centre for dredging, and to the IHC Offshore Technology Institute. The three hundred or so employees who work there develop new expertise and new products, such as a one-man operated bridge, which makes it possible for just one man to steer a ship *and* dredge at the same time. Royal IHC's innovation strategy is to develop existing technology further. Entirely new technology is acquired from outside or comes from the firm's own start-ups. Goof Hamers says that, 'if we don't have the knowledge, we buy it.'

When he came, Hamers was confronted with a management that had been there for a long time. 'This had resulted in stagnation setting in. It had all gotten in a bit of a mess. I switched from a cautious approach, which concentrated on what you had to do if things went wrong, to a more opportunistic approach, whereby you actually looked for the possibilities in the market.' As he himself says, he 'opened the gates to outside'. What he means by this is that he showed employees the different interesting activities and market territories that were possible. 'I believe that the role of the man at the top in this kind of business is to impress upon the people what kinds of opportunities there are. A bit like, take a look at the firm from this angle. I spread this message quite a lot, I give speeches, New Year's meetings, reviews, but I also just walk in on people. There are many ways of communicating with your organization.'

Going against tradition, Hamers also brought in people from outside, to get fresh ideas and different competences into the organization. More attention was given to management development: in addition to a trade school, the firm also has its own management school. New employees throughout almost all tiers of the organization are given several days of induction. Those in managerial positions are expected to complete at least one module at the management school every year, in subjects such as logistics, strategy, finance, project management, and supply chain management. The courses are almost all given by the firm's own people, including Hamers: 'Together with a colleague from organizational development, I give courses in strategy. My colleague in Finance gives finance courses, a salesperson gives sales lessons, and so on. It creates a huge impulse, on both sides. People really like hearing me tell how strategy works and why we do things the way we do. The introductory course ends with a conversation with me. Then I have twenty people for an hour each at my table. They can ask everything, and I can get my message over. People often ask: "Why do you do that?" Well, this is one way I also get to hear things. And I can ram the message home, to put it that way. I believe the people side of the firm is the most important thing there is. Without people, you have nothing.'

Hamers also changed the firm's remuneration policy, ensuring specialists could earn just as much as managers. His aim was to create a career path for them with the firm so that their specialist expertise could be retained within Royal IHC, and they did not feel impelled to take on managerial roles to which they were perhaps not well-suited. He also deliberately allowed a third of the variable remuneration to be determined by the profit of Royal IHC as a whole, not just that of the employee's particular unit. This is to underline the internal interwovenness. Another third of the remuneration is determined by the individual's own performance, and the final third by whether you have met a particular goal.

No really different management *style* was introduced at Royal IHC. The firm is still run in a reasonably transactional manner. It has chosen to follow a different route, and is led by a visionary and communicative leader.

One aspect of the culture at Royal IHC which struck Hamers was the aversion to making a lot of money. This sentiment originally came from customers who were critical of the high profits, but it also spread to the employees.

'The first time I published good figures here, I received comments like: "Should you really show that, do we earn that much money, that isn't possible, is it?" Rubbish, of course. That has disappeared now. Our salespersons have to say, at the right moment: "No, I won't drop my price any further." It is a matter of atmosphere, culture, and a bit of internal competition to get everyone to understand that there's nothing wrong with earning money.'

A second element of the Royal IHC culture which stood out to Hamers was that employees tended to focus on their own particular part of the business, even though the company was providing integrated solutions. Employees needed to join forces to realize integrated solutions, but, as Hamers notes, this turned out to be a challenging task: 'A disadvantage was that people concentrated on their own square metre. Their attitude was, I do not care about others outside my domain. [...] We have to deliver that model of integrated equipment. That means that very different business units have to collaborate on every product. If a dredger is delivered, it has a dredge pump from IHC Parts and Services, automation systems from IHC Systems, and so on. All those people have to work together in a way which is good for IHC. We have to create value with one another, and that is very demanding. We place a high priority on improving cooperation, because everyone is used to working only on his or her own little patch. But cooperation remains pretty much the most difficult thing for everyone to do together, I think.'

The company prioritized internal collaboration as one of its most important strategic objectives. It introduced the One IHC project to increase internal collaboration both within groups, and between units and clusters, with the aim of achieving synergies between them. Eventually, this project should shorten the time-to-market and reduce costs. One IHC is about creating uniform processes, procedures, and systems. The company considers a culture of more internal collaboration to be a requirement for operating more successfully and in a more uniform way. Under the umbrella of the One IHC programme, the company has started a number of subprojects such as the One Process, which is designed to harmonize business processes so that all parts of the company will eventually be using the same ERP (enterprise resource planning) system. IHC in the end abolished seventeen separate ERP platforms, and replaced them with one platform. Objectives for individual employees have also been reformulated so that they are now strongly related to the performance of the company as a whole. This has become an essential part of individual appraisals and the company's financial compensation system.

The balance sheet

- Royal IHC has changed from a strategy-driven replicator into a customer-driven renewer. Existing activities have been scaled up, particularly through internationalization, and new markets such as deep-sea mining have been opened up, often via joint ventures.

- A defensive strategy ('as long as the slipways are full') has been exchanged for an offensive one: the firm now actively seeks new business and value creation.

- With the appointment of Goof Hamers as president, the firm started operating more proactively. New and very promising market segments have been opened up by putting a lot of time, money, energy, and manpower into them.

- A clear new vision has been set out, and this has been accompanied by organizational changes such as the formation of divisions and product–market combinations. Rather than being a collection of separate shipyards and equipment firms, Royal IHC has now become more of a single entity.

- Hamers has tried to be an inspiring example and paid a lot of attention to learning (from fellow employees) and open communication.

- Remuneration and bonuses have been brought in line with the new organizational goals.

- Based on the idea 'think global, act local', the sales, production, and service activities have been relocated close to local markets.

- The firm's own innovation is incremental: it builds on existing knowledge and products. The firm acquires the knowledge needed to enter new markets or market segments from joint ventures and takeovers or from its own start-ups.

Figure 6.6 shows the business model transformation trajectory that Royal IHC has gone through. Table 6.4 outlines the essential areas of focus for top and middle managers.

How the levers affect business model transformation

The case studies presented here show how business model transformation can be realized by moving between the various quadrants of our matrix

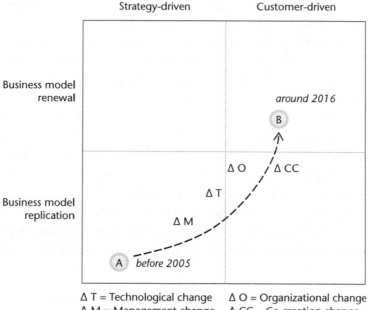

Figure 6.6 Business model transformation at Royal IHC

Table 6.4 Management roles in business model transformation: Royal IHC

	Trajectory A > B
Top management	• from transactional to transformational leadership • responding to environmental developments • initiating changes in levers: new organizational forms and new technology • internationalization and customer focus • management development of middle and frontline management
Middle management	• implementing divisional structure • implementing product–market combinations • strengthening internal cooperation and knowledge-sharing

(see Figure 6.7). This results in different trajectories. For example, at the start of its transformation trajectory DSM was in the bottom-left quadrant (strategy-driven replication), and after the transformation it ended up in the top-left quadrant (strategy-driven renewal). Figure 6.7 shows the three levers of strategy-driven renewal which played an important part in the

DSM case: renewal of technologies (Δ T), renewal of management practices (Δ M), and renewal of organizational forms (Δ O).

NXP shifted from the bottom-left quadrant to the bottom-right. This migration from strategy-driven to customer-driven replication came about not only through the firm's management, organization, and co-creation, but also by improving the complementarity between these three levers.

In the Royal IHC case, the firm's transformation trajectory also started in the bottom-left quadrant. By continual improvements of its technology, management, and organization, and then undertaking renewal through co-creation, Royal IHC shifted from strategy-driven replication to customer-driven renewal via customer-driven replication.

The Port of Rotterdam Authority also started its transformation trajectory in the bottom-left quadrant. Undertaking renewal using management and organization as the levers, and following this with co-creation, resulted in

	Strategy-driven	Customer-driven
Business model renewal	ΔT, ΔM, ΔO	ΔCC, ΔM, ΔO
Business model replication	Improvement of levers and complementarity of T, M, and O	Improvement of levers and complementarity of CC, M, and O

Key:
complementarity: relationship between different levers which increase the joint effect

T: technologies lever	Δ T: new technologies
M: management practices lever	Δ M: new management practices
O: organizational forms lever	Δ O: new organizational forms
CC: co-creation lever	Δ CC: new forms of co-creation

Figure 6.7 Underlying levers in the four types of business model transformation

a new business model—customer-driven renewal—which places the Port Authority in the top-right quadrant. In this case, the firm's trajectory took it through our top-left quadrant, strategy-driven renewal.

Wrap-up

The four cases in this chapter show that transformation trajectories can be set in motion by different factors. At DSM, embracing new technology played an important part, while at NXP the change of ownership was crucial. At both Royal IHC and the Port of Rotterdam Authority, the arrival of a new CEO was important. But the most noticeable thing is that each time the management lever occupies such a central place in the transformation trajectory. In the next chapter we will look in more detail at the role of top and middle management in business model innovation.

7

Managing Business Model Transformation

HOW TOMTOM, WIDELY SYNONYMOUS WITH NAVIGATION SYSTEMS,
JUMPED FROM BUSINESS MODEL TO BUSINESS MODEL

In 1991 two young men who had just left university started Palmtop in Amsterdam, a company which would make applications for the first generation of handheld computers. Those applications included things such as dictionaries, games, and route planners. This laid the basis for the TomTom of today, a forerunner in mobile navigation and now a multinational firm employing 3,500 people in thirty-five countries.

The key to TomTom's success is visionary and transformational management. Carlo van de Weijer, Vice-President of Traffic Solutions at TomTom, compares his firm to a fighter aeroplane operating in a highly unstable environment. 'When the engines and onboard computers fail on a normal plane, it will keep gliding and be able to land one way or another; it is stable. The design of a fighter plane is by definition unstable. That means it can veer and turn very fast. But once the computers fail, it crashes. That's how TomTom has been put together. Not much structure, but the firm can adapt easily, so it can change rapidly.' That ability to change rapidly is very much needed, given the huge competition, the very short product life cycles, and the continually changing customer demands in mobile navigation. There is very little market data that can be used to set a course—the vision of management is therefore vital for steering the company forward.

That vision comes down to this: precisely because everything changes so fast, you should only do what you are good at. At TomTom this is R&D, marketing, customer support, and organization of the entire process. That is why TomTom has built the firm around those functions. Despite its current size, the firm has not become sluggish—it remains a flat and flexible organization, imbued with an innovative and entrepreneurial spirit. What TomTom cannot do, it outsources; whenever it lacks knowledge, it hires in people who have it; and whatever it needs, it buys. Thus when it needed the map-maker TeleAtlas, it acquired the company. What is important in all this, says Van de Weijer, is that you are well aware of what you are not good at and that you acknowledge that openly.

Its great flexibility meant it was relatively easy for TomTom to make the shift from one business model to another. While it started as a software developer, the firm subsequently became a supplier of consumer electronics. Having recently established itself in the business-to-business market as supplier to the car industry, TomTom is now trying to enter a different market—that of business-to-government, by selling traffic information to the government.

Vision and versatility were an essential part of what helped TomTom make its initial breakthrough with navigation systems in 2002. Very shortly after the Clinton government had released GPS for civilian use, TomTom was able to put a navigator for palmtop computers on to the market. Luck? Yes, but not just luck. TomTom had already been straining at the leash. The firm was fully equipped to put the navigator into production swiftly and to market it. Carlo van de Weijer: 'of course TomTom was lucky. But being lucky is also a matter of being prepared for the right moment. That is a talent you have, that you are ready when the circumstances demand it and that you can adapt fast. TomTom was well prepared and took risks, but this was based on vision. The same applies to the current turn towards automotive and governments.' This latest change of direction was driven partly by the fact that the market for 'separate' mobile navigation has been declining rapidly since the arrival of smartphones.

Despite the growth, nothing has actually changed in the management style, organization, or technology at TomTom. In terms of technology, it is still a case of being able to present large amounts of data clearly on small screens. And yet the business model is changing continually: renewal was followed by replication, then again by renewal, and the end is undoubtedly not yet in sight. This makes TomTom a good example of how an enterprise can transform its business model with a visionary CEO as the enabler.

. . . .

Introduction

Central to this chapter are management and the management activities needed to achieve business model transformation. This is not without good reason. Many publications on business models and business model innovation pay little or no attention to management. Those publications describe business models as a coherent set of components which are changed and regrouped in business model innovation. It is as if they are simply pieces of a puzzle which just have to be put down again in a different configuration. There is little or no discussion as to whose responsibility this might be.

In their book *Business Model Generation,* Alexander Osterwalder and Yves Pigneur devote very little space to management in their nine building blocks for a business model. Even the *key resources* building block does not refer to management. This is striking, because in modern business and management literature, management is said to be *the* key resource of any organization (e.g. Hansen et al., 2004; Roberts, 2004; Sirmon et al., 2011). At the end of their book, Osterwalder and Pigneur do dedicate two short pages to management, but they do not address the crucial role played by the top management team (TMT) and middle management (MM) in business model innovation, for example.

In this chapter, we intend to fill that gap by tackling a number of important management topics. Firstly we discuss the roles of top and middle management in business model transformation. We also discuss the specific management tasks involved in getting the levers and enablers of business model innovation to work. If these tasks are not undertaken and warning signs are ignored, firms will continue too long with their existing business model and fall into a business model trap. That is why we highlight the key things that top management and the CEO must watch out for so they can start replicating or renewing their business model in good time. We conclude this chapter by analysing business model innovation at the business sector level and show that here there are repeating cycles of replication and renewal. The question is, if firms are able to combine replication and renewal at the same time, what enables them to do so successfully? We therefore close by looking at the features of a dual business model. These kinds of dual business models can often be found in large multi-unit firms such as the BMW Group and Randstad.

. . . .

DUAL BUSINESS MODELS AT THE BMW GROUP

The BMW Group has three divisions: cars, financial services, and motorbikes. BMW focuses especially on the premium market. The car division designs, builds, and sells passenger cars and off-road vehicles under the BMW, Mini, and Rolls-Royce brands.

BMW acquired the Mini brand in 2001. Since then there has been an explosion in sales. Sales for the Mini have increased from 25,000 in 2001 to more than 232,000 in 2008. The Mini is even catching on in countries which have their own strong local car industries. The five countries where the Mini sells best are Great Britain (45,000 cars in 2008), the United States (41,000), Germany (29,000), Italy (22,000), and Japan (13,000).

BMW has positioned its Mini as more than just a car: it stands for a lifestyle. The firm offers a wide range of accessories and other items to support this, such as clothing and key fobs. In addition, the Mini has its own online social network or 'urban initiative', called Mini Space. These give the brand more meaning. People who buy a Mini can have their car assembled in the way they want. There are 372 interior options and 319 exterior options, making the Mini one of the most customized cars in its class.

Marketing initiatives capitalize on the cheeky image of the brand. BMW is associated traditionally with larger and premium-priced cars, and ownership of the Mini brand therefore gave the company a completely new way of creating value. With the Mini, BMW entered a very different segment of the car market, one so different that there was very little risk of damage to their existing brand. The takeover also offered opportunities for growth, in both product development and brand development. The Mini enabled BMW to enter the highly competitive small hatchback market and compete with cars such as the Volkswagen Golf, the Audi A3, and the Ford Fiesta. With BMW, Mini, and Rolls Royce, the BMW Group now has a large market share in the various segments of the car market which the group covers.

Source: Volberda et al. (2011)

· ·

· ·

VARIOUS BUSINESS MODELS AT RANDSTAD

Randstad Netherlands also uses a number of different business models. Thus Tempo-Team is the firm's more aggressive and action-oriented brand, providing mainstream HR services, Yacht focuses on the recruitment, selection, and secondment of more highly qualified people, Randstad Inhouse Services provides several HR functions for large firms, and the premium-label Randstad employment agency offers temporary staffing, permanent placement, and specialist HR services. This means that Randstad is active in three broad markets: 'regular' temporary job placement and secondment, provision of services to professionals, and assisting employees in their career transition, through services such as reorganization and outplacement. The core business in all of these business models remains that of matching supply and demand on the labour market.

Randstad is not the best or the biggest in all these markets. The strength of the group lies in its size and scope. 'Some niche players, such as Young Capital, are doing very well, but only in their niche. In contrast to the niche players, Randstad is capable of supplying volume, also outside of the traditional job placement,' says Chris Heutink, managing director at Randstad Netherlands.

Being 'big' also has its advantages behind the scenes. 'We have really come a long way in HR planning systems, digitalization, portals, and suchlike. As an intermediary or consultant it is important to have a good understanding of what the customer wants,' according to Heutink. He believes that the strength of Randstad lies in understanding properly what the customer wants and having people whose work is of a very high level. A large database is indispensable for this.

Having a number of different business models requires coordination. What the customer does not need is for each unit within Randstad to send a separate representative. The customer must also have a clear understanding of the different concepts. René Schripsema, director of Randstad Inhouse Services, describes what happened. 'We were used to working from the position of the business lines, from the inside out. We had five product–market combinations and we had given them a name internally. We believed in this so much that it also turned into a name externally. So it was no longer Randstad, but Randstad Professionals. Then you see the customer thinking, do I also have to call Randstad Professionals if I need a temporary worker? No, we said. They didn't understand it at all. For the customer, it is all just Randstad. Now we've said, it is all Randstad—all you need to do is call us. We will arrange it so that you end up with the right people. Well, for us that was a real shift in thinking. We have to think much more in terms of what the customer wants, rather than on the basis of our internal organization.'

This customer-driven approach had large implications according to Schripsema: 'Then the question arose: how attractive is it to keep several brands in the air at the same time? There was no real reason any more to keep doing things separately. So we pushed everything together again under the same brand. That makes it a lot clearer for the customer and quite a bit more efficient internally.' It entailed lay-offs, since in many positions there was more than one person. Randstad achieved significant economies of scale by setting up shared service centres.

The internet played an important part in this process. It has made the sometimes complicated requests from customers more transparent and has allowed them to be grouped together. Requests come in via portals and are then classified. This provides an easier one-stop shop for customers than was possible either by telephone or by direct contact in branch. Now it no longer matters that the production workers come from Randstad Inhouse Services (formerly Capac), the secretaries from Randstad's temporary worker branch, and the engineers from Yacht.

. . . .

These examples from BMW and Randstad show that it can pay to have several business models, but decisions have to be taken as to how to capitalize on the potential advantages and deal with any conflict between the models. This is a task for the CEO and top management.

The role of top and middle management in replication and renewal

If we recall the four firms featured in our business model innovation matrix in Chapter 6 (Figure 6.2), we now want to focus in more detail on what top and middle managers had to do to allow those firms to undertake their particular transformation journeys. How did DSM, for example, manage to move over a period of fifteen years from a focus on strategy-driven replication (bottom-left quadrant in our matrix) to a focus on strategy-driven renewal (top-left quadrant)? In this section we will go into more detail on the necessary change in involvement of top and middle management in business model transformation, that is, in the shift from one quadrant to another.

Figure 7.1 shows the degree of involvement of top and middle management in the various modes of business model innovation. We can see from the matrix below that there is more centralized decision-making in renewal than in replication, as was evident earlier in Chapter 4. Compared to

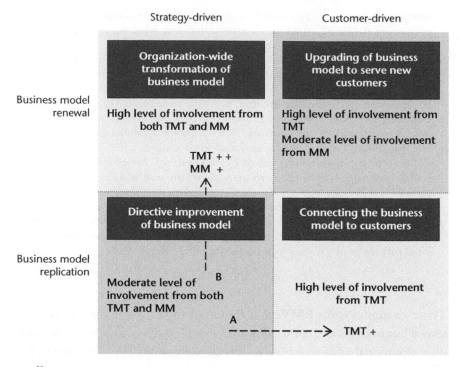

Figure 7.1 Level of involvement of the top management team and middle management in replication and renewal

customer-driven renewal, strategy-driven renewal requires greater involvement from middle management.

With strategy-driven replication in which the firm wants to perfect the existing business model, top management has to ensure that there are sufficient internal checks and balances and adequate control systems to keep the organization focused on maintaining and improving the existing levers. Middle management should be more active than top management in coordinating improvements in the various levers. Typically, middle management is charged with implementing further upgrades of the existing technology and fine-tuning the management practices and organizational structure. With customer-driven replication, top management is more involved.

Top management has the task of deciding which will be the best customer segments for the firm to serve and which of its existing customers warrant the most investment.

Transformation trajectories in the business model innovation matrix

We explain two of the trajectories shown in Figure 7.1 in more detail: the horizontal arrow A and the vertical arrow B. The journey indicated by arrow A, from a directive form of replication to connecting one's business model closely to clients, requires a high level of involvement from top management. The question is whether this kind of trajectory can be undertaken by the existing top management (Holmqvist, 2003). The existing top management is likely to have a strong internal orientation. Making a change to the composition of the top management team—for example, by bringing in a new CEO and/or new management members from outside the organization—can help to make this kind of trajectory even more successful (Day and Schoemaker, 2004). The NXP case in Chapter 6 shows how one firm replaced almost all of its management team with outsiders in order to effect this type of change.

Our second trajectory (arrow B) from directive business model improvement to organization-wide transformation of the business model requires a much greater step-change in the level of involvement from both top and middle management. Both top and middle management go from a moderate to a high level of involvement. Undertaking a trajectory of this kind takes its toll on top management, and there are thus likely to be more significant changes to the top management team. The DSM and Port of Rotterdam Authority cases illustrate this.

Also, the firm's existing middle management may be less well suited to completing this kind of trajectory. After all, some of those middle managers may have spent a large part of their career focusing on replication (Sheaffer et al., 1998). A context of renewal demands new management practices and processes (Heyden et al., forthcoming; Foss and Saebi, 2015). The trajectory of arrow B will almost certainly be accompanied by changes in middle management, as happened in the case of the Port of Rotterdam Authority.

Managing business model transformation: the tasks for top and middle management

How can top and middle managers ensure that the right levers are used, and that the firm can use the enablers of business model innovation to its advantage? Chapters 4, 5, and 6 showed that management plays a key role in this. Here we consider what the various tasks for top and middle managers may be, and what is needed to make best use of the various levers. Which enablers and which management activities demand particular attention?

Management of the levers

Top management plays a key role in determining whether business model innovation will take place and which direction it will take (replication or renewal) (Foss and Saebi, 2015; Markides, 2015). Top management has a strong influence on how employees are motivated. With business model replication, top managers should consistently focus on *improving* the existing levers; this requires more practices designed specifically to provide extrinsic motivation, such as setting clear targets for improvement, frequent monitoring of results, and tangible rewards in the form of financial incentives and rewards for performance. With renewal, top management will have to fundamentally change the levers by adopting new technologies, applying new management practices, changing the organizational form, and co-creating with new partners. Moreover, top managers have to pay more attention to intrinsic motivation (Avolio et al., 1999; Bass, 2003) by encouraging employees to take ownership of new initiatives, commit to new challenges, and look beyond self-interest to the common good.

The results of our survey reveal a number of striking issues. First, with both replication and renewal, the management lever makes the largest contribution. In other words, adopting new management practices plays a key role in both forms of business model innovation. But new management practices do not come out of thin air. They demand huge commitment from the top management. For successful business model replication, top managers have to ensure, for instance, that decision-making becomes more decentralized (Sheaffer et al., 1998); employees at all levels of the organization have a vital role to play in refining and strengthening the existing business model. For business model renewal, by contrast, top managers should centralize decision-making (e.g. Fulop, 1991; Hamel and Prahalad, 1989) and take responsibility for articulating an energizing vision and challenging the existing business model(s) of the firm.

Second, with all of the combinations of levers we have looked at, new management practices have to be adopted. Top management thus has responsibility for choosing the order in which those levers are activated. As shown both by the survey and by some of our other recent research (e.g. Heij, 2015; Volberda et al., 2013), if the new technologies lever is used without complementary changes in the management processes and practices, either simultaneously or at an earlier stage, it will not be effective. Business model renewal will not be successful, and company performance will not improve.

Third, middle management is also involved in managing the levers, not only top management. Middle managers are the ones with the most current knowledge and expertise and are closer to sources of information and to customers. In particular, integral business model renewal, the approach which requires the use of all of the levers, presents an enormous challenge to both top and middle management. Middle managers will be involved in implementing the change, deciding on the timing and order of that change, and managing the interaction between the various levers (e.g. Volberda and Lewin, 2003). For example, to enable a firm to engage in more co-creation with outside stakeholders, middle managers will need to ensure that there is more sharing of technology and knowledge, and to create practices that encourage open innovation. They will also need to work on making organizational processes more transparent, and to bring in flatter organizational structures.

Managing the factors which enable business model transformation

In Chapter 5 we explored a number of key factors that can act as an enabler in business model transformation. The findings from that chapter form the basis of Table 7.1. Thus the first factor listed below, transformational leadership, contributes to both replication and renewal. The second factor, CEO tenure, has a different influence. Although CEO tenure has no significant impact on replication, the same is not true for renewal. A CEO who remains in charge for too long is not as prepared to change course, and will not be able to do so as effectively. This is an issue which the top management and Supervisory Board (SB) must remain alert to.

Table 7.1 The involvement of the top management team and middle management in managing the factors which enable business model transformation

Factors that enable business model transformation	Replication	Renewal
1 transformational leadership	task of the TMT	task for the TMT + SB
2 CEO's length of tenure in the organization	shown to have no significant effect[a]	ensuring the tenure is not overlong: task for TMT + SB
3 knowledge-absorptive capacity of the organization	task of MM to promote this	task for MM to promote this
4 listening to what existing customers want	task of the TMT and MM	TMT needs to break free of this
5 organizational identity	task of the TMT to monitor this	shown to have no significant effect[a]
6 innovative culture	shown to have no significant effect[a]	task of the TMT and MM to promote this
7 internal cooperation	task of MM to promote this	task of the TMT to break through this if necessary

[a] on the basis of our analysis and/or the literature

TMT = top management team   MM = middle management   SB = Supervisory Board

Another key factor is 'listening to existing customers', and with replication this is something for which top and middle managers have a joint responsibility. Middle managers have the most direct contact with account managers and can thus act in a coordinating role. Their interactions with the market and with demanding clients spur them to strengthen and expand the firm's links with current customers, helping to embed the existing business model within the firm. Top managers will need to keep stimulating further improvements to the levers, attempting to fulfil the wishes of the most important existing customers. This allows the top management to persist in replicating the business model and to make incremental improvements in the firm's revenue model or cost structure. In an effort to ensure they understand and meet the demands of current customers, they often focus solely on leveraging the existing business model to boost uptake of upgraded products and services. However, when the limits of business model replication are reached, customers no longer value further improvements to products, even though they may not yet have articulated other needs which might be used by the firm to drive new business models (Paap and Katz, 2004). With renewal, it is the task of top management in particular to break free from the influence exerted on the organization by its most important existing customers (Govindarajan and Kopalle, 2006; Smith et al., 2010), often referred to as 'the tyranny of the served market'. They may do this, for example, by creating a separate organizational unit designed to bring in new customers and develop new customer value propositions. It is important that top managers should allocate part of the firm's resources to finding new areas of business, rather than focusing solely on developing the best products for existing customers (Christensen, 1997; Hamel and Prahalad, 1994). To attract new customers or serve new markets, top management should invest in disruptive technologies, experiment with new organizational forms, and co-create with new partners such as new entrants or start-ups (Ansari et al., 2016).

The last item in Table 7.1, internal cooperation, is particularly important for renewal. Here, top managers need to play an important role, in that they need to break down any fixed patterns of behaviour that may hinder change. Strong horizontal ties between departments, units, and line and staff managers require a lot of coordination and seriously limit the room for 'out-of-the-box thinking' and creation of new business models. This so-called tight coupling is more appropriate for exploiting a current business model (replication). Loose coupling (Weick, 1982), on the other hand, gives an organization the flexibility it needs to explore future business models (renewal). Thus, to promote business model renewal, top management should make tightly coupled organizations looser in structure by using autonomous self-contained units that are not reliant on one another. Loose coupling of this kind allows multiple initiatives for business model innovation to take place simultaneously. Top management can also decide to take up new organizational forms that involve collaboration with outsiders—for example, strategic alliances—in order to circumvent the *not invented here* problem (Geroski, 1999).

Early warning signs and how to spot them

We have discussed the roles and specific tasks of top and middle management extensively for both replication and renewal and in relation to various business model transformation trajectories. But how do you *know* whether you have held on to your existing business model for too long? And how do you avoid the danger of the business model trap? Retaining an existing business model for too long reduces your chances of developing a new business model in time and competing effectively against the rivals who have done this successfully. We discuss various warning signs which can help management to spot a potential trap. Of course, we acknowledge that a firm can also be proactive in experimenting with new business models (McGrath, 2010) and can disrupt an industry in order to take advantage of technology and solutions developed internally or in collaboration with external partners (e.g. Chesbrough, 2007; Johnson et al., 2008; McGrath, 2010). Nonetheless, in this section we focus on a number of 'red flags' that can signal to management that its existing business model is becoming obsolete. Recognizing these signs in good time reduces the chances that an organization will put its very survival at risk (Cunha and Chia, 2007; Day and Schoemaker, 2004). Early detection may help a firm to see where its future advantages may lie, which sectors of industry offer the company the most scope to effect disruption, and which business models it needs to build. D'Aveni (1994: 246) calls this 'strategic soothsaying', and explains that this involves interpreting the soft signals about how markets and technologies may evolve in ways that offer firms new opportunities to serve current or new customers. In a similar way, Hamel and Prahalad (1994) used the word 'industry foresight' to mean an ability to synthesize the collective impact of competitive forces which allows firms to imagine the future and to develop appropriate business models. Early detection of warning signs helps firms to develop viable business models before their rivals have been able to take action. Uber, Airbnb, Google, and Apple are all firms that have created successful first-mover business models based on superior industry foresight, thereby causing disruptive change for their rivals.

Early warning signs

Firms that monitor the flow of information relating to new markets (demand side) and emerging technologies (supply side) are better able to understand competitive actions, including those taken by disruptive new entrants (Geroski, 1999). In more stable and predictable environments, extrapolation from past phenomena and trends provides a means of identifying any potential changes ahead to markets or technologies, and of assessing the likely impact of those changes. Forecasting and planning tools like scenario planning can be used for those assessments (Kaivo-oja, 2012). However, extrapolation from past phenomena and trends does not provide a way of detecting discontinuities brought about by disruption to markets or technologies, for example, precisely because here there is no past that can be drawn upon (Holopainen and Toivonen, 2012; McGrath, 2010; Nunes and Breene, 2011). In particular, dynamic and unpredictable environments require managers to be more alert to the early warning signs which are often hard to spot with conventional forecasting and scanning tools (Harris and Zeisler, 2002; Holopainen and Toivonen, 2012). For example, while many telecommunication companies were focusing on the launch of 3G mobile phone services and on obtaining the licences required, offering certain ringtones on mobile phones emerged as a profitable business for ringtone providers, a business that would have been hard to anticipate beforehand. This development was rather unexpected for those telecommunication companies (Drew, 2006).

In this context, an early warning sign is the first weak and ill-defined symptom of a possible change in a market or technology that could take place in the near future (Cunha and Chia, 2007). It is not a clear message, but rather a set of perceptions regarding processes, events, or issues that might suggest a future development (Rossel, 2009). Such signs are often vague and fragmented symptoms of discontinuities in markets and technologies (Holopainen and Toivonen, 2012; Sheaffer et al., 1998) that are difficult to distinguish from other signals and noise (Bradley and O'Toole, 2016; Coffman, 1997; Harris and Zeisler, 2002). From the recipient's point of view, an early warning sign is often surprising and new, and in most cases is not taken seriously by experts in the established domains. The signs typically take some time to become widely recognized, and they provide huge opportunities for the firm to reinvent its business model (Coffman, 1997). When first detected by management, a sign might indicate something that appears to be relatively inconsequential, but the impact on a firm's existing business models could turn out to be far greater than first anticipated (Rossel, 2009). Yamaha, for example, noticed that the limited space available in a typical Japanese home meant that there was little room for a conventional piano, and also that playing a piano was typically something for adults, not for children. Using these observations the company came up with smaller electronic pianos and started to run music schools for children (Nonaka and Zhu, 2012).

As more information, including quantitative information, about markets or emerging technologies is generated and can be accessed more easily over time, weak signals start to become stronger and indicative of a more serious and increasingly obvious issue. Forecasting and scanning tools can then be used to complement early warning signals (Harris and Zeisler, 2002; Holopainen and Toivonen, 2012). Using early warning signs as the basis for action may be the best approach when a firm needs to begin putting together a new business model so that this can be implemented in time—namely, before the impact of the new development begins to be felt. Here it may be that waiting for a stronger signal would simply take too long. However, if there is deemed to be sufficient time to select, develop, and implement a new business model before that change in market or technology is likely to take effect, then it may be better to wait for a stronger signal, and to use that to decide what action to take (Ansoff, 1980; Rossel, 2009).

As we noted before, high-performing firms start to renew their business model before their financial performance actually starts to decline: they are also much more focused on invisible S-curves of strategic performance (Nunes and Breene, 2011). Typically organizational decay starts at the strategic level, and is followed by a drop in operational performance over time (Müller, 1985; Scherrer, 1988). Aggregate performance data such as market share or sales do not provide real early warning signs, because they often reflect the effect of disruptions instead of the cause of them. Factors such as sufficient slack resources, a benign environment in the form of large and loyal customers, or a protective government can all lead to there being long delays before disruptions to markets or technologies start to be reflected in performance metrics (Weitzel and Jonsson, 1989).

Market- and technology-related warning signs of disruption

Early warning signs of potential disruption to a firm's business model can involve the demand side (established customers no longer value the services or products offered) or the supply side (emerging technologies make the firm's business model redundant). Often it is a combination of various elements from both sides (Danneels, 2004; Gans, 2016). Table 7.2 highlights various market- and technology-related signs that warn of potential disruption. In addition to assessing possible disruptions from the firm's own perspective, managers can also attempt to gauge what effects these might have on others (e.g. rivals or new entrants) and whether it is likely that a particular

Table 7.2 Technology- and market-related warning signs of disruption

Various areas where warning signs can emerge	
Technology-related warning signs of disruption	• Changes in resource availability (Roberts, 2004; Weitzel and Jonsson, 1989) • Mature, existing technologies fit less well to customer needs (Meyers, 1990; Paap and Katz, 2004) • New technological developments to address related problems (Danneels, 2004; Paap and Katz, 2004) • Recruitment and training programmes do not ensure a sufficient number of well-qualified personnel (Bertolini et al., 2015; Weitzel and Jonsson, 1989) • Sharp increase in employee turnover (Nunes and Breene, 2011; Scherrer, 1988)
Market-related warning signs of disruption	• Customer needs and preferences, in particular emerging needs, are inadequately served (Govindarajan et al., 2011; Johnson et al., 2008) • Customers do not fully embrace a solution because it is too complicated or too expensive (Anthony and Christensen, 2005; Christensen et al., 2002) • Competitive changes by new entrants or rivals (Johnson et al., 2008; Roberts, 2004) • The firm's position within its ecosystem is becoming weaker (Bertolini et al., 2015; Scherrer, 1988) • Macro-economic developments relating to a firm's markets (Casadesus-Masanell and Ricart, 2011; Govindarajan and Trimble, 2005)

market player will change its business model to go in a different direction (Geroski, 1999).

Recognizing market disruptions before they actually become serious requires one to be close to the market and to quickly make sense of what is happening (Day and Schoemaker, 2004; Müller, 1985). Sales, customer service, and frontline staff typically have an advantage over managerial staff in spotting early warning signs (Weitzel and Jonsson, 1989) and identifying untapped customer needs or unsolved problems. Frontline staff working on activities at the periphery of the company, or at the intersection between R&D, marketing, production, and purchasing, and those with a wide range of internal contacts may be the ones most likely to pick up on weak signals (Holopainen and Toivonen, 2012; Nunes and Breene, 2011).

However, internal information often does not reach top managers on time. In particular, indications that there may be trouble ahead often do not travel easily up the organization, because most incentive systems reward news that is positive, rather than negative (Levitt and Snyder, 1997). To circumvent this problem, Daimler-Benz Aerospace developed an early warning system which taps into a broad range of internal and external information sources (Tessun, 2001). This system has improved the management's ability to filter out the most important warning signs by analysing information from a broad range of sources such as branch meetings, opinions of expert leaders, or the internet. As key staff members and managers from the firm's various product divisions are involved in detecting signs and deciding on which to prioritize for action, this helps to ensure that Daimler-Benz Aerospace takes heed of troubling news, even if that then involves some painful decisions (Tessun, 2001).

The periphery of a firm's market or industry is where new opportunities for a firm arise, including disruptive ones, and is thus often the place to get foresight information (Cunha and Chia, 2007; Day and Schoemaker, 2004; Harris and Zeisler, 2002). Or, as Andy Grove from Intel said, 'when spring comes, snow melts first at the periphery, because that is where it is most exposed' (Grove, 1999). The periphery that may impact on a firm's business models includes not only the intersection between markets or industries, but also the undefined space at the intersection between technologies, mindsets, and industries (Cunha and Chia, 2007). However, only a few of the seemingly endless combinations between these dimensions provide interesting and profitable opportunities for a firm (Geroski, 1999). Uber is just one example of a firm that has been successful in exploring new areas at the intersection between a technology (an app) and an industry (the taxi industry). When Apple and Nike joined forces to bring in the Nike+, a running shoe with a sensor which transmits data on the jogger's speed, distance, etc. to an iPod, they were exploiting an opportunity that lay at the intersection between the sports, health, and personal entertainment markets (Ofek and Wathieu, 2010).

The peripheries of complex business ecosystems are particularly rich areas in which to spot weak signals of disruption (Harris and Zeisler, 2002). A business ecosystem is a network of organizations that interact with one another, and share skills and assets, in order to produce technologies and products focused on addressing particular needs of end-users (Eisenhardt and Galunic, 2000; Zahra and Nambisan, 2012). Such ecosystems can facilitate a 'butterfly effect' (Cunha and Chia, 2007; Rossel, 2009) in which combinations of small events reinforce one another in unexpected ways (Kaplan and Mikes, 2012). Over time, unexpected competitors with new business models that build on new technologies and satisfy a new market

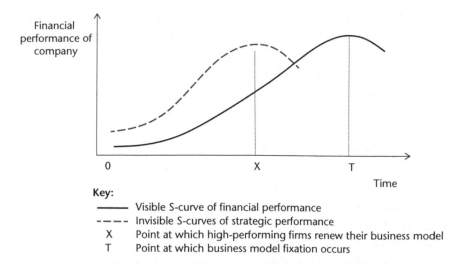

Key:

— Visible S-curve of financial performance
- - - Invisible S-curves of strategic performance
X   Point at which high-performing firms renew their business model
T   Point at which business model fixation occurs

Figure 7.2 S-curves of financial performance and strategic performance
Source: adapted from Nunes and Breene (2011)

Reprinted by permission of *Harvard Business Review*.

From *Reinvent Your Business Before It's Too Late* by P. Nunes & T. Breene, 89(1/2)/ 2011. Copyright © 2017 by the Harvard Business School Publishing Corporation; all rights reserved.

need may come in stealthily to the centre of a market from its furthest periphery (Cunha and Chia, 2007).

Nunes and Breene (2011) have identified three invisible S-curves of strategic performance which start to decline before a firm's financial performance does (see also point X on the horizontal axis of Figure 7.2): the firm's competitive position curve, its distinctive skills and capabilities curve, and its talent curve. Long before a successful business model hits its revenue peak, its competitive position starts to become eroded. When a new business model is first introduced, the financial performance is initially still relatively low, due to the substantial level of investments made and the low volumes of sales (Johnson et al., 2008; McGrath, 2010). However, if it is successful, there is usually a strong and quite rapid increase in performance. Over time price and turnover pressure occur, partly due to the competition, pushing the financial performance downwards (see Figure 7.2). Any TMTs and CEOs who manage their business from an economic perspective, looking almost exclusively at turnover, costs, and overall financial performance, will perhaps only review the business model for a particular product or service at year T (or even later) in Figure 7.2 (Nunes and Breene, 2011).

Research (Nunes and Breene, 2011) has shown that high-performing firms renew their business model much earlier, at around point X in our figure. There is a gap of several years between points X and T, and the number of years will depend on the dynamism and competition in a particular sector. What do these high-performing firms do differently to the firms which pay attention only to the financial S-curve? Research shows that they are much more focused on the three invisible S-curves of strategic performance. Those curves reach their peak earlier, sometimes much earlier, than the financial performance S-curve. For convenience's sake, the three strategic performance S-curves are represented by a single curve in our figure.

The first of the three invisible S-curves relates to the firm's strategic competitive position. Newcomers and existing rivals can cause that position to be undermined earlier than is shown by the turnover figures of the firm concerned. A second, similarly invisible, S-curve shows the same progression, and concerns the distinctiveness of the firm's core skills and capabilities. The third invisible S-curve relates to the talent within the firm: the employees and managers who possess the capacity to develop new business. In firms that are driven by financial performance, managers will look very closely at costs in order to ramp up the performance of a given business model even more. In this kind of exploitation-oriented context, talented individuals may be let go or may themselves decide to leave the firm (Nunes and Breene, 2011).

Detection and assessment of early warning signs, and resulting managerial action

Early warning signs are relatively easy to detect with hindsight; the value lies in detecting them and assessing their potential impact at the time, and this can be quite difficult (Harris and Zeisler, 2002). The challenge for managers is to scan the periphery of the market and emergent technology fields just broadly enough, identify alternative business models quickly, and capitalize on those business models (Day and Schoemaker, 2004).

Early warning signs of market threats or of disruptive technologies that could harm a firm's existing business model should be given the most attention (Johnson et al., 2008; Markides and Oyon, 2010; Ofek and Wathieu, 2010). Nintendo, for example, was able to develop its successful Wii business model partly because it had spotted several signs of potential disruption to its existing model (passive computer games) at the intersection between the games and fitness markets. They recognized, for example, that professional people have only limited time for playing games, that parents are happier when their children play computer games with other children rather than on their own, and that more attention is being given to sport and to the health of young children. The firm also took note of the blurring of the gaming and fitness markets, and of a strongly held view among non-gamers that video games are a waste of time, and bad for your brain and your health (Nonaka and Zhu, 2012).

Early warning signs of competing markets and disruptive technologies can be many-sided (Day and Schoemaker, 2004); they can even come from sci-fi movies (Hiltunen, 2008). For instance, movies such as *Star Wars* and *Back to the Future* have provided many ideas for market- and technology-related changes. Management may challenge its employees to detect, understand, and share emerging signs of disruption. For instance, they can facilitate dialogue or organize camp sessions, brainstorming seminars outside the workplace, and even drinking sessions (Nonaka and Takeuchi, 1995). Those signs of potential disruption are often shared in firms via informal networks (Fischbacher-Smith and Fischbacher-Smith, 2014) or during discussions at coffee time (Holopainen and Toivonen, 2012). For example, Rabobank challenges its employees to look out for emerging signs of disruption in the financial sector. The Rabobank 'Attack your own Bank' initiative stimulates its employees to spot new opportunities which might form the basis of viable new business models.

Detecting market and technology signs of disruptive developments that could potentially have a considerable impact on a firm's business model initially requires the use of qualitative and rather unstructured tools such as the Delphi methodology (expert meetings), interviews with radical thinkers, and consultation with different people with a broad knowledge base (Harris and Zeisler, 2002; Holopainen and Toivonen, 2012; Kaivo-oja, 2012). These days, companies can also spot possible signs of disruption on social media networks such as Facebook, Pinterest, and Twitter (Harrysson et al., 2014).

Nonetheless, many firms may have a natural tendency to overlook what is happening at the fringes of the market or of new technology fields, because their predominant focus is on their existing activities or they simply do not have a proper understanding of these fringes (Cunha and Chia, 2007; Day and Schoemaker, 2004). Current attitudes and mindsets, and inbuilt biases in the search for future developments, act as filters and obfuscate these signs (Harris and Zeisler, 2002). Ansoff (1984) referred to these kinds of filters as 'surveillance filters'.

However, if early warning signs pass through these surveillance filters, then firms need to take action in response. Signs of changes that could potentially have a very significant impact on the firm should not only be identified in time but should also be carefully monitored and addressed appropriately (Harris and Zeisler, 2002; Rossel, 2009). For instance, how could a smaller company like Canon manage to make such a huge dent in Xerox's market share? While Xerox focused on expensive photocopiers, Canon took over Xerox's position as the global leader in that market by introducing cheaper and smaller machines (Gilad, 2003). Apparently, Xerox did not keep abreast of trends that suggested there was an unmet need for small, low-cost copiers. One should keep in mind, though, that the estimated impact of a change on a firm's business model can increase or decrease over time: events that had been previously judged as likely to have a greater impact should then be given less managerial attention, and fewer resources should be allocated to them, while the reverse applies for an event that was previously thought to be less relevant.

However, firms may not fully appreciate the importance of an early warning sign, because they are relying on their past experiences. This phenomenon is also known as a 'mentality filter' (Holopainen and Toivonen, 2012). At an individual level, perceptual filters can cause employees to ignore information that does not reaffirm and validate their beliefs and expectations. At a group level, groupthink (Janis, 1972) and other defensive processes increase the pressures on organizational members to downplay the importance of independent opinion-making. At an organizational level, over time a dominant logic develops that may be hard to change: it is often focused very much on the existing business model and ignores competing technologies and potential or unserved markets. Logics of this kind are based on collective mental maps which managers have developed unconsciously as a result of their experience with a core business model. These maps often prevent managers from looking at markets and technologies in other ways and exploring possible new business models (Cunha and Chia, 2007). For instance, why was Sharp more successful in the electronic calculator business than the more experienced Texas Instruments? When Sharp entered the electronic calculator business, it did not have an established logic in the home appliance business, its main business. The calculator division of Sharp thus enjoyed a high degree of freedom and was able to refine its dominant logic independently. While Sharp was able to refine its logic, Texas Instruments could not change its dominant logic. Texas Instruments had developed a strong dominant logic in the semiconductor business, and its electronic calculator business was heavily dependent on its semiconductor division. When applied to the new business, that dominant logic which worked so well in the semiconductor business led to failure. And even if a signal passes through a firm's surveillance and mentality filters, a 'power filter' may then block a warning signal. A power filter refers to the power of key decision-makers in an organization to neutralize or eliminate warning signals, either intentionally or unintentionally (Holopainen and Toivonen, 2012). Fear of cannibalization is one factor that may drive the power filter.

If a firm faces untapped customer needs or rival technologies that may seriously impact its existing business model, then the question is how a firm responds, or fails to respond, to such disruptions (Harris and Zeisler, 2002; Ofek and Wathieu, 2010). Broadly speaking, if the management of a firm wants to use early warning signs as a basis for action, there are three possible ways it can do so:

- It can augment its existing business model by incorporating elements of the new technology or by targeting the new or emerging market. For example, in response to increased customer concerns about the environment, Tesco augmented its existing retail offering by introducing its Greener Living programme. As part of a wider drive to significantly cut carbon emissions, customers can earn green points by recycling printer cartridges, for instance, and can redeem those points for cash.

- It can renew its business model by combining elements of the current model with new elements that fit with the anticipated new developments. For example, by introducing the Nike+ sports web interface and kit, Nike offered a new value proposition to digital customers. Sports shoes remained an important part of its business model.

- It can reaffirm its distinctive values by replicating its business model to counteract the expected negative effects indicated by the early warning signs. For example, by introducing a prepaid debit card ('Current Card') for teenagers, the American internet-based Discover Bank reaffirmed its core business: facilitating convenient and responsible spending. In this way, the bank was able to help parents ensure that teenagers did not get into debt by spending excessive sums when shopping online (Ofek and Wathieu, 2010).

Making an early response to indications of change gives an organization more time to address the new market need or new technology, and more opportunities to influence the new markets or rival technologies to its advantage. It may also help it to prevent the disruption from escalating by working out ways in which to minimize the disruptive effect on the firm's business model (Kaivo-oja, 2012; McGrath, 2010). On the other hand, focusing exclusively on a narrow range of early warning signs that all point in the same direction—in terms of a competing market or a disruptive technology—can be quite dangerous (Day and Schoemaker, 2004; Drew, 2006). Testing out a new business model using low-cost experiments before moving to full implementation might mitigate against this danger (Day and Schoemaker, 2004; McGrath, 2010). However, given the uncertainty and other risks, incumbents often let others take action first in response to early warning signs (Ofek and Wathieu, 2010).

Acting too quickly or waiting too long before acting upon warning signs are both risky options (Bradley and O'Toole, 2016; Ofek and Wathieu, 2010). The challenge for a firm is to detect the signs of potential disruption and to change its business model appropriately before other players in the market (Geroski, 1999; Nunes and Breene, 2011). Honda is an example of a first-mover firm that senses and seizes technology-related opportunities for new business models. It envisioned a future in which society would place more value on the environment, and became a pioneer in designing robots and fuel-cell cars that emit only water vapour (Nonaka and Zhu, 2012). Having a vision for the future and taking the right course of action in response to early weak signs increases the chances that a firm itself will become a disruptor (Cunha and Chia, 2007). Imagining what the future might look like helps firms to adopt disruptive technologies and to build new business models with which to address changing customer needs (Tellis, 2006). For example, Starbucks transformed the coffee business by being the first to recognize that what consumers were looking for was a 'café experience' (Harris and Zeisler, 2002).

Management thus plays a crucial role in detecting early warning signs, either directly or indirectly, responding accordingly, and reducing the negative impact of the various filters and barriers. If managers overestimate the value of the firm's existing business model and underestimate the significance of warning signs, this may stop them from considering business model innovation. Early warning signs are often not regarded as a managerial priority, because they may appear unimportant and also because it is uncertain whether and when something might actually happen.

Business model traps

Perhaps even more important than spotting early warning signs is deciding when it is appropriate to undertake business model innovation, and what action senior managers should take. As Ofek and Wathieu (2010: 129) state, 'putting off action can be as risky as responding too quickly.' Holding on to an existing business model for too long by ignoring or underestimating early warning signals reduces the chances of developing a new business model at the right point and competing effectively with rivals who have managed to do so. Introducing new business models too quickly or intensively by acting too quickly or too boldly on early warning signs reduces the potential value to be derived from it (e.g. Roberts, 2004). This brings us to two business model traps:

* focusing too much on financial performance, with the result that the firm holds on to its existing business model for too long
* focusing too much on the future, so that the firm is unable to obtain appropriate value from its existing business models.

Focusing too strongly on financial performance: the fixation trap

Management is under great pressure to focus on short-term performance and hold on to its existing business model (e.g. Govindarajan and Trimble, 2011; Voelpel et al., 2005; Yoon and Deeken, 2013). Many top managers 'have a tendency to discount the future' (Kaplan and Mikes, 2012: 60). Success with an existing model can lead an organization to fall victim to the 'success-breeds-failure' syndrome. Building on that success reinforces established beliefs and mental models, and encourages organizational inertia (Ofek and Wathieu, 2010). For example, firms are likely to promote managers who have been involved in making that business model successful and to invest the resources they accumulate in keeping that model going.

Firms that do this are preoccupied with existing customer needs and technologies and they develop a strong internal focus (Cunha and Chia, 2007; Geroski, 1999). For example, when Coca-Cola was focusing intensely on its main rival Pepsi, it failed to pay sufficient attention to the growth in bottled water (Gilad, 2003). Factors such as overconfidence, existing mental filters, a tendency to give more weight to existing assumptions, and a dislike of ambiguity create organizational filters, thereby reducing the breadth of areas which a firm scans for potential market or technology disruptions and/or the intensity with which it does so (Day and Schoemaker, 2004). Because of these filters, warning signs are not detected, are not sufficiently understood or fully appreciated, or are simply ignored (Day and Schoemaker, 2004). In fact, they are treated as 'false alarms rather than alerts to imminent danger' (Kaplan and Mikes, 2012: 52). For example, many firms consider themselves to be providers of products within certain well-defined categories (e.g. newspapers) and they stop paying sufficient attention to what type of content consumers may actually be looking for (e.g. media content). As a result, they miss opportunities at the periphery of the market (Ofek and Wathieu, 2010) and are taken by surprise. This happened to many news-papers, retail firms, travel agencies, and banks, who initially did not regard online activities as being part of their market.

Even where firms do spot and understand emerging signs of disruption, they may not necessarily be inclined to take appropriate action. These firms may not be able to respond because their 'power filters' limit the type of action they can take or because they are unwilling to give up their existing business model (Cunha and Chia, 2007; Voelpel et al., 2005). As a result, the firms may end up 'doing all the right things to meet their existing customers' needs' (Geroski, 1999: 112), so that it becomes increasingly difficult for them to change path. Over time, existing customers may switch to other firms that did take proper action.

Firms of this kind do not start on business model innovation immediately after early warning signs become apparent. They may only become willing to start taking action at the point when their actual performance is showing signs of decline. When combined with monitoring tools and financial incentives, short-term performance orientation has been referred to as one of the most important 'innovation killers' (Christensen et al., 2008).

If a firm wants to change its business model at the appropriate point, it should carefully analyse three invisible S-curves. The first S-curve may become discernible if top management scans broadly to spot signs of potential disruption from emerging technologies and at the periphery of the market (e.g. Anthony and Christensen, 2005; Ofek and Wathieu, 2010). This allows the firm to identify customer value propositions which have not been attended to, customer needs which have not been recognized, or technology options which have not been considered. Frontline employees, research teams in far-flung parts of the company, and line managers all have a crucial role in detecting important shifts in the market or the emergence of competing technologies. Employees and managers who already have some knowledge of the fringes of the market or some affinity with unknown technologies are often not involved in strategy processes (Day and Schoemaker, 2016). It is they who form the far corners of the organization, as it were. To reinvent their business models, companies should bring the edges of the market and emerging technologies to the centre. In this 'edge-centric' approach, multiple stakeholders are involved in the business model innovation process (Nunes and Breene, 2011).

The second invisible S-curve of distinctiveness of the firm's core skills and capabilities requires that the capacities of the top management itself also have to be reviewed (Holmqvist, 2003). If the advanced production capacities become less distinctive and the market is approached with a fundamentally different proposition, this has consequences for the composition of the top management as far as expertise is concerned. This will lead to a change at the top (see Table 7.3).

Top management can tackle the third invisible S-curve of available talent within the firm by making an effort to cultivate and retain that talent. This kind of policy is aimed at the long term. Talented employees bind themselves to the firm mainly on the basis of intrinsic motivation. They are given the chance to bring promising projects to fruition and develop

Table 7.3 Actions required by top management to identify invisible S-curves

Identifying invisible S-curves		Action required by top management
1	Edge-centric strategy	Investigate the invisible S-curve of a firm's strategic competitive position; take seriously any signals from the furthest corners of the market and furthest periphery of the organization, and incorporate them into strategy formation.
2	Change at the top	Change the composition of the top management in time, based on the invisible S-curve of distinctive core capabilities; business model renewal requires new capabilities and skills.
3	Surplus talent	Use proactive talent management to stop the invisible S-curve of talent from dipping downwards.

Source: based on Nunes and Breene (2011)

themselves further through this. Creating a surplus of talent is a necessary condition for completing business model innovation trajectories more rapidly and successfully (Nunes and Breene, 2011).

The factors which enable business model transformation can help CEOs and top management teams to keep those three invisible S-curves in sight. We discuss three of these factors. The first, transformational leadership, helps in identifying the invisible S-curve of firm competitiveness and definitely also that of talent. Transformational leaders are quicker to notice the early departure of talented employees, and this will prompt them to take action earlier as well.

The second factor is CEO tenure. CEOs who have stayed in post for too long are more likely to retain the existing business model for longer than is advisable (Wu et al., 2005). CEOs who have just been appointed will take a more critical look at the existing business model (Day and Schoemaker, 2004; Holmqvist, 2003). But if new CEOs take the most notice of the financial performance, they also run the risk of the firm ending up in the fixation trap (Hope and Fraser, 2013).

The third factor, listening to existing customers, makes a firm more firmly wedded to its existing business model, and that increases the chances of falling into the trap.

Focusing too strongly on the future: the renewal trap

The second trap involves focusing too much on the future. CEOs and top management teams who are continuously analysing warning signs and developing a rapid succession of new business models miss out on the returns which come from the replication phase (Levinthal and March, 1993). When there is too much business model renewal, a firm dismantles its existing sources of competitive advantage without finding any adequate replacement (Aspara et al., 2013) and does not derive the full value from its business model (Davis et al., 2009). That results in a situation where there is a great deal of renewal, but insufficient financial resources to make a success of the new business model, for example, by acquiring appropriate distribution channels or positioning the product better in the market. The firm 3M, which excels at exploring new opportunities, found that investing too heavily in business model renewal did not work to its advantage. Substantial investment in people yielded no result; a culture grew up in which people were encouraged to work around and even defy their superiors, and it developed into a wait-and-see enterprise which was strongly dependent on the initiatives of its researchers. The company had no explicit strategy, and this led to losses in the magnetic storage market (disks, video tapes, and cassette tapes). A well-articulated business model could have helped 3M to resolve the long-standing problems in its imaging and electronic storage business.

Business model renewal can lead to instability as a result of overreactions to market or technology changes or elaborate search processes which waste money. The organization exaggerates the importance of local changes and becomes oversensitive to early warning signs, hype, and fashions (Massay and Wu, 2005; Volberda, 1998). This chronic form of business model renewal destroys the firm's identity and its shared norms and values. A downward spiral arises which ends in a renewal trap, characterized by conflict, unclear responsibilities, inadequate control systems, a lack of direction and collective ideology and, ultimately, inefficiency.

The renewal trap also occurs with CEOs and top management teams in firms which focus too much on the start of the three invisible S-curves and not enough on the financial returns in the replication phase. Those firms start working on a new business model way before point X in Figure 7.2, and are already pulling out of the existing model by that point. They are already looking ahead to the next generation of technologies and product/market combinations way before the financial performance of their business model reaches maturity. They jump, as it were, from one S-curve to the next too early. Jumping too soon to the next financial performance S-curve thus leads to the renewal trap, while jumping too late leads to the fixation trap.

Cycles of replication and renewal at the sector level

Development of business models in a sector

The dedication to large and loyal customers (mostly laggards) and financial key performance indicators in established firms work like a filter so that improvements which are profitable in the short term are adopted more readily than radical changes to the business model. The new products or services presented in a disruptive business model are initially likely to have lower margins and to be of lower quality. Most of the lucrative customers will not be all that prepared to buy the new product or service and often do not have a direct need for a fundamentally new solution. It is precisely the less lucrative customers who embrace the new product or service (Govindarajan and Kopalle, 2006; Govindarajan et al., 2011).

Disruptive new technologies are often put initially on to emerging markets or markets that are deemed to be less important. Many firms listen to the most lucrative customers and look for the most profitable products in the short term. This can make a company decide that the disruptive technology they have invented or adopted is not worth pursuing, and so they turn against it. This is how that works, according to Christensen (1997):

- A disruptive technology is developed in established firms;
- The marketing units in these firms ask leading customers for their reactions to the new technology and decide against rolling it out;
- The established firms carry on trying to make further developments to existing technologies;
- New firms are set up, and through trial and error they find markets for the disruptive technology;
- The newcomers scale up the market;
- Established firms make the switch to the new technology too late to be able to retain customers.

The problem for established firms is not so much the development of disruptive technologies. Often it is the established firms themselves which develop those technologies. But by allocating too many resources and their best people to projects for their main customers and business model replication, the firms are left with insufficient resources to develop these disruptive technologies further (Christensen, 1997). The story of Kodak, as discussed in our introductory chapter, is a perfect illustration of this.

It is remarkable that it often costs more to develop improved technologies than it does to develop new technologies, even though the risks are lower (Christensen, 1997). If a disruptive technology is used rarely or not at all, employees become frustrated and set up their own firm to try to commercialize the technology. Once the start-up has found a new market and invested in developing the technology further, it can address an unserved market need (Agarwal et al., 2007). The start-up searches for potentially lucrative customers, many of whom will already be customers of the established firms. As the start-up attempts to lure away those customers, this then disrupts the business model of the established players (Govindarajan et al., 2011).

If customers of the established firms start to see the benefits of the new concept, they may gradually switch to the start-up. The established players then start to protect their customer base. Because of the advantages which the start-up has built up in the meantime—such as more experience and cost advantages—the established players eventually have to withdraw from the new market or be satisfied with a smaller market share (Christensen, 1997). Where they settle for a smaller share, the established firms can sometimes survive by targeting a new and more sustainable niche in their existing market with their existing technology. Paradoxically, this new niche becomes apparent because the new technology exposes the diversity of customer demands (Adner and Snow, 2010).

An excessive focus on replication alone is therefore dangerous for the viability of firms in the long term. The rise of start-ups is part of the natural process of evolution, consisting of variation, selection, and retention. Disruptive technologies which are not developed further and commercialized by an established firm offer space for new start-ups (variation). Not every start-up has a long life (selection), but those which survive the selection process can develop further and become successful (retention). The new market created by the start-up also attracts new players (variation). A shake-out then takes place (selection), because a particular design has become dominant in the market, for example (e.g. Klepper, 1996).

However, start-ups are not the only ones to disrupt existing technologies or markets. Established companies can also disrupt existing markets via a low-end foothold, offering a new product at a lower price which initially attracts a more price-sensitive segment (Govindarajan and Kopalle, 2006). They can introduce a low-budget or a prize-fighter business model in different markets or market segments to cater for needs that were not being properly taken care of by other incumbents in those markets (who were initially focused on their most profitable and demanding customers). Examples include the arrival of Southwest Airlines as an alternative to the regular airlines and the creation of Randstad's low-budget 'Tempo-Team' business model as a competitor to other regular employment agencies.

Apart from disruption via low-cost competition, established companies can also disrupt existing markets by creating a market or market segment which did not exist before, that is, a new market foothold. In this case, they initially target non-customers of an existing product or service and gradually obtain a strong position in the mainstream market of that existing product or service (Christensen et al., 2015). For example, automobile companies have introduced service-based business models rather than product-based business models. Car2go is part of Daimler AG, and provides car-sharing services by means of point-to-point rental services in over 29 cities around the world. Instead of having to go to centralized rental offices, customers can use an app to find the nearest car, and the rates they pay are calculated either daily, hourly, or even by the minute. Car2go allows Daimler AG to learn about how people move about in and close to cities, which is important information in the context of the potential market for self-driving cars. Autonomous driving provides many opportunities for car-sharing (Fortune, 2015). Accordingly, business models based on car-sharing could disrupt traditional business models that revolve around selling cars in urban areas or even the traditional business models of taxi companies. The American electric vehicle manufacturer Tesla Motors introduced a roadside assistance service and can make certain repairs by updating a car's software remotely. This reduces the need to send a mechanic to the customer's vehicle and may in time disrupt the business model of traditional roadside assistance organizations (e.g. ADAC in Germany and ANWB in the Netherlands).

Carglass started as a wholesale car window business, and broadened its scope to car window repair and replacement. Later on, it disrupted the car window repair and replacement market by becoming a subcontractor for insurance companies. By sorting out insurance issues relating to car windows, Carglass drew customers away from other established car window repair and replacement companies. Also, by repairing tiny fractures Carglass was able to avoid the costs of replacing the windows, making it a more attractive subcontractor for insurance companies.

Unexpected but successful new entrants to the market who operate with new business models behave rationally, and can thus be identified by incumbents who are able to make use of the information flow from their market. There are three particular sources of information that can be used to detect almost all potential new entrants: related product markets (e.g. substitutes, complementary products), actors up and down the value chain (e.g. suppliers and customers), and actors with similar or related competencies which enable them to perform a similar function to the firm in question (Geroski, 1999). The firm itself can use these sources to exploit opportunities by means of business model innovation (Drew, 2006). Several different kinds of 'disruptors' can be distinguished: total newcomers, autonomous ventures by

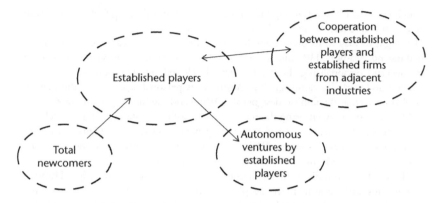

Figure 7.3 Established players and different types of newcomers
Source: based on Hensmans et al. (2001)

established players, and existing firms from other industries which cooper-ate with established firms (such as Ahold which entered the financial market in collaboration with Aegon) (see also Figure 7.3) (Hensmans et al., 2001).

Besides newcomers, established players can also reduce the value of a rival's business model, and vice versa. Introducing a new business model and subsequently replicating it increases the firm's operating income. But a counter-attack by a rival can reduce that income and give the firm a reason to develop yet another new business model. The competitive race between Hewlett-Packard and Dell is a good example of this. It shows how compe-tition makes cycles of business model renewal and replication follow one another in increasingly rapid succession; renewal by one player leads to replication by the other, and vice versa (Volberda et al., 2011).

. . . .

CYCLES OF RENEWAL AND REPLICATION: DELL VERSUS HEWLETT–PACKARD

Towards the end of 2009, Hewlett-Packard (HP) had a market share of 19.9 per cent on the global PC market, while Dell's share had dropped to 12.9 per cent. Dell's shares had dropped in price by 32 per cent, while HP's price had doubled. Dell had become big on the basis of its original concept of producing and supplying without using intermediaries. This concept, known as the 'Dell way', has been called 'one of the most revolutionary business models of the end of the twentieth century'. But here, too, past results do not guarantee future success. Reactions by rivals made the Dell way less valuable. Dell used its model more and more as a way of reducing costs and, with that, the price of its products.

HP has succeeded in reinventing itself in the past few years. After investigating the firm's own business model, Todd Bradely, head of PC Operations, came to the conclusion that HP was fighting the wrong battle. HP was fighting Dell on the points at which Dell excelled: direct sales via the internet and telephone. Bradely believed HP ought to play to its own strengths, sales via retailers, an area in which Dell was making no headway. HP shifted the focus by developing close relationships with retailers and 'personalizing' the PC. The firm developed unique products for different retailers and started a campaign, 'the computer is personal again', with the help of celebrities such as the fashion designer Vera Wang and the hip-hop artist Jay Z.

Dell responded by entering the retail sector as well. Dell started selling notebook computers and desktops in Japan through a Japanese retailer (Bic Camera Inc.). In addition, Dell invested more in R&D to create innovative products, and reminded consumers of the advantages of custom-made computers.

HP and Dell both diversified in order to retain their competitive edge. Through acquisitions HP became more deeply involved in the market for services and network products. Thus it took over 3Com, a computer network firm, and EDS, a business and technological services firm. This new area of business made up 14 per cent of HP's turnover at the end of 2009. In the third quarter of 2009 Dell acquired Perot Systems, an IT service provider, to increase its activity in the services sector.

Source: Volberda et al. (2011)

. . . .

Imitation of business models in a sector

Successful radical renewal of the business model at the company level sets changes in motion elsewhere and is regarded by established firms as a disruption to the sector (Sabatier et al., 2012). Many established firms tend to imitate the newcomer's disruptive behaviour (Markides and Oyon, 2010), and this can be regarded as 'herd behaviour'. Research into Dutch and British financial service providers showed that firms in the same sector apply renewal to a similar degree (Volberda et al., 2001). This suggests that there are shared mindsets or shared cognitive approaches to management at the industry level. Imitating the business model of the 'disruptor' is a trap, however, and rarely results in success. When imitating the game of a 'disruptor', you are trying to play it better than the party which invented the game (Markides and Oyon, 2010), but without having any first-mover advantages. For example, when the low-cost carriers Ryanair and EasyJet came on to the market in the 1990s, this provoked a reaction from various established airlines. They also wanted a piece of the pie. But the initial forays into that market by KLM (Buzz), British Airways (GO), and Continental Airlines (Continental Lite) did not meet with the same kind of success as Ryanair and EasyJet had experienced (Markides and Charitou, 2004). The established carriers were not able to alter their cost and operating structures fast enough to compete with the low-cost carriers. Their slow response enabled these low-cost carriers to gain an even stronger position in the leisure market.

A more appropriate reaction for established firms is to use so-called 'buffer strategies', combined with gradual implementation of 'bridging strategies'. Using a buffer strategy to protect themselves against a disruptive business model enables incumbents to preserve their legitimacy with regard to external partners, rivals, customers, and regulators, while at the same time challenging the legitimacy and reliability of the disruptive business model and the newcomers (Hensmans et al., 2001; Van den Bosch and Van Riel, 1998). We can see an example of this with the Dutch postal delivery company PostNL. Lobbying the Dutch regulators, labour unions, and Dutch political parties enabled PostNL to retain for longer its monopoly on the delivery of parcels and letters up to fifty grams in the Netherlands. Similarly, many established taxi companies tried to prevent Uber from entering their local markets by stressing that the company did not comply with legal rules and regulations. The degree to which this obstruction was successful varied by region, and some taxi companies responded by introducing their own apps, using competing apps that asked for lower fees (e.g. Taxify), or collaborating with Uber.

Established players, often larger firms, buy time with buffer strategies so they can gradually implement strategies which will allow them to bridge the gap between the existing business model and the new model by making intensive changes in the organization. Often they choose an integral business model renewal trajectory for this, in which the levers of new technology, new management practices, new organizational forms, and co-creation are used. This increases the long-term viability of the entire organization. Such bridging strategies do require existing approaches within a firm to be brought up for discussion.

One example of a bridging strategy is the development of a business model which is new to the industry (and thus different to the business model being used by a disruptor) and to the firm itself. This type of approach is also known as 'disrupt the disruptor' (Markides and Oyon, 2010). Nintendo's reaction to Sony and Microsoft is a good example of this.

. . . .

NINTENDO'S BRIDGING STRATEGY IN THE GAMING INDUSTRY:
THE INTRODUCTION OF POKÉMON GO

Sony and Microsoft had introduced the Playstation and the Xbox, targeting teenagers and young adults, and both were devices with good graphics, functionality, and speed. In response to these disruptive business models, Nintendo introduced the Wii, aimed primarily at families. The emphasis of the Wii is on simplicity, ease of use, family experience, and fitness (Markides and Oyon, 2010).

Nowadays, the business model in gaming has moved from game computers to mobile games that can be accessed at any time, in any place. In this new disruptive business model, firms do not make money by selling consoles, games, and occasionally merchandise. Instead, a game on a smartphone can be downloaded for free or played gratis for a trial period. A firm makes money when players make purchases within the game, such as extra lives which allow them to continue playing the game. Nintendo was typically known for video game consoles such as the Wii and Nintendo 64 and for computer games such as Super Mario and Zelda. With the Pokémon Go app, Nintendo has entered the era of the smartphone. With augmented reality technology, virtual creatures appear on a smartphone as if they were actually on the street or at other locations.

Within twenty-four hours after its release in Australia, New Zealand, and in the United States, the app was topping the Android and iOS download charts. Only a couple of days after the launch of this app, Nintendo's market value had increased by over 50 per cent. However, the question is to what extent the Pokémon Go business model provides Nintendo with a sustainable competitive advantage. Smartphone games are often ephemeral: the hype that surrounds such games immediately after their release typically dies down quite quickly (NRC, 2016). Thus while Nintendo may have successfully bridged various developments in the gaming industry (e.g. from game computers to mobile games) with the introduction of Pokémon Go, it is only a matter of time until another wave of disruptions occurs in the gaming industry, meaning that Nintendo may no longer be able to capture the same value from its current business model.

. . . .

A player which enters the market with a fundamentally new business model creates opportunities as well as threats for established players (Gilbert and Bower, 2002). The new business model can, for instance, expose a segment in which a firm is not yet active but which may potentially be profitable. In the first instance the disruptive business model should be regarded by established players as a threat, so that top management will pay attention to it and release resources to combat the threat. If a new demand is subsequently identified, the new model can be seen as an opportunity and organizational resources can be released in phases to exploit it (Gilbert and Bower, 2002).

Developing a new business model in response to a disruptive business model of another party is not the only possible reaction. In this kind of situation a firm can also decide to make its existing business model more competitive, ignore the disruptor's business model, or copy elements of the disruptor's new concept in order to commercialize it on a larger scale (Charitou and Markides, 2003; Markides and Oyon, 2010). For instance, with its capsule-based Nespresso range, Nestlé copied several elements of successful business models from various other industries; their revenue model mirrors Gilette's razor blade model or HP's printer ink model, while their distribution model is a hybrid of closed direct customer relationships (as used by book clubs) and premium boutiques (as used by luxury fashion chains) (Mikhalkina, 2016). To reinvent their business model many companies engage in cross-industry imitation of various elements of iconic business models (Enkel and Mezger, 2013). Firms such as Airbnb, Amazon, eBay, Dell, McDonald's, and Uber are known worldwide for their innovative business models, which disrupted the established logic of value creation and capture in their industry sectors and quickly became iconic (Sabatier et al., 2010), and various elements of those business models have since been widely copied across other industries.

The dual business model: replication and renewal at the company level

Our survey showed that firms which are capable of replicating their existing business model as well as developing new business models deliver better performance (see also Chapter 3). A more detailed analysis reveals that these effects are not straightforward (see Figure 7.4). With firms that are fundamentally renewing their business model, company performance will grow at a fast pace if they also do more work on replication (see the broken line in Figure 7.4). This enables firms to escape the renewal trap by further refining new business models (over time or geographically). Organizations which work on a high degree of replication and develop few new business models will experience a temporary dip in the company performance if they start working more on renewal (see the continuous line in Figure 7.4). This dip is shaped like a J-curve; performance decreases at first before a continual improvement is achieved.

Strong leadership, extra resources, and a sense that rapid change is urgently needed are required to transform the initial drop in performance into better results (e.g. Roberts, 2004; Smith et al., 2010; Volberda et al., 2001). A similar sequence of falling performance followed by eventual improvement (J-curves) could be observed in the business model renewal at BP and Unilever after the two firms had initially concentrated solely on replication (Roberts, 2004; Volberda, 1998). But this kind of J-curve in company performance also

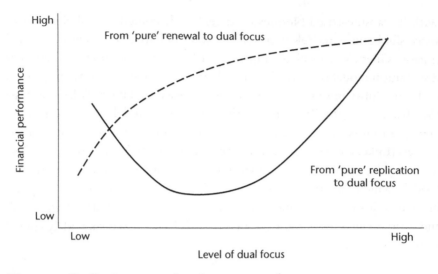

Figure 7.4 Replication, renewal, and company performance

occurred during the transformation of KLM Cargo's business model: generic transport activities were replicated, but the firm was also engaged in business model renewal through the provision of additional distribution and information services.

. . . .

KLM CARGO: INITIAL PROBLEMS WITH BUSINESS MODEL TRANSFORMATION

KLM Cargo made the switch from generic transport activities to customized services (for example, transporting chemicals or valuable paintings). The firm also attracted new customers and provided logistic services that were not transport-related (for example, the sub-assembly of components and stock management). This initially caused a great deal of friction within the organization. Up to that point, the most important freight activities for KLM Cargo had been generic transport activities for end-users. The profit margin on these generic services was slowly being eroded: carriers could only provide these services if efficiency was given the highest priority. KLM Cargo also did not know precisely who its final customers were, and the firm's immediate customers—the airfreight carriers—often turned out to be its rivals.

KLM Cargo's new business model was therefore based on serving the final customer, who is willing to pay extra for products with added value. Most important for the firm was to switch to a totally different way of thinking so that this new business model could be realized. KLM Cargo now had to see itself as a provider of integrated logistics services, not as an airline operator which supplied only transport and distribution services. This unlearning of the old business model and learning of a new model required significant investment by the firm to enable it to deliver a wide range of customized services that provided added value. The firm also decided on a fundamental organizational restructuring. The most obvious reasons for this were that it wanted to get closer to the customer, cut down on bureaucracy, and offer employees freedom ('empowerment') to act quickly and innovatively.

In less than a year KLM had succeeded in changing its geographical hierarchical structure into a flat dual structure, with central functional departments and autonomous business units. Those in management positions had to reapply for their jobs, and in many cases managers had to relocate to a different continent. The firm also created self-organizing teams on the work floor. To facilitate these fundamental changes, management organized awareness courses, training seminars, and interactive workshops.

Many mistakes were made initially in the primary process during this radical business model transformation at KLM Cargo, and company performance dropped for a time. The regular freight did not arrive at the right destination, there was no clear information about the new logistic services, employees felt uncertain about their future, and there were no coherent standards and values. There was also much resistance from lower-level managers who were not involved in the transformation process. What made the situation even worse was that the firm's freight market collapsed, just when two new freight planes had been bought.

With support from the management board and strong leadership from the division manager, the business model renewal eventually led to improved results. To roll out the new business model successfully alongside the existing business model, management standardized the services portfolio—grouping services into three categories, 'commodities', 'specialities', or 'customized'—and developed a more transparent structure. Within that structure a new Business Systems department was made responsible for more efficient coordination. Management also formulated a much sharper strategic vision and developed a code of conduct for communicating shared cultural values within KLM Cargo.

Source: Volberda et al. (2011)

. . . .

Creating a separate business model to run alongside the existing model

Having a series of different business models within a firm can lead to conflicts (Velu and Stiles, 2013). For example, disputes can arise over the allocation of resources, or the dominant logic can be subject to discussion. For the new business model, that logic has to be abandoned, at least in part, incurring resistance from supporters of the old model (Chesbrough, 2010). The outcome of this kind of conflict is usually that replication wins out over renewal. Because there is a danger that the new business model could canni-balize the existing model, the new model is given only a short time to prove its worth or is abandoned (Markides and Oyon, 2010). One way of resolving such conflicts is to create separate units that each have their own distinct business model. They need to have some kind of connection to one another so that synergies between them can be realized (Benson-Rea et al., 2013; Smith et al., 2010). It can be particularly valuable to set up separate units in this way when the following three factors apply (Markides and Oyon, 2010):

- The new customer segment demands a different set of activities from the value chain.
- The new market is so different to the existing market that the existing business model does not apply.
- The goal of top management is to approach the new market aggressively (rather than to reduce the risk of cannibalization).

Thus Randstad established a separate business unit, Randstad Inhouse Services (formerly Capac), in which the people appointed were mainly from the outside, except for a few Randstad managers. The purpose of Randstad Inhouse Services was to give further shape to the in-house concept of integrated HR solutions and to commercialize it. The unit was entirely separate from Randstad; initially, for example, no overheads were passed on to it. These kinds of separate units make it possible to have different cultures, structures, and processes operating within the one firm (see also Table 7.4) (Benner and Tushman, 2003; Markides, 2013; O'Reilly and Tushman, 2004).

Separate units also allow a firm to standardize replication processes and they also provide a firm with greater flexibility and variation that will help

Table 7.4 Differences between mainstream unit and business model innovation unit

Characteristic	Mainstream business (existing business model)	Separate business model innovation unit
Objective	costs, profit	innovation, growth
Competences	standardized and reliable	entrepreneurial and adaptive
Structure	more formal, mechanistic	more informal, organic
Culture	focus on efficiency and quality, risk-averse, and customer-driven	flexible, ready to take risks and to engage in experimentation

Source: adapted from O'Reilly and Tushman (2004)

in renewal. The separate units must have significant financial and operational autonomy, visionary and committed leadership, and their own director (Markides and Oyon, 2010; O'Reilly and Tushman, 2004). Dedicated units for experimenting and validating new business models have more inherent risks than units which target replication.

Combining replication and renewal: dual, oscillating, or network focus

How do organizations handle different business models? Do they develop a new business model while still continuing to exploit an existing business model, or do they abandon that earlier model? There are various ways of keeping the focus on both business model replication *and* business model renewal. Three variants are distinguished in this book:

- the dual business model, where both replication and renewal take place within the organization as discussed above. This is the most challenging option and has certain limits;
- the oscillating business model, where the firm moves over time from replication to renewal, and vice versa;
- the network business model, where the firm opts for a strong focus on either replication or renewal and outsources the other approach to partners within its network.

Dual business models

In the dual business model, one part of the firm focuses on the process of renewal and creating new added value, and another part focuses on replication and on ensuring that well-established routines and competences are put to optimal use (see Figure 7.5). For business model renewal, the firm uses a separate unit, which has been separated to a certain degree from its mainstream business. For example, the Nestlé Group experimented with its new capsule-based Nespresso business model in a completely separate unit (Markides and Charitou, 2004; Matzler et al., 2013). Also, when postal operators in various European countries were undertaking new ventures in which they were experimenting with new business models, these were to some extent separated from the companies' mainstream activities (Bogers et al., 2014). The basic

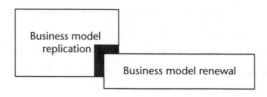

Figure 7.5 The dual business model

principle behind the dual business model focus is that the parent organization continues to concentrate on business model replication, while a separate sub-unit is tasked with working on business model renewal (e.g. Benner and Tushman, 2002, 2003). This enables a firm to focus on different market segments and customer needs, and gives it multiple ways of commercializing its technologies (Benson-Rea et al., 2013). One may think of a service-based business model being used alongside a production-based model (Nenonen and Storbacka, 2010) or a software-based model used alongside a business model relating to a hardware model (Adner and Kapoor, 2010). The firm's existing models typically remain at arm's length from the new business models so that the focus on existing operations can be maintained (Aspara et al., 2013; Markides, 2013; Orton and Weick, 1990).

Having multiple business models within a firm also provides opportunities for synergies between them—for instance, through the sharing of value chain activities and branding (Markides and Oyon, 2010). For managers, it is extremely difficult to determine what the right degree of integration may be between a new business model and existing models (Markides and Oyon, 2010; O'Reilly and Tushman, 2008). On the one hand, there needs to be sufficient integration between the new business model and the existing business models to ensure adequate coordination between them and to create synergies between them. On the other hand, the integration should not go too far, as the firm needs to ensure that cannabilization does not occur or conflicts between the various models. It is also important to prevent the new business model from losing whatever makes it distinctive from the firm's other business models (Markides and Charitou, 2004; Markides and Oyon, 2010; Velu and Stiles, 2013).

A dual business model represents a partial response by an entire firm to market or technological disruptions. If the new business model developed in one of a firm's units does not meet its objectives, having a dual business model decreases the risks for the firm as a whole. But if the entire organization is affected by disruption, a comprehensive response is needed, not a partial one (Massa and Tucci, 2014; Volberda, 2017). Creating a separate unit for business model renewal accelerates progress in the new areas of opportunity, but it often leads to problems of integration with the parent organization (Andriopoulos and Lewis, 2009). That is why exploiting new opportunities can be a slow and frustrating process. Sometimes a dramatic transformation of the entire firm is needed to make business model renewal possible.

Oscillating business models

In the oscillating business model the focus is on alternating cycles of business model replication, characterized by further refinement and sharpening of the levers of technology, management, and organizational forms, and business model renewal, based on the application of new technologies, new management practices, and new organizational forms (Khanagha et al., 2014; Markides, 2013; O'Reilly and Tushman, 2008) (see Figure 7.6). With this type of model, the firm is moving from an extreme mode of business model renewal which stimulates the development of new business models, then back to another mode of business model replication which enables the business model to be adopted on a much wider scale across the organization.

In making the distinction between the two different phases of replication and renewal, it is widely agreed that, during periods of replication, a firm can adopt some new business model components while still exploiting its existing business model. However, there will be times where replication and renewal cannot co-exist; these will occur when the firm is facing disruption of its technologies and markets. At these moments, the organization cannot simultaneously exploit and improve its existing model *and* develop a new model, but faces a stark choice: either to renew its business model or to face rapid decline.

This continual alternation between renewal and replication over time is part and parcel of the existence of small, entrepreneurial firms and it forms

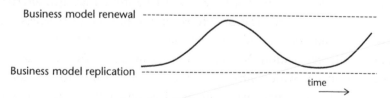

Figure 7.6 The oscillating business model

the basis of their competitive advantage (Smith and Lewis, 2011; Smith and Tushman, 2005; Volberda, 1998). Their relatively flexible resource base and low sunk costs allow them to implement business model transformation more easily (Nooteboom, 1994). For larger, diversified firms, it is much more complicated to transform their business model completely, and sometimes it can be almost impossible. The liabilities that often come with age and tradition seriously constrain well-established firms when they are confronted with disruption. For instance, large mail-order firms with a long history of using paper catalogues are being outcompeted by pure internet competitors such as Zalando, Amazon, and Sarenza. Although these well-established mail-order firms tried to migrate from an offline catalogues to a fully integrated online webshop business model, their progress in this has been slow and they have met with little success. Neckermann.com is moving from failure to failure. Otto.nl is making huge losses, and sales have dropped by half. Even Wehkamp, more successful than all other long-standing European mail-order firms in making the full switch to internet retailing, has not achieved an increase in sales that is comparable to the 15 per cent growth of the online fashion shops. Wehkamp's online business model was based on a limited assortment of products, and for a long time their offering did not include popular fashion brands such as G-star and Levi's, while the online fashion shop Zalando had a broad product base right from the start. Most other mail-order firms started the migration from replication to renewal too late and have not been able to catch up. It takes years before logistics and other processes are up to standard, and the hybrid business models of some mail-order firms have resulted in resources being wasted on offline distribution channels.

Nonetheless, there are examples of large corporations that have successfully alternated between business model replication and renewal, even though the triggers for renewal may have come from many quarters and the response to them may have been slow. The histories of large capital-intensive enterprises which operate in cyclical industries, such as Shell, DSM, and Unilever, show that they have successfully managed alternating cycles of renewal and replication. However, the periods of business model renewal were infrequent and relatively short compared to the periods of business model replication (Volberda and Lewin, 2003; Volberda, 2017).

These company-wide shifts in orientation over time from renewal to replication, and vice versa, were discussed extensively in Chapter 6, with revealing examples from DSM, Royal IHC, and Port of Rotterdam Authority.

This business model oscillation generally takes place at the firm level. Companies such as IKEA, McDonald's, and Ryanair started by creating new business models from scratch (renewal), and improved and extended their new business model over time (replication) in order to realize their growth strategy (Jonsson and Foss, 2011). Of course, when the opportunities for replication are exploited, firms should shift back to business model renewal. For instance, since McDonald's has been facing serious disruption from organic and eco food outlets in advanced Western economies, it has been trying to undertake a partial renewal of its business model by systematically introducing a company-wide sustainability programme, strengthening its partnerships with suppliers in order to create shared value, and focusing more on nutrition and well-being.

However, the sequence of business model renewal and replication can also begin lower down the organization (Dunford et al., 2010; Sosna et al., 2010). For example, the ING Group swiftly transferred the 'ING Direct' concept to banking units in other countries in order to leverage this completely new business model successfully in banking (Dunford et al., 2010). Similarly, the Dutch retail store Hema opened a branch in Barcelona. Unlike the low-budget business model used by this large superstore chain, the Barcelona branch is relatively small, has a 'boutique' feel, and features products from around the world (e.g. coffee-related products). The success of this new, boutique business model triggered its top management to replicate the concept across all its existing branches.

With the growing number of disruptions in many industries, lengthy replication is becoming extremely difficult for more and more firms, while the need for frequent business model renewal is increasing. During the process of moving from replication to renewal, or vice versa, firms have to avoid 'going too far' in either direction (Volberda, 1998). In practice firms often renew some elements of their business model, while replicating other elements (Aspara et al., 2013).

With an oscillating business model procedures are needed to manage the transformation from business model replication to business model renewal (or vice versa). Since in any given period organizations are either working mainly on business model replication or on business model renewal, they are inclined to invest more in that particular activity than in making the switch (O'Reilly and Tushman, 2008). This can cause delays in the switch from business model replication to business model renewal (or vice versa) and it can become more expensive to implement.

Network business models

Many firms find it difficult to combine the discipline of business model replication with the openness required for business model renewal. In a network business model, the firm accepts the tensions between replication and renewal, but does not believe that the differences between replication and renewal can be dealt with. That is why the organization outsources one of the two forms of activity (see Figure 7.7). In this type of business model, the firm cooperates more with other firms and becomes more of a broker of business model renewal and replication, which are linked in a variety of complex ways (Volberda, 1998). For example, the firm can develop a new business model itself and outsource activities relating to the previous model to low-cost subcontractors (Cliffe and McGrath, 2011). One example of a firm which uses a network business model is Nike. In its business model this sportswear manufacturer has focused on the design and marketing of products, something which it is able to do very rapidly, and has outsourced the production and distribution to pure replicators. The Dutch firm ASML, one of the world's leading manufacturers of chip-making equipment for the semiconductor industry, also uses a network business model. Because of the speed of technological developments and the short life cycles of chip machines, partners in ASML's network have to innovate continuously. ASML works with hundreds of technology companies that supply most of the components in its systems and often does substantial research and development work itself. In this network ASML orchestrates the production network, the R&D consortium, and the assembly process. The firm thus focuses on its role as a system architect and system integrator. Staying ahead of the technology curve and ensuring its products are not outdated before they are even launched requires ASML to share roadmaps, risk, and rewards with its partners. This means giving suppliers real responsibility and incentive to improve, learning from each other, and sharing knowledge so that partners can engage in joint thinking with ASML. The partners each have their own strategic competences, and the cooperation between ASML and its partners is intensive and designed for the long term.

Figure 7.7 The network business model

A firm can replicate its own business model in a network by improving or scaling up its cooperation with existing network partners (e.g. Easterby-Smith et al., 2008; Tsai, 2009). However, it can also renew its business model in the network by actively changing the composition of the network partners, for instance, by adding new parties (Zott et al., 2011). In a network business model, the different parties collaborate but also compete with each other. The cooperation provides stability and resources, while the competition serves as an engine for renewal (e.g. Volberda and Baden-Fuller, 1999; Bengtsson and Kock, 2000; Clarke-Hill and Davies, 2003). Cooperation—especially through the strong social connections between the different actors—can become a delaying factor for business model renewal. Established firms can reduce the likelihood of this by bringing in different network partners, especially by developing alliances with smaller, agile firms that serve new markets or promising start-ups that bring in new technologies.

In addition, there must be a balance between how much replication and renewal the organization undertakes itself and how much it leaves up to its network partners. Leaving too much to the network can have a detrimental effect on the unique business model of the organization itself. In this situation, the knowledge and skills within the organization in terms of innovating its business model relate mainly to integrating business model components from external parties or combining those components in new ways. This means that the organization loses the knowledge and skills required to develop a business model internally (Berchicci, 2013; Cassiman and Veugelers, 2006).

When it outsources business model renewal to its partner network, an organization should still undertake certain elements of the business model itself, otherwise it will become a 'hollow corporation'. Without internal renewal, an organization becomes less capable of selecting suitable partners and/or projects for business model renewal and putting them to effective use (e.g. Berchicci, 2013; Capron and Mitchell, 2009). Business model innovation in a network is a gradual process. If too much business model innovation is 'outsourced' to the network, over the long term certain partners can end up becoming rivals and taking over part of the firm's value chain (Christensen, 2001).

Thus Dell in the first instance outsourced the production of computer parts to a supplier. After all, this was that supplier's core competence, not Dell's. The supplier then also took over the integration from Dell as it could do this more cheaply. It seemed to be a win-win situation for Dell and the supplier. Dell lowered its costs, which was good for its margins. The supplier took over more activities, which was good for its profit. But when the supplier gradually started taking over the logistics as well, on the same win–win logic, the only core competence remaining for Dell was brand management. The supplier could then start delivering the same as Dell, but at a lower price. Dell was left with nothing to offer (Christensen, 2013). This is also known as the 'erosion effect'.

How can renewal *and* replication be realized within a firm?

The previous section already provided some insights into how an organization can manage different business models. But what are the particular characteristics of firms which have managed to combine both replication and business model renewal within certain areas of their business? And does that result in markedly better performance? Analysis of our data shows that organizations have to apply a high degree of replication as well as renewal in order to achieve solid company performance. Firms which do not pay much attention to replication and renewal suffer from *business model fixation* and perform much less well (as discussed in Chapter 3). The firms with a *dual business model* differ on various points from firms with a focus on fixation (see Figure 7.8). Organizations with a dual focus have a high capacity to absorb knowledge (29 per cent more than firms with a fixation mode).

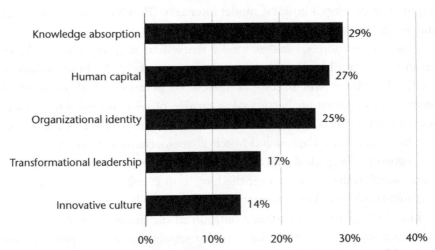

Scores on various characteristics of firms with a dual business model in comparison to those which suffer from fixation

Figure 7.8 Where do firms with dual business models focus their efforts on?

They also invest more in human capital (an additional 27 per cent) and they have a much stronger organizational identity (an additional 25 per cent). Transformational leadership (an additional 17 per cent) and an innovative culture (an additional 14 per cent) are also found much more in firms which have a dual focus (see Figure 7.8). A strong shared identity helps dual business model firms to deal with the inherent tensions and frictions between business model replication and renewal.

Having a separate unit for renewal running alongside units which focus on business model replication demands a shared vision, common values, and strong collaboration and cooperation between senior managers (Mihalache et al., 2014; O'Reilly and Tushman, 2008; Smith et al., 2010). These are areas that need to be taken care of by the top management team. Only shared leadership in which senior managers share responsibility for and fully participate in the task of leadership will encourage cooperation when the various business models present conflicting demands (Mihalache et al., 2014). Senior managers who engage in ongoing negotiation and role-sharing experience a stronger sense of commitment to the firm's overall success and, as such, are more likely to approach any conflicts between the new unit and the mainstream business as joint problems which require solutions that will benefit everyone. Frequent interactions between the different units are also needed to ensure knowledge will flow back and forth, and this can be achieved by using teams made up of employees from different departments, for example. As Markides and Oyon noted (2010), when setting up a separate unit the top management must make a number of important choices regarding:

- where the unit should be located (alongside the parent firm or elsewhere?)
- what it should be called (the same as the parent firm or a different name?)
- where the ownership should reside (should the parent firm be the sole owner or not?)
- what activities should form part of the value chain (should back-office functions be shared with the parent firm or not?)
- what type of organizational context is appropriate (should the unit develop its own values, culture, people, processes, and rewards, or adopt those of the parent firm?).

Organizations with a separate unit of this kind must integrate it to a certain degree with the mainstream business in order to create synergy. Not using this synergy entails considerably more risks and costs. As stated earlier, the task is twofold: there must be sufficient separation between the organizational units to avoid conflict, but the separation must not be so rigid as to lose the possibility of synergies. We identify six steps that managers can take to help realize synergies between the separate unit for renewal and the main part of the business (Markides and Oyon, 2010):

1. Appoint a common general manager who has supervisory responsibility for both new business and existing business

2. Foster stronger, shared values that will connect together people from different units

3. Appoint an active and reliable manager to take care of the integration

4. Develop a system of rewards to encourage cooperation between different units

5. Integrate activities which cannot be carried out properly in isolation from one another

6. Ensure that organizational resources and expertise are made available to the separate unit.

The degree of integration between the different units can vary over time. Capac, for example—the separate unit set up at Randstad, and the precursor of Randstad Inhouse Services—enjoyed a great deal of autonomy in the first instance, but was later integrated into Randstad in order to achieve more synergy. The introduction of cloud computing at Ericsson also went through various phases, with the new activity gradually shifting more towards the mainstream business (see Figure 7.9).

Figure 7.9 shows that there is a ripple effect in terms of the degree to which the new business model is integrated into the rest of the organization. Thus in the first phase Ericsson created cross-functional teams to determine what impact cloud computing would have on its existing business. This led to hardly any changes, either formal or informal. More resources were then freed up to experiment and to give more shape to the concept, and in the end Ericsson gradually integrated the new concept into the group (Khanagha et al., 2013).

Wrap-up

CEOs and management play a crucial role in business model transformation trajectories. They have to keep an eye on the S-curves of financial performance,

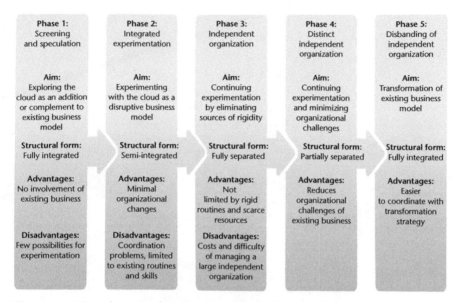

Phase 1: Screening and speculation	Phase 2: Integrated experimentation	Phase 3: Independent organization	Phase 4: Distinct independent organization	Phase 5: Disbanding of independent organization
Aim: Exploring the cloud as an addition or complement to existing business model	**Aim:** Experimenting with the cloud as a disruptive business model	**Aim:** Continuing experimentation by eliminating sources of rigidity	**Aim:** Continuing experimentation and minimizing organizational challenges	**Aim:** Transformation of existing business model
Structural form: Fully integrated	**Structural form:** Semi-integrated	**Structural form:** Fully separated	**Structural form:** Partially separated	**Structural form:** Fully integrated
Advantages: No involvement of existing business	**Advantages:** Minimal organizational changes	**Advantages:** Not limited by rigid routines and scarce resources	**Advantages:** Reduces organizational challenges of existing business	**Advantages:** Easier to coordinate with transformation strategy
Disadvantages: Few possibilities for experimentation	**Disadvantages:** Coordination problems, limited to existing routines and skills	**Disadvantages:** Costs and difficulty of managing a large independent organization		

Figure 7.9 Five phases in the adoption of a cloud computing business model of Ericsson

Source: adapted from Khanagha et al. (2014)

but also need to pay particular attention to the invisible S-curves of strategic performance. It is only by doing this that they can renew the business model effectively, neither too early nor too late. At the business sector level, existing rivals as well as newcomers may contribute to business model innovation, although herd behaviour also occurs among established players in a market. Firms can realize a high degree of replication and renewal, and thus perform well, by creating a separate unit for renewal, but this does require integration with the units which are engaged in replication. Firms can also choose to work with partners in a network and to focus on either replication or renewal. However, at times of extreme disruption, an organization cannot simultaneously replicate and renew, but has to go for full business model transformation.

8

Re-examining Business Model Innovation

Dos and Don'ts for Managers

. . . .

NOKIA HAD AN IPHONE EQUIVALENT ON THE SHELF, BUT
NEVER RELEASED IT TO ITS CUSTOMERS

'What? That is *our* product!' Frank Nuovo, telephone designer at Nokia knows exactly what he thought when Apple introduced the iPhone in 2007. Email, surfing on the internet, and downloading apps—Nokia's new phone had been first with all of these. But it lay on the shelf for years because Nokia's management did not believe there was a market for 'fun' products.

Nokia sold over a billion mobile phones in 2004. Ten years later, the story was over and Microsoft took over the mobile division. How is it possible that a world leader in mobile phones simply ceased to exist seven years after the introduction of the iPhone? And it was not only Nokia that went down: the whole Finnish economy suffered as a result of Nokia's collapse, as this pioneering mobile phone company had been one of the main pillars of the country's knowledge-based economy.

Politicians knew where to point the finger. 'Apple is to blame for the loss of the Finnish economy,' declared the Finnish President Alexander Stubb, in an interview with CNBC. 'The iPhone killed Nokia and the iPad killed the Finnish paper industry.' But this is too simple, according to analysts and former Nokia employees. Frank Nuovo, who was involved in the development of mobile phones right from the start, knows that in the early years the company was a creative breeding ground for new ideas. 'We made telephones with rounded corners and put a camera in them.' This really was business model renewal. It was the same with the concept of coloured faceplates. This idea emerged following one of many bar sessions enjoyed by Nokia engineers, when they became so drunk that they mixed up their phones. Having removable fronts was thus a way of ensuring they could better identify their own phone.

This was typically Nokia: business model innovation was part of its DNA. Originally founded as a processing plant for wood pulp, Nokia then ventured into the rubber industry before finally becoming a leading player in the telecommunications industry. Nokia's immense success with mobile phones was in the end the source of its failure. The company was focusing on refinements to its existing profitable offering—mobile phones—instead of developing new products and services. In 1996 Nokia invented the Nokia Communicator, one of the first smartphones in the world. This underwent further development in the laboratory, but was never introduced on to the market. Frank Nuovo argued that telephones should become more fun, but managers responded that Nokia was not about fun, but about high-tech. These managers, often former bankers, were much more powerful than the creative designers, and were convinced that a device of this kind would only be of interest to a small audience. Nokia's intensive focus on its existing offering reduced its interest in the smartphone. By the time the firm introduced its own smartphone in 2011, the market was already divided between other companies such as Apple and Samsung (the 'winner takes all' effect). Nokia was too late with the smartphone, despite having first invented it. To make matters worse, intense competition from low-cost Chinese companies in Nokia's existing market—the mobile phone—ate into its profits. This combination was in the end fatal for Nokia.

Sources: Vuori and Huy (2016); Laamanen et al. (2016)

. . . .

Introduction

When faced with increasing disruption, how do you reinvent your business model? Most firms fail by doing the very things that have made them successful in the past. Kodak, Polaroid, Blockbuster, and Nokia are all examples of this. But precisely where did they go wrong? It was not that these firms did not invest in disruptive technologies, or that they were poorly managed, complacent, or fraudulent. They clearly suffered from business model fixation; they focused only on short-term financial performance, missed early signs of disruption, and were in thrall to their existing customers.

Our research has provided some important insights into how firms can cope with disruption or even reinvent their business model in such a way that they themselves become disruptors. In this final chapter, we present our key findings on how business models can be reinvented. We group these into four main areas, each with its own set of key questions and management issues: the two main types of business model innovation and why firms might choose one over another, the levers of business model innovation, the business model transformation process, and the role that top and middle managers play in this process. We conclude by discussing the more practical dos and don'ts, and we also present an online business model innovation scan.

The two basic types of business model innovation

How do firms weigh up the two basic types of business model innovation: replication and renewal?

Disruption makes existing business models obsolete and requires new ones to be developed. Firms can innovate their business models in different ways. They can scale up and improve their existing business model through replication, either geographically and/or over time in the way that McDonald's and IKEA did. It is a way of maintaining or improving the firm's competitive position. The risks involved in replication are limited in the short term, but do increase over the long term. Quite often, firms fail to recognize in time the new means of value creation which are taking over in the market.

Firms can also change their business model far more radically, through renewal. DSM did this, by switching from mining to petrochemicals and then to life sciences. A move of this kind allows firms to establish a new and more sustainable competitive position. The risks attached are quite high, but not undertaking this journey may erode a firm's competitive position.

Which strategies for business model innovation do firms use?

Findings from our large-scale survey suggest that 14 per cent of firms are able to adopt a dual focus, both replicating their existing business model to a high degree and also developing a new business model. Three out of ten firms concentrate to a moderate degree on refining their existing business model and developing a new model. Few, if any, firms focus purely on renewal (0.3 per cent) or replication (2 per cent). One in ten firms works hardly at all on either renewal or replication, and is what we call 'trapped in business model fixation'.

Which sectors are most and least active in business model innovation?

Business model renewal and replication occur to a high degree in the life sciences and information and communication (ICT) sectors and in the food industry. The sectors which undertake the least replication or renewal are energy supply, government and government-related, and construction.

What are the performance benefits of business model innovation?

Firms that suffer from business model fixation show relatively low growth in turnover (on average 1 per cent growth per year) and poor company performance. Firms which aim mainly at renewal perform on average 8 per cent better than firms trapped in fixation, but their turnover drops slightly after they have engaged in renewal (on average a decrease of 1 per cent per year). Firms which aim mainly at replication perform 13 per cent better than firms trapped in fixation and have an average growth in turnover of 7 per cent. The firms with a dual focus perform 18 per cent better than firms that suffer from fixation, and their turnover grows on average by 11 per cent each year. Firms which move from replication to a dual focus experience a (temporary) dip in the company performance during that transformation. Firms which switch from 'pure renewal' to a dual business model focus enjoy a swift increase in company performance. They are able to scale up and commercialize their 'unique formula'.

The levers of business model innovation

Which levers should managers use in replication and renewal?

We have distinguished four levers of business model innovation in this book: technology, management practices, organizational forms, and co-creation. Adopting disruptive technologies such as the Internet of Things, big data, robotics, and 3D printing helps firms to transform input into output more effectively, and this can thus contribute to fundamentally new ways of value creation and appropriation (business model renewal). For instance, Airbus's vision of applying innovative technologies to design and manufacturing enabled it to use 3D printing to develop improved aircraft parts. In this way, Airbus was able to reduce its production lead times and its raw material requirements and to increase its aircraft efficiency. However, a business model is about more than just technology or R&D. As Chesbrough (2007: 12) rightly remarked, 'a better business model often will beat a better idea or technology.' Teece (2010) and Baden-Fuller and Haefliger (2013) also share the view that it is important to distinguish between business models and technology. New technologies can boost new business models, but business model innovation can also occur without new technologies. Of the four levers, adjustment of management practices makes the most powerful contribution to both business model renewal and replication. Replication in particular requires a system-wide improvement of organizational forms. While replication of the business model often goes hand in hand with organic growth, renewal requires a delicate balance between organic growth and cooperation with external parties.

Which combinations of levers have a positive effect on business model innovation and on company performance?

Our research showed four complementary effects which arise from effective combinations of the levers. When the right levers are combined, they have a mutually strengthening effect on the degree of business model renewal. In *technologically oriented business model renewal*, it is the combination of new technologies and new management practices which enables organizations to reap the benefits of business model renewal. When technology, management practices, and organizational forms are used in combination, this strengthens *internally oriented renewal*. Renewal of the business model can be technology-driven in the first instance (e.g. Ericsson and cloud computing), but can also be driven by new management practices and new organizational forms (e.g. the disintermediation of Dell). Adopting outstanding management practices and redesigning the organization ensures that the potential of new technologies can be exploited more effectively.

When a combination of co-creation, management practices, and organizational forms is used, this also serves to strengthen renewal, in this case *externally oriented renewal*. One example of this is the Port of Rotterdam Authority which set up the joint venture Multicore together with Vopak Chemical Logistics in order to construct a system of short underground pipelines for the petrochemical and gas industries. Also, P&G's connect-and-develop programme helped the firm to reinvent its business model and to absorb 50 per cent of its innovations from outside the company. Collaboration with external partners gives organizations opportunities for value creation which they would not be able to realize independently or only at a slower pace.

Using all four levers together to achieve what we have called *integral renewal* occurs in organizations which have a superior capacity to absorb knowledge both from within their own industry and from related industries, and even from industries which are only beginning to take shape. This capacity to recognize the need for change is especially beneficial for renewal. The steps taken by DSM to make the switch from petrochemicals to life sciences and then to material sciences provide a good example of this. DSM turned a peripheral technology (life and material sciences) into its core technology, especially through takeovers, and divested itself of the old core technology (petrochemicals).

In the end, for successful business model innovation all four levers have to be taken into account. The leading tyre manufacturer Michelin, for instance, invested heavily in a new disruptive technology, namely the Internet of Things, and collaborated with completely new partners. With smart sensors and in-vehicle telematics, Michelin is no longer simply selling tyres, but also providing solutions for fleets of trucks, buses, and commercial vehicles in a wide range of areas: tyre management, vehicle productivity, and fuel efficiency. They use new technologies from the Internet of Things to collect extremely accurate data on a wide range of topics such as tyre pressure. Once the data have been analysed, the company's engineers and technicians can make various recommendations, typically on how to improve the safety and profitability of a fleet of vehicles. Michelin has a road usage laboratory which gives its analysts access to real-time traffic data. Smart sensors have been fitted to 2,800 vehicles throughout Europe, belonging to drivers with varying levels of experience. The data collected are not reserved exclusively for developing services, but are also used to mastermind new products so that Michelin can continually break new ground in the market. In this way, the firm is extending its traditional business model and providing a wider range of services for its customers; it is helping them to save more on fuel, reducing their CO_2 emissions, and minimizing vehicle downtime for fleets of trucks, buses, and commercial vehicles. By creating the new unit Michelin Solutions the firm has been able to shift its business model from selling mainly tyres to providing other services designed to improve the performance of its clients' vehicle fleets. In its new business model, Michelin makes contractual agreements with customers to meet pre-defined targets under a multi-year contract and is remunerated from the savings made. If the savings are achieved, they are then shared. If not, the customer receives compensation. It is definitely a new means of value creation and capture which has helped Michelin to achieve better customer satisfaction, greater loyalty, and higher margins. Initially, Michelin started this digital transformation internally (through new technology), but the company soon realized that in some critical areas, such as big data analytics or infrastructure, it needed to partner with external experts (through co-creation). Michelin's organizational structure is also changing, and it is currently working with small mixed teams, because the Internet of Things requires the firm to be extremely agile. The risks inherent in changing the business model were mitigated since Michelin Solutions was created as a stand-alone entity (new organizational form) and the company decided to test the new services with several pilots. Cultural change and new management skills (new management practices) were other prerequisites for managing this business model transformation successfully.

Nonetheless, most new business models start with technology as the most important driver. For instance, by leveraging digital technologies Lego was able to transform its old plastic brick business model and become one of the world's most successful toymakers. After a period of expansion between 1970 and 1991 Lego suffered a steady decline, and by 2004 it was close to bankruptcy. However, the company was able to renew its business model by launching new digitally based products and services such as movies, Lego Mindstorms, video games, and applications which are connected to their traditional building bricks but more appealing to digitally savvy customer groups. The company's design capabilities have been increasingly handed over to its fans through the Digital Designer, a web-based 3D design tool which allows customers to create their own designs (co-creation). Lego has recovered steadily since 2005 and is now seen as the Apple of the toy industry.

Which factors enable the replication and/or renewal of a business model?

The survey and our case studies show various factors which have an enabling or an inhibiting effect on business model innovation. Transformational leadership, for instance, can have an enabling effect on both renewal and replication. A strong organizational identity also stimulates replication, while an innovative culture will promote renewal (e.g. 3M's motto, 'thou shalt not kill ideas'). The result of listening to existing customers can be that firms refine their existing business models, but this inhibits the development of new skills and capabilities and thereby also renewal. How long a CEO has been in the organization also influences renewal. The risk with CEOs who lead the same organization for a long time is that they want to continue building on business models which have brought them success in the past.

That comes at the expense of renewal. CEOs who spend only a short time in an organization will have already left before the potential benefits can be realized. And that means that they do not focus as much on renewal. CEOs who work for an organization either too long or not long enough therefore have an adverse effect on business model renewal. Our research shows that the optimal length of time is around thirteen years.

Business model transformation

How do firms transform their business model?

Both replication and renewal can be either internally driven (by strategy) or externally driven (by customers). This produces four possible combinations. The approaches in each quadrant each have their own specific levers, environmental characteristics, and enablers and inhibitors (see also Figure 8.1). With *strategy-driven renewal* (a transformation of the business model which

	Strategy-driven	Customer-driven
Business model renewal	**Explore and dominate:** *organization-wide transformation* 1. Transformational leadership 2. Commitment of top and middle management 3. Innovative culture 4. Internal knowledge absorption 5. Dynamic environment 6. New internal identity	**Explore and connect:** *upgrading to new customers* 1. Transformational leadership 2. Commitment of top and frontline management 3. Innovative, customer-driven culture 4. External knowledge absorption 5. Dynamic environment 6. New external identity
Business model replication	**Exploit and improve:** *directive improvement* 1. Transactional leadership 2. Commitment of top managers 3. Less innovative culture 4. Internal knowledge absorption 5. Competitive pressure 6. Strong internal identity	**Exploit and connect:** *linking with existing customers* 1. Transactional leadership 2. Commitment of top management 3. Customer-driven culture 4. External knowledge absorption 5. High competitive pressure 6. Strong external identity

Figure 8.1 The business model innovation matrix

affects the entire firm), renewal takes place from the inside out, via the levers of technology, management practices, and organizational forms. Both top management and middle management are involved intensively in this. DSM, for example, used these three levers to move from strategy-driven replication to strategy-driven renewal. This type of move places a heavy burden on senior managers, and is thus likely to result in some major changes to the top management team. The substantial involvement required from middle managers generally means that this type of trajectory may be more difficult to complete satisfactorily with the firm's existing middle managers still in place. After all, some of those middle managers may have spent a large part of their career focusing on replication.

With *customer-driven replication* (strengthening the business model by linking it more to existing customers), the improvement comes mainly from engaging in co-creation with customers, adjusting management practices, and redesigning the organization—activities which are particularly powerful in combination. The level of involvement required from top management is less than for strategy-driven renewal, but nevertheless more than for strategy-driven replication. The role of top management is to consider issues such as which types of customer segment to serve or which of the firm's existing customers are most important to invest in.

How do firms change their business model over time?

When managers assess their business models, financial performance is clearly an important consideration. This performance will typically follow an S-shaped curve over time, which means that managers start to consider business model renewal once the curve starts to head downwards. A business model may already have become outdated before this, however, through the actions of rivals or disruptive moves by new entrants. In a highly competitive environment especially, managers should begin the process of renewal in good time. In an environment with little dynamism, there is less need for renewal.

If managers only renew the business model once financial performance is already dropping, this leads to a *business model trap*. The firm has taken action too late. In a highly competitive market, profitability is not a good indicator of the sustainability of the existing business model. Although there may be fewer outward signs of what is happening, strategic performance will already have begun to dip earlier on (see Figure 8.2). Here there are three other S-curves, often referred to as invisible S-curves, which may be

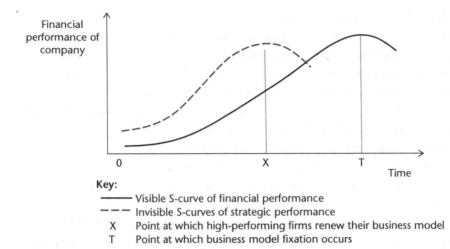

Key:
——— Visible S-curve of financial performance
— — — Invisible S-curves of strategic performance
X   Point at which high-performing firms renew their business model
T   Point at which business model fixation occurs

Figure 8.2 S-curves of financial performance and strategic performance
Source: adapted from Nunes and Breene (2011)
Reprinted by permission of *Harvard Business Review*.
From *Reinvent Your Business Before It's Too Late* by P. Nunes & T. Breene, 89 (1/2)/ 2011. Copyright
© 2017 by the Harvard Business School Publishing Corporation; all rights reserved.

harder to detect. These relate to (1) the strategic competitive position,
(2) the core skills and capacities, and (3) the existing talent. The CEO, top
management, middle management, and Supervisory Board must respond
promptly to any early signs that these particular S-curves are starting to dip
downwards. Before the financial performance of a business model actually
starts to decline, there may be various early indicators, both internally and
externally, of impending disruption to the firm's existing business model.
Quite often managers do not detect these indicators, or they simply ignore
or discount them. On the other hand, if they become oversensitive to such
signs, or act too quickly or too boldly in response to fads and fashions long
before any decline in financial performance, then existing sources of competitive advantage may be dismantled without any adequate replacement.
A firm may then end up in a *renewal trap*.

Managerial actions

What are the roles and activities of top and middle
management in business model innovation?

The CEO, top, and middle management have different roles and activities
in business model transformation. With replication, top management has to

strengthen the organizational identity, while middle management must promote internal cooperation. For renewal, however, top management may need to discourage internal cooperation. With replication, one of the tasks of top and middle management is to be very responsive to the firm's most important customers. For renewal, however, the firm should not focus merely on current customers and allocate all of its resources to finding the best solutions for them—often referred to as the 'tyranny of the served market' (Christensen, 1997; Hamel and Prahalad, 1994); a firm's largest customers will often be resistant to new technologies and products. To achieve renewal, top managers must free themselves of the influence of the most important customers, and may do this by establishing a separate organizational unit for new customers, for example.

Which signs should managers watch out for in order to avoid traps?

We have outlined four different business model traps. The first is business model fixation. The results of our survey show that it is mainly organizations in the energy supply, government and government-related, and construction sectors which fall into this category. Firms suffering from business model fixation have to contend with relatively low company performance. The second trap is where firms focus too much on financial performance and thus cling to their existing business model for too long. One example is the Dutch telecom provider KPN; the business model it adhered to for a long time (too long) was based on calls and SMS, while what customers began to want was digital data communication. It is the task of the CEO and top management to identify the invisible S-curves of strategic performance by paying more attention to early warning signs. They can do this by giving serious attention to signs from the periphery of their market and industry and from the 'far corners' of their own firm. They should also work to ensure that the firm's core skills and capacities are distinctive and that existing talent is retained. To detect potential disruption, top management should focus on 'what is happening with customer and operational needs' (Paap and Katz, 2004: 15).

The third trap is one in which the CEO and top management look to the future *too* much. Here the firm pays too much heed to early warning signs and fails to pay sufficient attention to the financial returns of replication. This results in a situation where there is plenty of renewal, but insufficient financial resources to make the new business model a success. In this case a company may then renew its business model too soon. The firm 3M fell into this trap. A failure to make sufficient use of its existing financial and intellectual resources and a determination to let the company follow wherever its scientists and customers led meant that the company pursued new inventions in a somewhat haphazard fashion. It did not have a clear business model: new products merely evolved. The lack of a distinctive business model led to losses for 3M in the magnetic storage market (disks, video tapes, and cassette tapes). Below we discuss the fourth trap, relating to the tensions between the independence and the integration of multiple business models within a single firm.

Is it possible to combine replication and renewal?

Some firms do indeed engage in a high level of both renewal and replication, and these are the firms which show the best company performance. They combine these two approaches in various ways:

- Renewal and replication take place in different units (dual business model).
- Replication and renewal alternate over time (oscillating business model).
- Replication and renewal no longer take place within the firm itself, but in a network of firms (network business model).

The fourth of our business model traps is linked especially to the dual business model approach, and involves ineffective integration of the different business models. If firms are capable of both replicating the existing business model and developing new models, top managers must ensure that there is adequate separation of the different models and that they are able to manage conflicts. On the other hand, the degree of separation should not be too great, because synergy between the different business models is still required. That demands leadership. Thus, after KLM had made various attempts (including Buzz) to develop a new low-cost business model as a complement to its existing quality-driven business model, it found a way of operating in the low-cost, low-fare market with Transavia.

What are the 'dos and don'ts' in business model innovation?

As we observed earlier in this book, in the literature on business model innovation little attention has been paid to the crucial role of management

Table 8.1 Seven dos and don'ts of business model innovation

Dos and don'ts of business model innovation
1 Do understand that business model innovation starts with leadership and thorough knowledge of your own organization.
2 Do ensure the composition of your management team is sufficiently diverse.
3 As a manager do watch out for warning signs other than the financial performance of your firm.
4 Don't separate business model innovation from environmental dynamism and competitive pressure.
5 Do manage conflicts resulting from a dual business model focus; don't avoid them.
6 Don't focus on one lever; do use several levers to renew your business model.
7 Do realize that communication and implementation make or break business model innovation.

in business model innovation. For that reason, and because the role of management in both renewal and replication should not be underrated, we invited seven managers from various firms to formulate with us a list of 'dos and don'ts' of business model innovation. These managers come from the firms which also feature as case studies in this book. We asked them questions such as: what kinds of things do you encounter in real life? What helped you achieve renewal or replication successfully? Which levers and enablers were of most use to you? What kind of obstacles did you encounter? This resulted in a set of seven 'dos and don'ts' which are accompanied by supporting information, explanation, and discussion (see Table 8.1).

. . . .

MANAGER PANEL PARTICIPANTS

Henk de Bruijn: Director of Corporate Strategy, Port of Rotterdam Authority

Goof Hamers: former President-Director, Royal IHC

Erik van der Liet: labour market specialist, Randstad Netherlands

Charles Smit: Vice-President and General Counsel, EMEA, NXP

Jeffrey Tierie: CEO, Claymount Technologies Group

Robert Witvliet: founder and director, WIAR Workplace Performance

Herman Wories: Vice-President, Global Business Incubator, DSM

. . . .

Business model innovation starts with leadership and thorough knowledge of your own organization

There was consensus among the panel on this point. Goof Hamers of Royal IHC: 'Renewal starts with leadership, and you don't get that from management books. As CEO you must have vision and have your feet firmly on the ground in the outside world. The same applies to your people. They have to be right in the middle of the market, talk with customers, and keep their ears and eyes open. I often miss that personal element in the ideas on renewal.'

Hamers adds that the kind of leadership he means is not coercive or stifling. The reason he stimulates employees is so that they will come up with ideas, and he gives them space and resources to pursue those ideas if they look promising. 'If you want to start something new, you have to do it right. But in the end it's me who decides whether something is given an opportunity. I do ask people to provide a basis for their ideas, but ultimately, it's intuition which is the decisive factor. It's difficult to formulate exact criteria for renewal.'

According to Charles Smit of NXP, the essence of leadership is decision-making and providing clarity—about what the organization will do and what it will not. 'That's what got NXP through everything. If we hadn't sold any units, and hadn't chosen very clearly for particular market segments, we would have gone bankrupt in 2009. Our new CEO flew around the entire world in two months. He is a very friendly person, who can explain the strategy patiently. But he always ended his talk with, "And if you don't like it, get the hell out of here."'

That culture, with a resolute management which constantly keeps people up to the mark, is still there at NXP. As Smit says, 'Every few months managers from all over the world fly in to make their reports and compare their performance with what they had announced previously.'

Jeffrey Tierie of Claymount Technologies Group keeps stressing the importance of examining your own organization properly. 'I think the internal impulses are more important than the external ones. Know your own organization. It is good to know what the trends and innovations on the market are. But what really counts is whether your own people are able to cope with them.'

Henk de Bruijn from the Port of Rotterdam Authority elaborates on the connection between internal and external: 'We make a distinction between *market attractivity* and *market access*. A development can look hugely interesting, but you have to be able to take it up. We pay more and more attention with our own people to their capacity to cooperate. That means that they have to be able to give way and to trust. This is essential for co-creation with customers and partners.'

Charles Smit endorses the remarks made by Tierie and De Bruijn: 'Your own people have to be convinced that the new business model will be a success. We once imagined that you could offer services alongside chips, and that would allow us a continuing stream of revenue. It didn't work, partly because our people didn't really believe in it. So I say, each man to his trade.'

Goof Hamers concludes: 'Thinking up a business model, anyone can do that. Implementing the business model, that is much more difficult. That is when you hit the human side, and that is much more important than is often imagined. For that reason, I don't invent business models from behind my desk. They mainly come about from talking with people.'

Charles Smit even goes a step further by stating that in the end the shared norms within a firm are decisive for the successful implementation of new business models. To echo the words of Peter Drucker (albeit in relation to strategy), 'culture eats business models for lunch.' In other words, you can come up with whatever business model you like, but in the end it will be the organizational culture that determines which will be the most viable.

Your management team has to have a sufficiently diverse composition

This insight arises spontaneously during the discussion, albeit quite late. This is not so much because the participants do not think this point is important, rather that they think it is self-evident. Goof Hamers says, 'I fall asleep if I do the same thing three times. You need someone like me in top management, because the renewal of your business model won't be coming from the bottom or the middle of your organization. But you don't want to have only these kinds of people; top management should be diverse. It should include renewers as well as replicators. You also need a good mix of people who look outwards and people who look inwards. That's what we have at Royal IHC. I am really involved with the outside world; my CFO [chief financial officer] by contrast pays more attention to what is happening inside the organization.'

Robert Witvliet, from the Dutch consultancy firm WIAR, adds, 'Diversity is very precise work. Because we were growing, we expanded our management team. But that disrupted the balance. I am good at setting up things;

my colleague is good at implementing them. When a third person came along, the balance was disturbed. We ended up going back to a two-person management team.'

As a manager, you have to watch out for warning signs other than the financial performance of your firm

Henk de Bruijn stressed the importance of keeping a close eye on what is going on within the organization: 'You have to be able to listen properly to the troublemakers in your organization, for instance. Don't avoid internal conflicts; they can be very good for you. Don't avoid them, *manage them*. Every organization needs its court jesters. You shouldn't get rid of them, you should have a workout with them. Consensus thinking is useless if what you want is renewal. I always say, be crazy, then you're normal enough, while often people say, be normal, then you're crazy enough. Give craziness a chance. That's only possible if the CEO joins in. You also need a leader who knows how to steer the craziness in the right direction.'

Herman Wories of DSM agrees with him: 'You even have to *organize* conflicts. And you have to keep asking yourself what you want. At DSM, we started on our renewal early every time. That was because we had a good look around us and the internal discussion was always about that. For instance, we saw how rivals grew very large while we weren't able to do that. And we were sensitive to the economic climate. At a certain moment you all look at the competitive landscape and wonder: do I still want to be out there?'

Charles Smit concurs that it is vitally important to be alert to possible dangers, even while the figures are good. 'If Apple asks us to submit a tender for the iPhone 6 and we don't get that order, it is a signal, more than falling turnover or profit, and definitely if something like that happens again. Reviews also tell you things. If you keep on being labelled as a follower [. . .] That's right, we don't like that, because we want to be the number one in our market segments.'

Goof Hamers adds, 'But you do have to have some tolerance for the things that go wrong. Nine out of ten ideas end up nowhere. Give it some space, don't punish it. And don't be satisfied. When I came to Royal IHC, we were up to our ears in orders. And yet we set out on renewal. And we had discussions with a customer who wanted to have a ship built overseas. Previously we would have chased him out of the building.'

Jeffrey Tierie stresses the importance of taking a longer-term view: 'Renewal needs time and space. The big players in my sector, like Philips, only look two years ahead. These days, long-term thinking has to come from suppliers like us. I actually have a horizon of ten to twelve years, and I use a six-year schedule. That way you allow yourself to entertain strange ideas.'

Do not separate business model innovation from environmental dynamism and competitive pressure

All the managers in our panel in some way or another raised the issue of growing environmental turbulence and how to cope with disruptive change, and how this made employees in their organization slightly nervous. Discussion of this point led to stories about the deepening economic crisis in much of Europe. According to Goof Hamers, despite the crisis ('which doesn't exist at all in most of the countries where we do business'), the sustainability of business models decreases exponentially under the pressure of growing competition. 'We are currently being overwhelmed by market and technological developments of various kinds. On the one hand, you shouldn't let that drive you crazy. On the other hand, you have to participate in it. The situation is very different to three or four years ago.'

Herman Wories points out that DSM is renewing its business model more and more frequently, often in cooperation with other parties. 'That means you have to deal with a large variety of business models. It makes it more complicated to develop a business model yourself.'

At the Port of Rotterdam Authority, the dynamism is increasing due to internal factors as well, says Henk de Bruijn: 'Apart from competing with other ports, we also now encourage more and more competition within our own port. That makes the picture more complicated.'

Charles Smit puts things into perspective by explaining how the chips industry works at several speeds. Mobile telephones become outdated after only a few months. 'But we also do a lot of work for the automotive industry and the changes there don't happen as fast. We are now looking particularly at the medical world. It is a matter of waiting until a "Steve Jobs of the life sciences" steps up, who will use technology to tackle the problems in healthcare, so you can get robots at the bedside and in the future just a drop of blood on a chip will replace all those tubes of blood having to go here and there for blood testing.'

Jeffrey Tierie adds his perspective on how the healthcare market is developing: 'The trend in healthcare now is that everything has to be done more cheaply. That kind of development trickles down through the entire chain to the bottom and eventually it ends up on our plate. Among other things, it has resulted in us combining digital and analogue technology.'

Manage conflicts resulting from a dual business model focus, do not avoid them

Business model renewal is regarded by the managers in our panel as being one of the most desirable but challenging options. However, a dual business model seems to be their preferred option since it allows them most scope to keep all other options open. Henk de Bruijn is emphatic: 'We are a hybrid organization. Renewal in our firm is both customer-driven and strategy-driven. Actually, you could say that we apply strategy to customers. For instance, we only allow large firms with sustainable operations in the new man–made seaport Maasvlakte 2. That's because they are the parties we want to do business with.'

Goof Hamers says that there has been a change in how Royal IHC approaches business model innovation: 'A few years ago we used to listen more to our customers. Dredging companies told us: "We need such and such." So that's what we made for them. Now we do more of the thinking ourselves about what is good for the customer.'

Do not focus on a single lever; use several to renew your business model

There is general consensus among the panel members that it is better to use several levers in combination, although some feel that one particular lever was initially the most important.

Goof Hamers says, 'Technology is the basis of our competitive model. Even now, we are one of the few in our field to do our own research and engineering. If a customer turns up with their own design, we refer them to China. What we don't have in-house in technology, we buy. That's why we acquired a pipe-laying firm: we didn't know much about it, and yet the ships we sell are used for that activity.'

But a structural change of direction was only achieved at Royal IHC by pulling on all the levers at once, according to Hamers. It was crucial to have different management for this. This change in management opened up new possibilities for business model renewal at Royal IHC, as Hamers explains: 'All our managers are given three kinds of objective every year; one of them relates to the future. You ask a financial manager, for instance, whether he can think up a new financial product for customers. It's how you anchor the renewal in your system.' DSM even aims to have 20 per cent of its turnover coming from new business.

In the end, Hamers believes that co-creation with the customer is the most important lever. 'We adapted our entire organization to this, through vertical integration but also by taking over component suppliers, which enables us to talk with our customers about all the parts. It is true that the customer is not always after business model renewal in the first place. But you have control of that partly yourself, by the way you get in and the people you talk with. If you discuss an order only with their purchasing department, they will try to compare you with five Chinese shipyards.'

Erik van der Liet from Randstad adds, 'Our customers are used to paying for the number of employment agency hours, not for extra services. That means we also have to talk with people other than HR management at the customer's firm—operations, for instance—to convince customers they should pay for new concepts. That requires an internal change of culture as well. We are not yet used to approaching the customer that way either.'

Communication and implementation make or break business model innovation

The managers emphasize that the implementation process and good communication are extremely important. On the floor, that is where it happens, they say, in all kinds of ways. Charles Smit says, 'In parts of our organization there used to be space for people's own "hobbies". Technically we were very good, but our people didn't always have the right focus. Now we set very clear goals—for example, that we want to supply more high-performance products. Take cars: these days they have to be able to drive in the desert as well as in the north of Norway. That imposes high demands on our chips. That kind of sharp focus requires a lot of good communication. No, I don't believe that communication is important just for business model replication; it's definitely also important for renewal! Otherwise everyone heads off in different directions.'

Jeffrey Tierie adds, 'Communication also means provoking a reaction, daring people to think and act *out of the box*.'

Herman Wories qualifies this view: 'But not everyone in your organization has that capacity to go crazy. You have to separate the departments
which are renewing from the ones which are replicating. At our firm,
experimentation with fundamentally new business models takes place in
the Innovation Centre. There is a great deal of freedom there, while in
operations things are much tighter.'

In the words of Robert Witvliet: 'Give those people that dare to dream of
new business models room and space to act as entrepreneurs; that's what it
comes down to. Dare to dream it.'

From offline to online: the Business Model Innovation Scan

The discussion and case studies presented in this book have provided some
insights into the paths that firms might take to transform their business
models, and which levers may be the most helpful to them in that process.
But, of course, you may still have your own questions about the best route
for you. How do you reinvent your business model? Are you really facing
disruption? What levers are most effective for developing a new business
model? And what are the specific enablers or inhibitors of business model
innovation in your company?

To assist you in this, we have therefore developed an online tool to support
you in your attempts to innovate your business model. This Business Model
Innovation Scan can be found at www.reinventingbusinessmodels.com.
This tool has been tested with firms across a variety of sectors, and within
small businesses as well as multinationals. We hope that after reading this
book many readers will fill in the scan, after which they will receive valuable feedback on how to reinvent their business model, be it replication,
renewal, or a combination of the two. In this way, we as authors are practising what we preach: ours is a dual business model in which we combine an
offline model, a book, with an online model in the form of an online scan.

Appendices

GLOSSARY

Business model: a collection of activities which are carried out to meet market needs. A business model consists of various components and describes the relationships between those components. It analyses how value creation takes place and how the firm captures that, and it sets out clearly how the components and their interrelationships contribute to the competitive strategy.

Business model innovation: a collective term for the two fundamental ways of changing a business model: business model replication and business model renewal.

Business model innovation matrix: an overview of four types of business model innovation (renewal versus replication, and strategy-driven versus customer-driven) with corresponding organizational, management, and environmental features.

Business model replication: refining and perfecting an existing business model by leveraging its existing components or strengthening the interdependencies between these components to create and capture more value.

Business model renewal: introducing new business model components or new interdependencies between those components which go beyond the framework of an existing model in order to create and capture new value.

Business model transformation: switching from business model replication to business model renewal, or vice versa.

Dual focus: working on both business model replication and business model renewal.

Focus on fixation: working on neither business model replication nor business model renewal.

Levers: the elements which drive business model innovation: technology, management practices, organizational forms, and co-creation.

Levers for technologically oriented renewal: a combination of new technologies and new management practices.

Levers for internally oriented renewal: new technology, new management practices, and new organizational forms.

Levers for externally oriented renewal: new management practices, new organizational forms, and co-creation.

Levers for integral renewal: new technology, new management practices, new organizational forms, and co-creation.

Enablers or disenablers of business model innovation: internal or external factors which facilitate or inhibit the development of new business models or the improvement of existing business models.

DEFINITIONS OF BUSINESS MODELS

Business model description	Authors
'The heuristic logic which connects technological potential with the realisation of economic value.'	Chesbrough and Rosenbloom (2002)
'Management's hypothesis about what the customer wants, and how an enterprise can best meet those needs, and get paid for doing so.'	Teece (2007)
'A business model articulates the logic, data and other evidence that support the value proposition for the customer, and has a viable structure for revenue and costs of a firm to deliver that value.'	Teece (2010)
'A business model is a reflection of the firm's realised strategy.'	Casadesus-Masanell and Ricart (2010)
'An architecture of the product, service and information flows, including a description of the various business actors and their roles; a description of the potential benefits for the various business actors; a description of the sources of revenue.'	Timmers (1998)
'A business model explains how the activities of a firm work together to execute its strategy.'	Richardson (2008)
'The method by which a firm builds and uses its resources to offer its customers better value and to make money doing so.'	Afuah and Tucci (2001)
'A business model depicts the content, structure and governance of transactions designed so as to create value through the exploitation of business opportunities.'	Amit and Zott (2001)
'Stories that explain how firms work. They answer the following questions: who is the customer? What does the customer value? How do we make money in this business? What is the underlying economic logic that explains how we can deliver value to the customer at an appropriate cost?'	Margretta (2002)
'Designing interdependent systems which create and sustain a competitive advantage.'	Mayo and Brown (1999)
'A set of interlocking elements which create and deliver value.'	Johnson et al. (2008)

'A concise representation of how an interrelated set of decision variables in the areas of strategy, architecture and economy of a firm are addressed to create sustainable competitive advantage in defined markets.'	Morris et al. (2005)
'a set of generic level descriptors of how a firm organizes itself to create and distribute value in a profitable manner'	Baden-Fuller and Morgan (2010)
'the business model as a system that solves the problem of identifying who is (are) the customer(s), engaging with their needs, delivering satisfaction, and monetizing the value.'	Baden-Fuller and Haefliger (2013)
'The sum of material, objectively existing structures and processes as well as intangible, cognitive meaning structures at the level of a business organization'	Tikkanen et al. (2005)
'Business models stand as cognitive structures providing a theory of how to set boundaries to the firm, of how to create value, and how to organize its internal structure and governance'	Doz and Kosonen (2010)
'The pattern of cause-effect relations that, in top managers' or entrepreneurs' understandings, link value creation and value capture activities'	Furnari (2015)

RESEARCH ACCOUNTABILITY

The organizations which worked with us on this research:

1. Claymount Technologies Group
2. DSM*
3. Ericsson
4. NXP*
5. Port of Rotterdam Authority*
6. Randstad
7. Roche Diagnostics Netherlands
8. Royal IHC*
9. TomTom

* *More extensive case studies for these firms are provided in Chapter 6. The case studies concerned were carried out by Henk Volberda, Frans van den Bosch, Kevin Heij, Diana Perra, Milos van Moorsel, Rick Hollen, and Benjamin Wörner.*

Before holding semi-structured interviews with managers from these organizations, we undertook document analysis for each organization, using a standard case study protocol. This analysis covered the period from 2000 to 2016, and involved examination of various documents, including annual reports, and also media articles relating to the organization.

PARTICIPATING FIRMS AND INTERVIEWEES

Claymount Technologies Group	Jeffrey Tierie—CEO
DSM	Robert Kirschbaum—former Vice-President, Open Innovation Rob van Leen—Executive Director and Chief Innovation Officer Hein Schreuder—former Executive Vice-President, Corporate Strategy & Acquisitions
Ericsson	Manfred Dasselaar—Practice Manager, Technology Consulting
NXP	Guido Dierick—Executive Vice-President, General Counsel and Country Manager Maarten Dirkzwager—Vice-President and Manager of Corporate Strategy Office Theo Kedzierski—Director of Technology Licensing John Schmitz—Senior Vice-President, Intellectual Property and Licensing
Port of Rotterdam	Henk de Bruijn—Director of Social Affairs, former Director of Corporate Strategy Pieter van Essen—Project Director, Rotterdam Climate Initiative Caroline Kroes—Corporate Strategist Bram van der Staaij—Senior Advisor, Corporate Strategy Mare Straetmans—Managing Director of PortXL, Innovation Program Manager
Randstad	Chris Heutink—member of the Executive Board Alje Kuiper—Director of Strategy & Innovation Mark de Lat—former Director of Consultancy René Schripsema—Director of Randstad Inhouse Services
Roche	Josefien van der Meer—Communications Manager
Royal IHC	Goof Hamers—former CEO Arjan Klijnsoon—Executive Director, Shipbuilding Martijn Schouten—Executive Sales Director
TomTom	Roland van Venrooy—Director of Advanced Engineering Carlo van de Weijer—Vice-President, Business Development Traffic Solutions

SURVEY ACCOUNTABILITY

The main constructs used in the survey and presented in this book are shown below, together with the academic articles from which the items used in the constructs originate.

Construct	Source
Company performance	Jaworski and Kohli (1993)
Business model renewal	Heij et al. (2014); Jansen et al. (2006)
Business model replication	Heij et al. (2014); Jansen et al. (2006)
New technologies	Average investment in R&D and ICT during the previous three years (as a percentage of sales)
New management practices	Covin and Slevin (1989); Vaccaro et al. (2012a)
New organizational forms	Vaccaro et al. (2012a)
Co-creation	Volberda et al. (2001)
Environmental dynamism	Jansen et al. (2006)
Environmental competitiveness	Birkinshaw et al. (1998)
Centralization of decision-making	Hage and Aiken (1967)
Current management skills versus required management skills	Capron and Mitchell (2009)
Current marketing skills versus required marketing skills	Capron and Mitchell (2009)
Human capital	Youndt et al. (2004)
Innovative culture	Volberda et al. (2012)
Internal connectedness	Jaworski and Kohli (1993)
Knowledge-absorptive capacity	Jansen et al. (2005)
Organizational identity	Kottasz et al. (2008)
Process innovation	Belderbos et al. (2004)
Transformational leadership	Rafferty and Griffin (2004)

The large majority of our main constructs are based on perceptual scales, because how executives perceive the external environment will determine what they do with their firm's business model (Demil and Lecocq, 2010; Smith et al., 2010). This approach is in line with other measures of business model innovation (e.g. Aspara et al., 2010; Zott and Amit, 2007) and of firm performance (e.g. Berthon et al., 2004; Volberda et al., 2012). We adopted existing measures wherever possible.

We compared the scales we adopted for business model renewal and business model replication with other constructs used in the research in order to verify that the concept was robust. We found that business model renewal correlates significantly with other scales, namely those for strategic focus on renewal[1] ($r = 0.46$; $p < 0.01$) and corporate venturing[2] ($r = 0.50$; $p < 0.01$). Corporate venturing is about the development of new business within existing organizations (e.g. Burgers et al., 2009). Our measure of business model renewal also correlates strongly with the sales from

1. This scale originates from Aspara et al. (2010).
2. This scale originates from Burgers et al. (2009).

new products and services measured as a percentage of total sales ($r = 0.29; p < 0.01$). The scale for business model replication correlates significantly with the scale for strategic focus on improvement[3] ($r = 0.25; p < 0.01$), and with the measure of sales from improved products and services as a percentage of the total sales ($r = 0.25; p < 0.01$). More information about the scales we used to measure business model replication and renewal can be found in Heij et al. (2014) and Heij (2015).

To check for non-response bias, we randomly selected around one hundred organizations from our observations and collected data from the Company.info database on their profitability in the year 2012. A t-test indicates no significant difference ($p > 0.05$) between the average profitability of this selection of companies and that of Dutch companies included in the database. There is thus no serious indication of non-response bias.

In our findings, we often refer to there being a high or low degree of a particular construct within a particular sector or across a particular group of firms. A high degree refers to the top 25 per cent of survey organizations with high scores for the construct in question, and a low degree pertains to the bottom 25 per cent of organizations with low scores for that construct. We also use the terms 'above average' and 'below average', and here the same logic applies, although in this case above average is used to mean the top 50 per cent of survey organizations with high scores for the construct in question. Below average then indicates the bottom 50 per cent of organizations with low scores for that construct.

The differences in percentage that are discussed in Chapters 3, 5, and 7 were tested for significance.[4] The type of test did vary, however. Thus t-tests were used to test whether a significant difference exists between the scores on a particular construct in various settings. For example, the scores on business model renewal and business model replication per industry compared to the national average score on those constructs (Chapter 3) were tested with one-sided t-tests. Since we are interested in general terms in whether a particular construct is present to a greater or lesser degree, we usually ran one-sided t-tests. Although the significance effect was stronger for most of the constructs, a p-value of 0.10 is regarded as the lower limit. Besides t-tests, we also used ordinary least squares analysis to test the effects of constructs on a dependent variable. For example, this form of analysis was used to test the effects of the levers of business model replication and renewal which we presented in Chapter 4.

3. This scale originates from Aspara et al. (2010).
4. The only exception to this was a small number of univariate analyses in which we looked at how respondents were grouped into particular constructs or a combination of constructs. This applies, for instance, to the findings presented in Figure 3.1.

References

Acs, Z. J., and Audretsch, D. B. 1988. 'Innovation in large and small firms: An empirical analysis.' *The American Economic Review,* 78 (4): pp. 678–90.

Adner, R., and Kapoor, R. 2010. 'Value creation in innovation ecosystems: How the structure of technological interdependence affects firm performance in new technology generations.' *Strategic Management Journal,* 31 (3): pp. 306–33.

Adner, R., and Snow, D. 2010. 'Old technology responses to new technology threats: Demand heterogeneity and technology retreats.' *Industrial and Corporate Change,* 19 (5): pp. 1655–75.

Afuah, A., and Tucci, C. 2001. *Internet business models and strategies.* Irvine: McGraw-Hill.

Agarwal, R., Audretch, D., and Sarkar, M. B. 2007. 'The process of creative construction: Knowledge spillovers, entrepreneurship, and economic growth.' *Strategic Entrepreneurship Journal,* 1 (3/4): pp. 263–86.

Aghion, P., Bloom, N., Blundell, R., Griffith, R., and Howitt, P. 2005. 'Competition and innovation: An inverted-U relationship.' *Quarterly Journal of Economics,* 120 (2): pp. 701–28.

Ahuja, G., and Lampert, C. M. 2001. 'Entrepreneurship in the large corporation: A longitudinal study of how established firms create breakthrough inventions.' *Strategic Management Journal,* 22 (6–7): pp. 521–43.

Ahuja, G., Lampert, C. M., and Tandon, V. 2008. 'Moving beyond Schumpeter: Management research on the determinants of technological innovation.' *The Academy of Management Annals,* 2 (1): pp. 1–98.

Albert, S., Ashforth, B. E., and Dutton, J. E. 2000. 'Organizational identity and identification: Charting new waters and building new bridges.' *Academy of Management Review,* 25 (1): pp. 13–17.

Amit, R., and Zott, C. 2001. 'Value creation in E-business.' *Strategic Management Journal,* 22 (6–7): pp. 493–520.

Amit, R., and Zott, C. 2012. 'Creating value through business model innovation.' *MIT Sloan Management Review,* 53 (3): pp. 41–9.

Andries, P., DeBackere, K., and Van Looy, B. 2013. 'Simultaneous experimentation as a learning strategy: Business model development under uncertainty.' *Strategic Entrepreneurial Journal,* 7 (4): pp. 288–310.

Andriopoulos, C., and Lewis, M. W. 2009. 'Exploitation-exploration tensions and organizational ambidexterity: Managing paradoxes of innovation.' *Organization Science,* 20 (4): pp. 696–717.

Ansari, S. S., Garud, R., and Kumaraswamy, A. 2016. 'The disruptor's dilemma: TiVo and the US television ecosystem.' *Strategic Management Journal*, 37 (9): pp. 1829–53.

Ansoff, H. I. 1980. 'Strategic issue management.' *Strategic Management Journal*, 1 (2): pp. 131–48.

Ansoff, H. I. 1984. *Implanting strategic management*. Englewood Cliffs, New Jersey: Prentice-Hall.

Anthony, S. D., and Christensen, C. M. 2005. 'How you can benefit by predicting change.' *Financial Executive*, 21 (2): pp. 36–41.

Antorini, Y. M., Muñiz Jr, A. M., and Askildsen, T. 2012. 'Collaborating with customer communities: Lessons from the LEGO Group.' *MIT Sloan Management Review*, 53 (3): pp. 73–9.

Aragón-Correa, J. A., Hurtado-Torres, N., Sharma, S., and García-Morales, V. J. 2008. 'Environmental strategy and performance in small firms: A critical perspective.' *Journal of Environmental Management*, 86 (1): pp. 88–103.

Argyris, C., and Schön, D. A. 1996. *Organizational learning II: Theory, method and practice*. Reading, MA: Addison-Wesley.

Aspara, J., Hietanen, J., and Tikkanen, H. 2010. 'Business model innovation vs. replication: Financial performance implications of strategic emphases.' *Journal of Strategic Marketing*, 18 (1): pp. 39–56.

Aspara, J., Lamberg, J. A., Laukia, A., and Tikkanen, H. 2013. 'Corporate business model transformation and inter-organizational cognition: The case of Nokia.' *Long Range Planning*, 46 (6): pp. 459–74.

Atuahene-Gima, K., Slater, S. F., and Olson, E. M. 2005. 'The contingent value of responsive and proactive market orientations for new product program performance.' *Journal of Product Innovation Management*, 22 (6): pp. 464–82.

Avolio, B. J., Bass, B. M., and Jung, D. I. 1999. 'Re-examining the components of transformational and transactional leadership using the Multifactor Leadership Questionnaire.' *Journal of Occupational and Organizational Psychology*, 72 (4): pp. 441–62.

Avolio, B. J., Walumbwa, F. O., and Weber, T. J. 2009. 'Leadership: Current theories, research, and future directions.' *Annual Review of Psychology*, 60: pp. 421–49.

Baden-Fuller, C., and Mangematin, V. 2013. 'Business models: A challenging agenda.' *Strategic Organization*, 11 (4): pp. 418–27.

Baden-Fuller, C., and Morgan, M. S. 2010. 'Business models as models.' *Long Range Planning*, 43 (2–3): pp. 156–71.

Baden-Fuller, C., and Volberda, H. W. 2003. 'Dormant capabilities, complex organizations and renewal.' In R. Sanchez (Ed.), *Knowledge management and organizational competence*: pp. 114–36. Oxford: Oxford University Press.

Baden-Fuller, C., and Winter, S. 2007. 'Replicating knowledge practices: Principles or templates.' Working paper, *Cass Business School*.

Barney, J. 1991. 'Firm resources and sustained competitive advantage.' *Journal of Management*, 17 (1): pp. 99–120.

Barrett, S. D. 2000. 'Airport competition in the deregulated European aviation market.' *Journal of Air Transport Management*, 6 (1): pp. 13–27.

Bass, B. M. 1985. *Leadership and performance beyond expectations.* New York: Free Press; Collier Macmillan.

Bass, B. M. 2003. 'Face to face — power to change: A conversation with Bernard M. Bass.' *Leadership in Action,* 23 (2): pp. 9–11.

Bass, B. M., Avolio, B. J., Jung, D. I., and Berson, Y. 2003. 'Predicting unit performance by assessing transformational and transactional leadership.' *Journal of Applied Psychology,* 88 (2): pp. 207–18.

Belderbos, R., Carree, M., and Lokshin, B. 2004. 'Cooperative R&D and firm performance.' *Research Policy,* 33 (10): pp. 1477–92.

Bengtsson, M., and Kock, S. 2000. '"Coopetition" in business networks — to cooperate and compete simultaneously.' *Industrial Marketing Management,* 29 (5): pp. 411–26.

Ben-Menahem, S. M., Van den Bosch, F. A. J., Volberda, H. W., and Kwee, Z. 2013. 'Strategic renewal over time: The enabling role of absorptive capacity in aligning internal and external rates of change.' *Long Range Planning,* 46 (3): pp. 216–35.

Benner, M. J., and Tushman, M. L. 2002. 'Process management and technological innovation: A longitudinal study of the photography and paint industries.' *Administrative Science Quarterly,* 47 (4): pp. 676–707.

Benner, M. J., and Tushman, M. L. 2003. 'Exploitation, exploration, and process management: The productivity dilemma revisited.' *Academy of Management Review,* 28 (2): pp. 238–56.

Benson-Rea, M., Brodie, R. J., and Sima, H. 2013. 'The plurality of co-existing business models: Investigating the complexity of value drivers.' *Industrial Marketing Management,* 42 (5): pp. 717–29.

Berchicci, L. 2013. 'Towards an open R&D system: Internal R&D investments, external knowledge acquisition and innovative performance.' *Research Policy,* 42 (1): pp. 117–27.

Berg, P. 1986. 'Organization change as a symbolic transformation process.' In P. J. Frost, L. F. Moore, M. R. Louis, C. L. Lundberg, and J. Martin (Eds.), *Organizational culture*: pp. 281–301. Beverly Hills: Sage.

Berthon, P., Hulbert, J. M., and Pitt, L. 2004. 'Innovation or customer orientation? An empirical investigation.' *European Journal of Marketing,* 38 (9/10): pp. 1065–90.

Bertolini, M., Duncan, D., and Waldeck, A. 2015. 'Knowing when to reinvent.' *Harvard Business Review,* 93 (12): pp. 90–101.

Bezemer, P. J., Van den Bosch, F. A. J., and Volberda, H. W. 2012. *Aandeelhouderswaarde versus stakeholderwaarde: Een analyse van de ontwikkelingen in Nederland (1992–2009).* In M. Luckerath-Rovers, B. Bier, H. van Ees, and M. Kaptein (Eds.), *Jaarboek Corporate Governance 2012–2013*: pp. 17–28. Deventer: Kluwer.

Bezemer, P. J., Zajac, E., Naumovska, I., Van den Bosch. F. A. J., and Volberda, H. W. 2015. 'Power and paradigms: The Dutch response to pressures for shareholder value.' *Corporate Governance: An International Review,* 23 (1): pp. 60–75.

Birkinshaw, J. 2010. *Reinventing management.* Chichester: John Wiley & Sons.

Birkinshaw, J., Hamel, G., and Mol, M. J. 2008. 'Management innovation.' *Academy of Management Review,* 33 (4): pp. 825–45.

Birkinshaw, J., Hood, N., and Jonsson, S. 1998. 'Building firm-specific advantages in multinational corporations: The role of subsidiary initiative.' *Strategic Management Journal*, 19 (3): pp. 221–41.

Björkdahl, J., and Holmén, M. 2013. 'Editorial: Business model innovation – the challenges ahead.' *International Journal of Product Development*, 18 (3/4): pp. 213–25.

Bloom, N., Sadun, R., and Van Reenen, J. 2010. 'Does product market competition lead firms to decentralize?' *The American Economic Review*, 100 (2): pp. 434–8.

Bloom, N., and Van Reenen, J. 2007. 'Measuring and explaining management practices across firms and countries.' *Quarterly Journal of Economics*, 122 (4): pp. 1351–408.

Bock, A. J., Opsahl, T., George, G., and Gann, D. M. 2012. 'The effects of culture and structure on strategic flexibility during business model innovation.' *Journal of Management Studies*, 49 (2): pp. 279–305.

Bock, L. 2015. *Work rules! Insights from inside Google that will transform how you live and lead*. New York: Twelve.

Bogers, M., Sund, K. J., and Villarroel, J. A. 2014. 'The organizational dimension of business model exploration: Evidence from the European postal industry.' In N. J. Foss and T. Saebi (Eds.), *Business model innovation: The organizational dimension*: pp. 269–88. Oxford: Oxford University Press.

Bonaccorsi, A., Giannangeli, S., and Rossi, C. 2006. 'Entry strategies under competing standards: Hybrid business models in the open source software industry.' *Management Science*, 52 (7): pp. 1085–98.

Bonner, J. M., and Walker, O. C. 2004. 'Selecting influential business-to-business customers in new product development: Relational embeddedness and knowledge heterogeneity considerations.' *Product Innovation Management*, 21 (3): pp. 155–69.

Bower, J. L., and Christensen, C. M. 1995. 'Disruptive technologies: Catching the wave.' *Harvard Business Review*, 73 (1): pp. 43–53.

Bowman, C., and Ambrosini, V. 2003. 'How the resource-based and the dynamic capability views of the firm inform corporate-level strategy.' *British Journal of Management*, 14 (4): pp. 289–303.

Bradley, C., and O'Toole, C. 2016. 'An incumbent's guide to digital disruption.' *McKinsey Quarterly*, 52 (3): pp. 76–85.

Brandenburger, A. M., and Nalebuff, B. J. 2011. *Co-opetition*. New York: Doubleday.

Brown, S. L., and Eisenhardt, K. M. 1997. 'The art of continuous change: Linking complexity theory and time-paced evolution in relentlessly shifting organizations.' *Administrative Science Quarterly*, 42 (1): pp. 1–34.

Brown, S. L., and Eisenhardt, K. M. 1998. *Competing on the edge: Strategy as structured chaos*. Boston, MA: Harvard Business Press.

Burgelman, R. A. 2002. 'Strategy as vector and the inertia of co-evolutionary lock-in.' *Administrative Science Quarterly*, 47 (2): pp. 325–57.

Burgers, J. H., Jansen, J. J. P., Van den Bosch, F. A. J., and Volberda, H. W. 2009. 'Structural differentiation and corporate venturing: The moderating role of formal and informal integration mechanisms.' *Journal of Business Venturing*, 24 (3): pp. 206–20.

Burgers, J. H., Van den Bosch, F. A. J., and Volberda, H. W. 2008. 'Why new business development projects fail: Coping with the differences of technological versus market knowledge.' *Long Range Planning*, 41 (1): pp. 55–73.

Camisón, C., and Villar-López, A. 2014. 'Organizational innovation as an enabler of technological innovation capabilities and firm performance.' *Journal of Business Research*, 67 (1): pp. 2891–902.

Capron, L., and Mitchell, W. 2009. 'Selection capability: How capability gaps and internal social frictions affect internal and external strategic renewal.' *Organization Science*, 20 (2): pp. 294–312.

Carroll, L. 1946. *Through the looking glass & what Alice found there*. New York: Grosset & Dunlap.

Casadesus-Masanell, R., and Ricart, J. E. 2010. 'From strategy to business models and onto tactics.' *Long Range Planning*, 43 (2–3): pp. 195–215.

Casadesus-Masanell, R., and Ricart, J. E. 2011. 'How to design a winning business model.' *Harvard Business Review*, 89 (1/2): pp. 100–7.

Casadesus-Masanell, R., and Tarziján, J. 2012. 'When one business model isn't enough.' *Harvard Business Review*, 90 (1): pp. 132–7.

Casadesus-Masanell, R., and Zhu, F. 2013. 'Business model innovation and competitive imitation: The case of sponsor-based business models.' *Strategic Management Journal*, 34 (4): pp. 464–82.

Cassiman, B., and Veugelers, R. 2006. 'In search of complementarity in innovation strategy: Internal R&D and external knowledge acquisition.' *Management Science*, 52 (1): pp. 68–82.

Cavalcante, S., Kesting, P., and Ulhøi, J. 2011. 'Business model dynamics and innovation: (Re)establishing the missing linkages.' *Management Decision*, 49 (8): pp. 1327–42.

Chandy, R. K., and Tellis, G. J. 2000. 'The incumbent's curse? Incumbency, size, and radical product innovation.' *Journal of Marketing*, 64 (3): pp. 1–17.

Charitou, C. D., and Markides, C. C. 2003. 'Responses to disruptive strategic innovation.' *MIT Sloan Management Review*, 44 (2): pp. 55–63.

Chatterji, A. K., and Fabrizio, K. R. 2014. 'Using users: When does external knowledge enhance corporate product innovation?' *Strategic Management Journal*, 35 (10): pp. 1427–45.

Chesbrough, H., and Davies, A. 2010. 'Advancing services innovation: Five key concepts.' In P. P. Maglio, C. A. Kieliszewski, and J. C. Spohrer (Eds.), *Handbook of service science*: pp. 579–601. New York: Springer.

Chesbrough, H. W. 2003. *Open innovation: The new imperative for creating and profiting from technology*. Boston, MA: Harvard Business School Press.

Chesbrough, H. W. 2007. 'Business model innovation: It's not just about technology anymore.' *Strategy & Leadership*, 35 (6): pp. 12–17.

Chesbrough, H. W. 2010. 'Business model innovation: Opportunities and barriers.' *Long Range Planning*, 43 (2–3): pp. 354–63.

Chesbrough, H. W. 2011a. 'Why companies should have open business models.' *MIT Sloan Management Review*, 52 (2): pp. 68–74.

Chesbrough, H. W. 2011b. 'The era of open innovation.' *MIT Sloan Management Review*, 52 (2): pp. 35–41.

Chesbrough, H.W., Di Minin, A., and Piccaluga, A. 2013. 'Business model innovation paths.' In L. Cinquini, A. Di Minin, and R.Varaldo (Eds.), *New business models and value creation: A service science perspective*: pp. 45–66. Milan: Springer-Verlag.

Chesbrough, H.W., and Rosenbloom, R. S. 2002. 'The role of the business model in capturing value from innovation: Evidence from Xerox Corporation's technology spin-off companies.' *Industrial and Corporate Change*, 11 (3): pp. 529–55.

Christensen, C. M. 1997. *The innovator's dilemma: When new technologies cause great firms to fail*. Boston, MA: Harvard University Press.

Christensen, C. M. 2001. 'The past and future of competitive advantage.' *MIT Sloan Management Review*, 42 (2): pp. 105–9.

Christensen, C. M. 2013. 'Across the great divide: The role of theory as a bridge between academia and practice.' Presentation at SMS Special Conference, 22 March, Lausanne: IMD.

Christensen, C. M., Johnson, M.W., and Rigby, D. K. 2002. 'Foundations for growth: How to identify and build disruptive new businesses.' *MIT Sloan Management Review*, 43 (3): pp. 22–31.

Christensen, C. M., Kaufman, S. P., and Shih, C. 2008. 'Innovation killers – how financial tools destroy your capacity to do new things.' *Harvard Business Review*, 86 (4): pp. 98–105.

Christensen, C. M., Raynor, M. E., and Anthony, S. D. 2003. 'Six keys to creating new-growth businesses.' *Harvard Management Update*, 8 (1): pp. 3–6.

Christensen, C. M., Raynor, M. E., and McDonald, R. 2015. 'What is disruptive innovation?' *Harvard Business Review*, 93 (12): pp. 44–53.

Clarke-Hill, C., and Davies, H. L. 2003. 'The paradox of co-operation and competition in strategic alliances: Towards a multi-paradigm approach.' *Management Research News*, 26 (1): pp. 1–20.

Clausen, T. H., and Rasmussen, E. 2013. 'Parallel business models and the innovativeness of research-based spin-off ventures.' *The Journal of Technology Transfer*, 38 (6): pp. 836–49.

Cliffe, S., and McGrath, R. C. 2011. 'When your business model is in trouble.' *Harvard Business Review*, 89 (1/2): pp. 96–8.

Coffman, B. 1997. 'Weak signal research, part I: Introduction.' *Journal of Transition Management*, 2 (1), MG Taylor Corporation.

Cohen, W. M., and Levinthal, D.A. 1990. 'Absorptive capacity: A new perspective on learning and innovation.' *Administrative Science Quarterly*, 35 (1): pp. 128–52.

Cohen, W. M., and Levinthal, D.A. 1997. 'Reply to "comments on 'fortune favors the prepared firm'".' *Management Science*, 43 (10): pp. 1463–8.

Contractor, F. J. 2007. 'Is international business good for companies? The evolutionary or multi-stage theory of internationalization vs. the transaction cost perspective.' *Management International Review*, 47 (3): pp. 453–75.

Cortimiglia, M. N., Ghezzi, A., and Frank, A. G. 2016. 'Business model innovation and strategy making nexus: Evidence from a cross-industry mixed-methods study.' *R&D Management*, 46 (3): pp. 414–32.

Covin, J. G., and Slevin, D. P. 1989. 'Strategic management of small firms in hostile and benign environments.' *Strategic Management Journal*, 10 (1): pp. 75–87.

Crawford, C. B., Gould, L. V., and Scott, R. F. 2003. 'Transformational leader as champion and techie: Implications for leadership educators.' *Journal of Leadership Education*, 2 (1): pp. 1–12.

Cunha, M. P., and Chia, R. 2007. 'Using teams to avoid peripheral blindness.' *Long Range Planning*, 40 (6): pp. 559–73.

Currie, W. L. 1999. 'Revisiting management innovation and change programmes: Strategic vision or tunnel vision?' *Omega*, 27 (6): pp. 647–60.

Daft, R. L. 1978. 'A dual-core of organizational innovation.' *Academy of Management Journal*, 21 (2): pp. 193–210.

Damanpour, F., and Aravind, D. 2012. 'Managerial innovation: Conceptions, processes, and antecedents.' *Management and Organization Review*, 8 (2): pp. 423–54.

Damanpour, F., and Evan, M. E. 1984. 'Organizational innovation and performance: The problem of "organizational lag".' *Administrative Science Quarterly*, 29 (3): pp. 392–409.

Damanpour, F., Walker, R. M., and Avellaneda, C. N. 2009. 'Combinative effects of innovation types and organizational performance: A longitudinal study of service organizations.' *Journal of Management Studies*, 46 (4): pp. 650–75.

Danneels, E. 2002. 'The dynamics of product innovation and firm competences.' *Strategic Management Journal*, 23 (12): pp. 1095–121.

Danneels, E. 2003. 'Tight-loose coupling with customers: The enactment of customer orientation.' *Strategic Management Journal*, 24 (6): pp. 559–76.

Danneels, E. 2004. 'Disruptive technology reconsidered: A critique and research agenda.' *Journal of Product Innovation Management*, 21 (4): 246–58.

D'Aveni, R. 1994. *Hypercompetition: Managing the dynamics of strategic management.* New York: Free Press.

Davis, J. P., Eisenhardt, K. M., and Bingham, C. B. 2009. 'Optimal structure, market dynamism, and the strategy of simple rules.' *Administrative Science Quarterly*, 54 (3): pp. 413–52.

Day, G. S., and Schoemaker, P. J. 2004. 'Driving through the fog: Managing at the edge.' *Long Range Planning*, 37 (2): pp. 127–42.

Day, G. S., and Schoemaker, P. J. 2016. 'Adapting to fast-changing markets and technologies.' *California Management Review*, 58 (4): pp. 59–77.

De Boer, M., Van den Bosch, F. A. J., and Volberda, H. W. 1999. 'Managing organizational knowledge integration in the emerging multimedia complex.' *Journal of Management Studies*, 36 (3): pp. 379–98.

De Luca, L. M., Verona, G., and Vicari, S. 2010. 'Market orientation and R&D effectiveness in high-technology firms: An empirical investigation in the biotechnology industry.' *Journal of Product Innovation Management*, 27 (3): pp. 299–320.

Demil, B., and Lecocq, X. 2010. 'Business model evolution: In search of dynamic consistency.' *Long Range Planning*, 43 (2–3): pp. 227–46.

De Pelsmacker, P., Geuens, M., and Van den Bergh, J. 2007. *Marketing communications: A European perspective*, third edition. Harlow: Prentice Hall.

Dess, G. G., and Beard, D. W. 1984. 'Dimensions of organizational task environments.' *Administrative Science Quarterly*, 29 (1): pp. 52–73.

Dombrowski, C., Kim, J.Y., Desouza, K. C., Braganza, A., Papagari, S., Baloh, P., and Jha, S. 2007. 'Elements of innovative cultures.' *Knowledge and Process Management*, 14 (3): pp. 190–202.

Doz, Y. L., and Kosonen, M. 2010. 'Embedding strategic agility: A leadership agenda for accelerating business model renewal.' *Long Range Planning*, 43 (2): pp. 370–82.

Draulans, J., De Man, A. P., and Volberda, H. W. 2003. 'Building alliance capability: Management techniques for superior alliance performance.' *Long Range Planning*, 36 (2): pp. 151–66.

Drew, S. A. 2006. 'Building technology foresight: Using scenarios to embrace innovation.' *European Journal of Innovation Management*, 9 (3): pp. 241–57.

Drucker, P. 1985. *Innovation and entrepreneurship*. New York: Harper & Row.

Dunford, R., Palmer, I., and Benveniste, J. 2010. 'Business model replication for early and rapid internationalization.' *Long Range Planning*, 43 (5): pp. 655–74.

Dvir, T., Eden, D., Avolio, B. J., and Shamir, B. 2002. 'Impact of transformational leadership on follower development and performance: A field experiment.' *Academy of Management Journal*, 45 (4): pp. 735–44.

Dyer, J. H., and Singh, H. 1998. 'The relational view: Cooperative strategy and sources of inter-organizational competitive advantage.' *Academy of Management*, 23 (4): pp. 660–79.

Easterby-Smith, M., Lyles, M. A., and Tsang, E. W. K. 2008. 'Inter-organizational knowledge transfer: Current themes and future prospects.' *Journal of Management Studies*, 45 (4): pp. 677–90.

Ebben, J. J., and Johnson, A. C. 2005. 'Efficiency, flexibility, or both? Evidence linking strategy to performance in small firms.' *Strategic Management Journal*, 26 (13): pp. 1249–59.

Eisenhardt, K. M., and Galunic, D. C. 2000. 'Coevolving: At last, a way to make synergies work.' *Harvard Business Review*, 78 (1): pp. 91–101.

Eisenhardt, K. M., and Martin, J. A. 2000. 'Dynamic capabilities: What are they?' *Strategic Management Journal*, 21 (10–11): pp. 1105–21.

Efron, L. 2017. *Purpose meets execution*. New York: Taylor & Francis.

Enkel, E., and Mezger, F. 2013. 'Imitation processes and their application for business model innovation: An explorative study.' *International Journal of Innovation Management*, 17 (1): pp. 1–34.

Erden, Z., Klang, D., Sydler, R., and Von Krogh, G. 2014. 'Knowledge-flows and firm performance.' *Journal of Business Research*, 67 (1): pp. 2777–85.

Ettlie, J. E., and Reza, E. M. 1992. 'Organizational integration and process innovation.' *Academy of Management*, 35 (4): pp. 795–827.

Eyring, M. J., Johnson, M. W., and Nair, H. 2011. 'New business models in emerging markets.' *Harvard Business Review*, 89 (1/2): pp. 88–95.

FD Outlook. 2012. 'Innovatieprikkels: slimme steun van de staat.' December: pp. 30–2.

Financieele Dagblad. 2016. 'Snelle groei? Besteed dan vooral extra aandacht aan de bedrijfscultuur.' 10 June.

Fine, C. H. 1998. *Clockspeed: Winning industry control in the age of temporary advantage.* New York: Basic Books.

Fischbacher-Smith, D., and Fischbacher-Smith, M. 2014. 'What lies beneath? The role of informal and hidden networks in the management of crises.' *Financial Accountability & Management*, 30 (3): pp. 259–78.

Fiss, P. C., and Zajac, E. J. 2004. 'The diffusion of ideas over contested terrain: The (non)adoption of a shareholder value orientation among German firms.' *Administrative Science Quarterly*, 49 (4): pp. 501–34.

Forbes. 2014. 'A look back at why Blockbuster really failed and why it didn't have to.' https://www.forbes.com/sites/gregsatell/2014/09/05/a-look-back-at-why-blockbuster-really-failed-and-why-it-didnt-have-to/

Foreman, P., and Whetten, D. A. 2002. 'Members' identification with multiple-identity organizations.' *Organization Science*, 13 (6): pp. 618–35.

Forsman, H. 2009. 'Improving innovation capabilities of small enterprises: Cluster strategy as a tool.' *International Journal of Innovation Management*, 13 (2): pp. 1–23.

Fortune. 2015. 'Car-sharing service car2go goes luxe with Mercedes.' http://fortune.com/2015/09/28/car2go-mercedes/

Foss, N. J. 2002. 'New organizational forms-Critical perspectives.' *International Journal of the Economics of Business*, 9 (1): pp. 1–8.

Foss, N. J., Husted, K., and Michailova, S. 2009. 'Governing knowledge sharing in organizations: Levels of analysis, governance mechanisms, and research directions.' *Journal of Management Studies*, 47 (3): pp. 455–82.

Foss, N. J., Laursen, K., and Pedersen, T. 2011. 'Linking customer interaction and innovation: The mediating role of new organizational practices.' *Organization Science*, 22 (4): pp. 980–99.

Foss, N. J., Lyngsie, J., and Zahra, S. A. 2013. 'The role of external knowledge sources and organizational design in the process of opportunity exploitation.' *Strategic Management Journal*, 34 (12): pp. 1453–71.

Foss, N. J., and Saebi, T. 2015. 'Business models and business model innovation: Bringing organization into the discussion.' In N. J. Foss and T. Saebi (Eds.), *Business model innovation: The organizational dimension*: pp. 1–23. Oxford: Oxford University Press.

Foss, N. J., and Saebi, T. 2017. 'Fifteen years of research on business model innovation.' *Journal of Management*, 43 (1): pp. 200–27.

Fulop, L. 1991. 'Middle managers: Victims or vanguards of the entrepreneurial movement?' *Journal of Management Studies*, 28 (1): pp. 25–44.

Furnari, S. 2015. 'A cognitive mapping approach to business models: Representing causal structures and mechanisms.' In C. Baden-Fuller and V. Mangematin (Eds.), *Advances in Strategic Management*, Vol. 33: pp. 207–39. Bingley: Emerald Group.

Galbraith, J. R. 1982. 'Designing the innovating organization.' *Organizational Dynamics*, 10 (3): pp. 3–24.

Galunic, D. C., and Rodan, S. 1998. 'Resource recombinations in the firm: Knowledge structures and the potential for Schumpeterian innovation.' *Strategic Management Journal*, 19 (12): pp. 1193–201.

Gambardella, A., and McGahan, A. M. 2010. 'Business-model innovation: General purpose technologies and their implications for industry structure.' *Long Range Planning*, 43 (2): pp. 262–71.

Gans, J. 2016. *The disruption dilemma*. Cambridge, MA: MIT Press.

Gebauer, H. 2011. 'Exploring the contribution of management innovation to the evolution of dynamic capabilities.' *Industrial Marketing Management*, 40 (8): pp. 1238–50.

Genc, A. A., Volberda, H. W., and Sidhu, J. S. 2017. 'Dynamic capabilities, innovation, and firm performance: The mediating effect of management innovation.' Working paper, *Rotterdam School of Management*, Erasmus University.

George, G., and Bock, A. J. 2011. 'The business model in practice and its implications for entrepreneurship research.' *Entrepreneurship Theory and Practice*, 35 (1): pp. 83–111.

Geroski, P. A. 1999. 'Early warning of new rivals.' *MIT Sloan Management Review*, 40 (3): pp. 107–16.

Giesen, E., Berman, S. J., Bell, R., and Blitz, A. 2007. 'Three ways to successfully innovate your business model.' *Strategy and Leadership*, 35 (6): pp. 27–33.

Giesen, E., Riddleberger, E., Christner, R., and Bell, R. 2010. 'When and how to innovate your business model.' *Strategy & Leadership*, 38 (4): pp. 17–26.

Gilad, B. 2003. *Early warning: Using competitive intelligence to anticipate market shifts, control risk, and create powerful strategies*. New York: AMACOM.

Gilbert, C., and Bower, J. L. 2002. 'Disruptive change: When trying harder is part of the problem.' *Harvard Business Review*, 80 (5): pp. 95–100.

Gilbert, R. J. 2006. 'Competition and innovation.' *Journal of Industrial Organization Education*, 1 (1): pp. 1–23.

Gilsing, V., Nooteboom, B., Vanhaverbeke, W., Duysters, G., and Van den Oord, A. 2008. 'Network embeddedness and the exploration of novel technologies: Technological distance, betweenness centrality and density.' *Research Policy*, 37 (10): pp. 1717–31.

Govindarajan, V., and Kopalle, P. K. 2006. 'Disruptiveness of innovations: Measurement and an assessment of reliability and validity.' *Strategic Management Journal*, 27 (2): pp. 189–99.

Govindarajan, V., Kopalle, P. K., and Danneels, E. 2011. 'The effects of mainstream and emerging customer orientations on radical and disruptive innovations.' *Journal of Product Innovation Management*, 28 (s1): pp. 121–32.

Govindarajan, V., and Trimble, C. 2005. 'Building breakthrough businesses within established organizations.' *Harvard Business Review*, 83 (5): pp. 58–68.

Govindarajan, V., and Trimble, C. 2011. 'The CEO's role in business model reinvention.' *Harvard Business Review*, 89 (1–2): pp. 108–14.

Grant, R. M. 1996. 'Toward a knowledge-based theory of the firm.' *Strategic Management Journal*, 17 (7): pp. 109–22.

Graves, S. B., and Langowitz, N. S. 1993. 'Innovative productivity and returns to scale in the pharmaceutical industry.' *Strategic Management Journal*, 14 (8): pp. 593–605.

Griffin, A., Josephson, B. W., Lilien, G., Wiersema, F., Bayus, B., Chandy, R., Dahan, E., Gaskin, S., Kohli, A., Miller, C., Oliva, R., and Spanjol, J. 2013. 'Marketing's roles in innovation in business-to-business firms: Status, issues, and research agenda.' *Marketing Letters*, 24 (4): pp. 323–37.

Grove, A. S. 1997. 'Navigating strategic inflection points.' *Business Strategy Review*, 8 (3): pp. 11–18.

Grove, A. S. 1999. *Only the paranoid survive: How to exploit the crisis points that challenge every company.* New York: Bantam/Currency.

Hacklin, F. 2007. *Management of convergence in innovation: Strategies and capabilities for value creation beyond blurring industry boundaries.* Leipzig: Springer.

Hage, J., and Aiken, M. 1967. 'Program change and organizational properties: A comparative analysis.' *American Journal of Sociology*, 72 (March): pp. 503–19.

Hamel, G. 1998. 'Bringing Silicon Valley inside.' *Harvard Business Review*, 77 (5): pp. 70–84.

Hamel, G. 2000. *Leading the revolution.* Boston, MA: Harvard Business School Press.

Hamel, G. 2006. 'The why, what, and how of management innovation.' *Harvard Business Review*, 84 (2): pp. 72–84.

Hamel, G. 2007. *The future of management.* Boston, MA: Harvard Business School Press.

Hamel, G., and Prahalad, C. K. 1989. 'To revitalize corporate performance, we need a whole new model of strategy.' *Harvard Business Review*, 55 (4): pp. 45–64.

Hamel, G., and Prahalad, C. K. 1994. 'Strategy as a field of study: Why search for a new paradigm?' *Strategic Management Journal*, 15 (S2): pp. 5–16.

Hamel, G., and Valikangas, L. 2003. 'The quest for resilience.' *Harvard Business Review*, 81 (9): pp. 52–65.

Hansen, M. H., Perry, L. T., and Reese, C. S. 2004. 'A Bayesian operationalization of the resource-based view.' *Strategic Management Journal*, 25 (13): pp. 1279–95.

Hansen, M. T. 2002. 'Knowledge networks: Explaining effective knowledge sharing in multiunit companies.' *Organizational Science*, 13 (3): pp. 232–48.

Harker, M. J., and Egan, J. 2006. 'The past, present and future of relationship marketing.' *Journal of Marketing Management*, 22 (1–2): pp. 215–42.

Harris, S. D., and Zeisler, S. 2002. 'Weak signals: Detecting the next big thing.' *The Futurist*, 36 (6): pp. 21–8.

Harrysson, M., Métayer, E., and Sarrazin, H. 2014. 'The strength of "weak signals".' *McKinsey Quarterly*, 1: pp. 14–17.

Hecker, A., and Ganter, A. 2013. 'The influence of product market competition on technological and management innovation: Firm-level evidence from a large-scale survey.' *European Management Review*, 10 (1): pp. 17–33.

Heij, C. V. 2015. *Innovating beyond technology: Studies on how management innovation, co-creation and business model innovation contribute to firms' (innovation) performance.* Rotterdam: Erasmus Institute of Management/Erasmus University Rotterdam.

Heij, C.V., Volberda, H. W., and Van den Bosch, F. A. J. 2014. *How does business model innovation influence firm performance: The moderating effect of environmental dynamism.* In J. Humphreys (Ed.), Proceedings of the 74th Annual Meeting of the Academy of Management, pp. 1502–7.

Helfat, C. E., and Winter, S. G. 2011. 'Untangling dynamic and operational capabilities: Strategy for the (n)ever-changing world.' *Strategic Management Journal*, 32 (11): pp. 1243–50.

Henderson, R., and Clark, K. 1990. 'Architectural innovation: The reconfiguration of existing product technologies and the failure of established firms.' *Administrative Science Quarterly*, 35 (1): pp. 9–30.

Hensmans, M., Van den Bosch, F. A. J., and Volberda, H. W. 2001. 'Clicks vs. bricks in the emerging online financial services industry.' *Long Range Planning*, 34 (2): pp. 231–47.

Heyden, M. L., Sidhu, J. S., and Volberda, H. W. (forthcoming). 'The conjoint influence of top and middle management characteristics on management innovation.' *Journal of Management*. doi: 0149206315614373.

Hill, C. W., and Rothaermel, F. T. 2003. 'The performance of incumbent firms in the face of radical technological innovation.' *Academy of Management Review*, 28 (2): pp. 257–74.

Hiltunen, E. 2008. 'Good sources of weak signals: A global study of where futurists look for weak signals.' *Journal of Futures Studies*, 12 (4): pp. 21–44.

Hitt, M. A., Ireland, R. D., and Lee, H. U. 2000. 'Technological learning, knowledge management, firm growth and performance: An introductory essay.' *Journal of Engineering and Technology Management*, 17 (3): pp. 231–46.

Hodgkinson, I. A., Hughes, P., and Hughes, M. 2012. 'Absorptive capacity and market orientation in public service provision.' *Journal of Strategic Marketing*, 20 (3): pp. 211–29.

Hofstede, G. 1990. *Cultures and organizations: Software of the mind*. New York: McGraw-Hill.

Hofstede, G., Neuijen, B., Ohayv, D. D., and Sanders, G. 1990. 'Measuring organizational cultures: A qualitative and quantitative study across twenty cases.' *Administrative Science Quarterly*, 35 (2): pp. 286–316.

Hollen, R. M. A., Van den Bosch, F. A. J., and Volberda, H. W. 2013. 'The role of management innovation in enabling technological process innovation: An interorganizational perspective'. *European Management Review*, 10 (1): pp. 35–50.

Holmqvist, M. 2003. 'A dynamic model of intra- and interorganizational learning.' *Organization Studies*, 24 (1): pp. 95–123.

Holopainen, M., and Toivonen, M. 2012. 'Weak signals: Ansoff today.' *Futures*, 44 (3): pp. 198–205.

Hope, J., and Fraser, R. 2013. *Beyond budgeting: How managers can break free from the annual performance trap*. Boston, MA: Harvard Business Press.

Hoskisson, R. E., Covin, J., Volberda, H. W., and Johnson, R. H. 2011. 'Revitalizing entrepreneurship: The search for new research opportunities.' *Journal of Management Studies*, 48 (6): pp. 1141–68.

Huston, L., and Sakkab, N. 2006. 'Connect and develop.' *Harvard Business Review*, 84 (3): pp. 58–66.

Hutzschenreuter, T., Pedersen, T., and Volberda, H. W. 2007. 'The role of path dependency and managerial intentionality: A perspective on international business research.' *Journal of International Business Studies*, 38 (7): pp. 1055–68.

Itami, H., and Nishino, K. 2010. 'Killing two birds with one stone: Profit for now and learn for the future.' *Long Range Planning*, 43 (2–3): pp. 364–9.

Janis, I. L. 1972. *Victims of groupthink: A psychological study of foreign-policy decisions and fiascoes*. Boston, MA: Houghton Mifflin.

Jansen, J. J. P., Van den Bosch, F. A. J., and Volberda, H. W. 2005. 'Managing potential and realized absorptive capacity: How do organizational antecedents matter?' *Academy of Management Journal*, 48 (6): pp. 999–1015.

Jansen, J. J. P., Van den Bosch, F. A. J., and Volberda, H. W. 2006. 'Exploratory innovation, exploitative innovation, and performance: Effects of organizational antecedents and environmental moderators.' *Management Science*, 52 (11): pp. 1661–74.

Jaworksi, B. J., and Kohli, A. K. 1993. 'Market orientation: Antecedents and consequences.' *Journal of Marketing*, 57 (3): pp. 53–70.

Jay, R., and Weintraub, J. 2013. 'How innovative is your company's culture?' *MIT Sloan Management Review*, 54 (3): pp. 29–37.

Jean, R. J., Sinkovics, R. R., and Kim, D. 2010. 'Drivers and performance outcomes of relationship learning for suppliers in cross-border customer-supplier relationships: The role of communication culture.' *Journal of International Marketing*, 18 (1): pp. 63–85.

Jean, R. J., Sinkovics, R. R., and Kim, D. 2012. 'Drivers and performance outcomes of supplier innovation generation in customer-supplier relationships: The role of power-dependence.' *Decision Sciences*, 43 (6): pp. 1003–38.

Johnson, M. W., Christensen, C. M., and Kagermann, H. 2008. 'Reinventing your business model.' *Harvard Business Review*, 86 (12): pp. 50–9.

Jonsson, A., and Foss, N. J. 2011. 'International expansion through flexible replication: Learning from the internationalization experience of IKEA.' *Journal of International Business Studies*, 42 (9): pp. 1079–102.

Kaivo-oja, J. 2012. 'Weak signals analysis, knowledge management theory and systemic socio-cultural transitions.' *Futures*, 44 (3): pp. 206–17.

Kalwani, M. U., and Narayandas, N. 1995. 'Long-term manufacturer-supplier relationships: Do they pay off for supplier firms?' *Journal of Marketing*, 59 (1): pp. 1–16.

Kanter, R. M. 1988. 'Three tiers for innovation research.' *Communication Research*, 15 (5): pp. 509–23.

Kaplan, R. S., and Mikes, A. 2012. 'Managing risks: A new framework.' *Harvard Business Review*, 90 (6): pp. 48–60.

Kaplan, R. S., and Norton, D. P. 1995. 'Putting the balanced scorecard to work.' In D. G. Shaw, C. E. Schneider, R. W. Beatty and L. S. Baird (Eds.), *Performance measurement, management, and appraisal sourcebook*: pp. 66–79. Amherst, MA: Human Resources Development Press.

Kaplan, S. 2012. *The business model innovation factory*. Hoboken, NJ: John Wiley & Sons.

Katila, R., and Ahuja, G. 2002. 'Something old, something new: A longitudinal study of search behavior and new product introduction.' *Academy of Management Journal*, 45 (6): pp. 1183–94.

Kauffman, S. A. 1995. 'Escaping the red queen effect.' *The McKinsey Quarterly*, 1: pp. 118–30.

Khanagha, S., Volberda, H. W., and Oshri, I. 2014. 'Business model renewal and ambidexterity: Structural alteration and strategy formation process during transition to a cloud business model.' *R&D Management*, 44 (3): pp. 322–40.

Khanagha, S., Volberda, H. W., Sidhu, J., and Oshri, I. 2013. 'Management innovation and adoption of emerging technologies: The case of cloud computing.' *European Management Review*, 10 (1): pp. 51–67.

Kim, W. C., and Mauborgne, R. 2005. *Blue ocean strategy: How to create uncontested market space and make the competition irrelevant.* Cambridge, MA: Harvard Business School Press.

Kindström, D., and Kowalkowski, C. 2014. 'Service-driven business model innovation: Organizing the shift from a product-based to a service-centric business model.' In N. J. Foss and T. Saebi (Eds.), *Business model innovation: The organizational dimension:* pp. 191–216. Oxford: Oxford University Press.

Klang, D., Wallnöfer, M., and Hacklin, F. 2014. 'The business model paradox: A systematic review and exploration of antecedents.' *International Journal of Management Reviews*, 16 (4): pp. 454–78.

Klepper, S. 1996. 'Entry, exit, growth, and innovation over the product life cycle.' *The American Economic Review*, 86 (3): pp. 562–83.

Klitsie, J., Ansari, S., and Volberda, H. W. 2016. 'The advantages of a lack of compliance: Relating regulatory fit to performance.' Working paper, *Rotterdam School of Management*, Erasmus University.

Kottasz, R., Bennett, R., Svani, S., and Ali-Choudhury, R. 2008. 'The role of corporate art in the management of corporate identity.' *Corporate Communications*, 13 (3): pp. 235–54.

Kwee, Z. 2009. *Investigating three key principles of sustained strategic renewal: A longitudinal study of long-lived firms.* Rotterdam: Erasmus Research Institute of Management/Erasmus University Rotterdam.

Kwee, Z., Van den Bosch, F. A. J., and Volberda, H. W. 2011. 'The influence of top management team's corporate governance orientation on strategic renewal trajectories: A longitudinal analysis of Royal Dutch Shell plc. 1907–2004.' *Journal of Management Studies*, 48 (5): pp. 984–1014.

Laamanen, T., Lamberg, J. A., and Vaara, E. 2016. 'Explanations of success and failure in management learning: What can we learn from Nokia's rise and fall?' *Academy of Management Learning & Education*, 15 (1): pp. 2–25.

Lambert, S. C., and Davidson, R. A. 2013. 'Applications of the business model in studies of enterprise success, innovation and classification: An analysis of empirical research from 1996 to 2010.' *European Management Journal*, 31 (6): pp. 668–81.

Laursen, K. 2012. 'Keep searching and you'll find: What do we know about variety creation through firms' search activities for innovation?' *Industrial and Corporate Change*, 21 (5): pp. 1181–220.

Laursen, K., and Salter, A. 2006. 'Open for innovation: The role of openness in explaining innovation performance among UK manufacturing firms.' *Strategic Management Journal*, 27 (2): pp. 131–50.

Lavie, D. 2006. 'The competitive advantage of interconnected forms: An extension of the resource-based view.' *Academy of Management Review*, 31 (3): pp. 638–58.

Leonard-Barton, D. 1992. 'Core capabilities and core rigidities: A paradox in managing new product development.' *Strategic Management Journal*, 13 (S1): pp. 111–25.

Leonard-Barton, D., Bowen, H. K., Clark, K. B., Holloway, C., and Wheelwright, S. C. 1994. 'How to integrate work and deepen expertise.' *Harvard Business Review*, 72 (5): pp. 121–30.

Levinthal, D. A., and March, J. G. 1993. 'The myopia of learning.' *Strategic Management Journal*, 14 (S2): pp. 95–112.

Levitt, B., and March, J. G. 1988. 'Organizational learning.' *Annual Review of Sociology*, 14: pp. 319–38.

Levitt, S. D., and Snyder, C. M. 1997. 'Is no news bad news? Information transmission and the role of "early warning" in the principal-agent model.' *The RAND Journal of Economics*, 28 (4): pp. 641–61.

MacDonald, S. 1995. 'Too close for comfort: The strategic implications of getting close to the customer.' *California Management Review*, 37 (4): pp. 8–27.

Management Scope. 2010. 'President-directeur Goof Hamers in gesprek met Ron H. Jansen, managing partner Ebbinge & Company.' 25 November: pp. 40–2.

March, J. G. 1995. 'The future, disposable organizations and the rigidities of imagination.' *Organization*, 2 (3/4): pp. 427–40.

Margretta, J. 2002. 'Why business models matter.' *Harvard Business Review*, 80 (5): pp. 86–92.

Markides, C. 2015. 'How established firms exploit disruptive business model innovation: Strategic and organizational challenges.' In N. J. Foss and T. Saebi (Eds.), *Business model innovation: The organizational dimension:* pp. 123–44. Oxford: Oxford University Press.

Markides, C., and Charitou, C. D. 2004. 'Competing with dual business models: A contingency approach.' *The Academy of Management Executive* (1993–2005), 18 (3): pp. 22–36.

Markides, C., and Oyon, D. 2010. 'What to do against disruptive business models (when and how to play two games at once).' *MIT Sloan Management Review*, 51 (4): pp. 26–32.

Markides, C. C. 2013. 'Business model innovation: What can the ambidexterity literature teach us?' *Academy of Management*, 27 (4): pp. 313–23.

Mason, K., and Spring, M. 2011. 'The sites and practices of business models.' *Industrial Marketing Management*, 40 (6): pp. 1032–41.

Massa, L., and Tucci, C. L. 2014. 'Business model innovation.' In M. Dodgson, D. M. Gann, and N. Philips (Eds.), *The Oxford handbook of innovation management*: pp. 420–41. Oxford: Oxford University Press.

Massa, L., Tucci, C. L., and Afuah, A. 2017. 'A critical assessment of business model research.' *Academy of Management Annals*, 11 (1): pp. 73–104.

Matusik, S. F., and Hill, C. W. L. 1998. 'The utilization of contingent work, knowledge creation, and competitive advantage.' *Academy of Management Review*, 23 (4): pp. 680–97.

Matzler, K., Bailom, F., Von Den Eichen, S. F., and Kohler, T. 2013. 'Business model innovation: Coffee triumphs for Nespresso.' *Journal of Business Strategy*, 34 (2): pp. 30–7.

Mayo, M. C., and Brown, G. S. 1999. 'Building a competitive business model.' *Ivey Business Journal*, 63 (3): pp. 18–23.

McGrath, R. G. 2010. 'Business models: A discovery driven approach.' *Long Range Planning*, 43 (2): pp. 247–61.

McGrath, R. G. 2012. 'How the growth outliers do it.' *Harvard Business Review*, 90 (1/2): pp. 110–16.

McGrath, R. G. 2013. *The end of competitive advantage: How to keep your strategy moving as fast as your business.* Boston, MA: Harvard Business Review Press.

Menguc, B., and Auh, S. 2010. 'Development and return on execution of product innovation capabilities: The role of organizational structure.' *Industrial Marketing Management*, 39 (5): pp. 820–31.

Mention, A. L. 2011. 'Co-operation and co-opetition as open innovation practices in the service sector: Which influence on innovation novelty?' *Technovation*, 31 (1): pp. 44–53.

Meuleman, M., Lockett, A., Manigart, S., and Wright, M. 2010. 'Partner selection in interfirm collaborations: The paradox of relational embeddedness.' *Journal of Management Studies*, 47 (6): pp. 995–1019.

Meyers, P. W. 1990. 'Non-linear learning in large technological firms: Period four implies chaos.' *Research Policy*, 19 (2): pp. 97–115.

Mihalache, O., Jansen, J. J. P., Van den Bosch, F. A. J., and Volberda, H. W. 2014. 'Top management team shared leadership and organizational ambidexterity: A moderated mediation framework.' *Strategic Entrepreneurship Journal*, 8 (2): pp. 128–48.

Mikhalkina, T. 2016. *Cognitive perspectives: Conceptualizing the business model.* PhD thesis, Cass Business School, City University London.

Miller, P. 1987. 'Strategic industrial relations and human resource management – distinction, definition and recognition.' *Journal of Management Studies*, 24 (4): pp. 347–61.

Mitchell, D., and Coles, C. 2003. 'The ultimate competitive advantage of continuing business model innovation.' *Journal of Business Strategy*, 24 (5): pp. 15–21.

Mol, M. J., and Birkinshaw, J. 2006. 'Against the flow: Reaping the rewards of management innovation.' *European Business Forum*, 27: pp. 24–9.

Mol, M. J., and Birkinshaw, J. 2009. 'The sources of management innovation: When firms introduce new management practices.' *Journal of Business Research*, 62 (12): pp. 1269–80.

Montgomerie, J., and Roscoe, S. 2013. 'Owning the consumer—Getting to the core of the Apple business model.' *Accounting Forum*, 37 (4): 290–9.

Morris, M., Schindehutte, M., and Allen, J. 2005. 'The entrepreneur's business model: Toward a unified perspective.' *Journal of Business Research*, 58 (6): pp. 726–35.

Morris, M. H., Shirokova, G., and Shatalov, A. 2013. 'The business model and firm performance: The case of Russian food service ventures.' *Journal of Small Business Management*, 51 (1): pp. 46–65.

Müller, R. 1985. 'Corporate crisis management.' *Long Range Planning*, 18 (5): pp. 38–48.

Mullins, J., and Komisar, R. 2009. *Getting to plan B: Breaking through a better business model*. Boston, MA: Harvard University Press.

Nadkarni, S., and Narayanan, V. K. 2007. 'Strategic schemas, strategic flexibility, and firm performance: The moderating role of industry clockspeed.' *Strategic Management Journal*, 28 (3): pp. 243–70.

Nelson, R. P., and Winter, S. G. 1982. 'The Schumpeterian trade-off revisited.' *The American Economic Review*, 72 (1): pp. 114–32.

Nenonen, S., and Storbacka, K. 2010. 'Business model design: Conceptualizing networked value co-creation.' *International Journal of Quality and Service Sciences*, 2 (1): pp. 43–59.

Nonaka, I., and Takeuchi, H. 1995. *The knowledge-creating company*. Oxford: Oxford University Press.

Nonaka, I., Von Krogh, G., and Voelpel, S. 2006. 'Organizational knowledge creation theory: Evolutionary paths and future advances.' *Organization Studies*, 27 (8): pp. 1179–208.

Nonaka, I., and Zhu, Z. 2012. *Pragmatic strategy: Eastern wisdom, global success*. New York: Cambridge University Press.

Nooteboom, B. 1994. 'Innovation and diffusion in small firms: Theory and evidence.' *Small Business Economics*, 6 (5): pp. 327–47.

NRC Handelsblad. 2016. 'Een tweede leven voor Nintendo?' 13 July.

Nunes, P., and Breene, T. 2011. 'Reinvent your business before it's too late.' *Harvard Business Review*, 89 (1/2): pp. 80–7.

Ofek, E., and Wathieu, L. 2010. 'Are you ignoring trends that could shake up your business?' *Harvard Business Review*, 88 (7–8): pp. 124–31.

O'Hern, M. S., and Rindfleisch, A. 2010. 'Customer co-creation'. In N. K. Malhotra (Ed.), *Review of marketing research*, Vol. 6: pp. 84–106. Armonk, NY: M. E. Sharpe.

O'Reilly, C. A., and Tushman, M. L. 2004. 'The ambidextrous organization.' *Harvard Business Review*, 82 (4): pp. 74–81.

O'Reilly, C. A., and Tushman, M. L. 2008. 'Ambidexterity as a dynamic capability: Resolving the innovator's dilemma.' *Research in Organizational Behavior*, 28 (1): pp. 185–206.

Orton, J. D., and Weick, K. E. 1990. 'Loosely coupled systems: A reconceptualization.' *Academy of Management Review*, 15 (2): pp. 203–23.

Osiyevskyy, O., and Dewald, J. 2015a. 'Explorative versus exploitative business model change: The cognitive antecedents of firm-level responses to disruptive innovation.' *Strategic Entrepreneurship Journal*, 9 (1): pp. 58–78.

Osiyevskyy, O., and Dewald, J. 2015b. 'Inducement, impediments, and immediacy: Exploring the cognitive drivers of small business managers' intentions to adopt business model change.' *Journal of Small Business Management*, 53 (4): pp. 1011–32.

Osterwalder, A., and Pigneur, Y. 2009. *Business model generation*. Amsterdam: Self Published.

Ouchi, W. G. 1981. *Theory Z: How American business can meet the Japanese challenge*. Reading, MA: Addison-Wesley.

Paap, J., and Katz, R. 2004. 'Anticipating disruptive innovation.' *Research Technology Management*, 47 (5): pp. 13–22.

Pascale, R. T. 1990. *Managing on the edge: How the smartest companies use conflict to stay ahead*. New York: Simon and Schuster.

Pascale, R. T. 1996. 'Perspectives on strategy: The real story behind Honda's success.' *California Management Review*, 26 (3): pp. 47–72.

Perra, D. B., Sidhu, J., and Volberda, H. W. 2017. 'How do established firms produce breakthrough innovations? Managerial identity-dissemination discourse and the creation of novel product–market solutions.' *Journal of Product Innovation Management*, 34 (4): pp. 509–25.

Perschel, A. 2010. 'Work-life flow: How individuals, Zappos, and other innovative companies achieve high engagement.' *Global Business and Organizational Excellence*, 29 (5): pp. 17–30.

Peters, T., and Waterman, R. H. 1982. *In search of excellence*. New York: Harper & Row.

Pohle, G., and Chapman, M. 2006. 'IBM's global CEO report 2006: Business model innovation matters.' *Strategy and Leadership*, 34 (5): pp. 34–40.

Posen, H. E., and Levinthal, D. A. 2012. 'Chasing a moving target: Exploitation and exploration in dynamic environments.' *Management Science*, 58 (3): pp. 587–601.

Prahalad, C. K., and Ramaswamy, V. 2004. 'Co-creation experiences: The next practice in value creation.' *Journal of Interactive Marketing*, 18 (3): pp. 5–14.

Prigogine, I., and Stengers, I. 1984. *Order out of chaos: Man's new dialogue with nature*. New York: Bantam New Age Books.

Rafferty, A. E., and Griffin, M. A. 2004. 'Dimensions of transformational leadership: Conceptual and empirical extensions.' *The Leadership Quarterly*, 15 (3): pp. 329–54.

Richardson, J. 2008. 'The business model: An integrative framework for strategy execution.' *Strategic Change*, 17 (5/6): pp. 133–44.

Ritter, T., Wilkinson, I. F., and Johnston, W. J. 2004. 'Managing in complex business networks.' *Industrial Marketing Management*, 33 (3): pp. 175–83.

Roberts, J. 2004. *The modern firm: Organizational design for performance and growth*. New York: Oxford University Press.

Robertson, B. J. 2015. *Holacracy: The revolutionary management system that abolishes hierarchy*. London: Penguin Books.

Rosenbloom, R. S. 2000. 'Leadership, capabilities, and technological change: The transformation of NCR in the electronic era.' *Strategic Management Journal*, 21 (10/11): pp. 1083–103.

Rossel, P. 2009. 'Weak signals as a flexible framing space for enhanced management and decision-making.' *Technology Analysis & Strategic Management*, 21 (3): pp. 307–20.

Rubera, G., and Kirca, A. H. 2012. 'Firm innovativeness and its performance outcomes: A meta-analytic review and theoretical integration.' *Journal of Marketing*, 76 (3): pp. 130–47.

Sabatier, V., Kennard, A., and Mangematin, V. 2012. 'When technological discontinuities and disruptive business models challenge dominant industry logics: Insights from the drugs industry.' *Technological Forecasting and Social Change*, 79 (5): pp. 949–62.

Sabatier, V., Mangematin, V., and Rousselle, T. 2010. 'From recipe to dinner: Business model portfolios in the European biopharmaceutical industry.' *Long Range Planning*, 43 (2–3): pp. 431–47.

Samuel, P. 2014. 'Head to head: Two academics tangle over "disruptive innovation".' BMGI Chief Innovator: http://www.chiefinnovator.com/structure-methods/head-head-two-academics-tangle-over-disruptive-innovation.

Schein, E. 1985. *Organizational culture and leadership*. San Francisco: Jossey Bass.

Scherrer, P. S. 1988. 'From warning to crisis: A turnaround primer.' *Management Review*, 77 (9): pp. 30–7.

Schilke, O. 2014. 'On the contingent value of dynamic capabilities for competitive advantage: The nonlinear moderating effect of environmental dynamism.' *Strategic Management Journal*, 35 (2): pp. 179–203.

Schmidt, G. M., and Druehl, C. T. 2008. 'When is a disruptive innovation disruptive?' *Journal of Product Innovation Management*, 25 (4): pp. 347–69.

Schneider, S., and Spieth, P. 2013. 'Business model innovation: Towards an integrated future research agenda.' *International Journal of Innovation Management*, 17 (1): pp. 1–34.

Schoemaker, P. J. H., Krupp, S., and Howland, S. 2013. 'Strategic leadership: The essential skills.' *Harvard Business Review*, 91 (1): pp. 131–4.

Schumpeter, J. A. 1942. *Capitalism, socialism and democracy*. New York: Harper.

Schwab, K. 2016. *The fourth industrial revolution* Geneva: World Economic Forum.

Schwab, K. 2017. *The global competitiveness report 2017–2018*. Geneva: World Economic Forum.

Selnes, F., and Sallis, J. 2003. 'Promoting relationship learning.' *Journal of Marketing*, 67 (3): pp. 80–95.

Sheaffer, Z., Richardson, B., and Rosenblatt, Z. 1998. 'Early-warning-signals management: A lesson from the Barings crisis.' *Journal of Contingencies and Crisis Management*, 6 (1): pp. 1–22.

Shell. 2016a. 'Liquefied natural gas (LNG).' http://www.shell.com/energy-and-innovation/natural-gas/liquefied-natural-gas-lng.html.

Shell. 2016b. 'More and cleaner energy.' http://www.shell.com/energy-and-innovation/the-energy-future/more-and-cleaner-energy.html.

Siggelkow, N. 2001. 'Change in the presence of fit: The rise, the fall, and the renaissance of Liz Claiborne.' *Academy of Management Journal*, 44 (4): pp. 838–57.

Sirmon, D., Hitt, M. A., Ireland, R. D., and Gilbert, B. A. 2011. 'Resource orchestration to create competitive advantage: Breadth, depth and life cycle effects.' *Journal of Management*, 37 (5): pp. 1390–412.

Slater, S. F., and Mohr, J. J. 2006. 'Successful development and commercialization of technological innovation: Insights based on strategy type.' *Journal of Product Innovation Management*, 23 (1): pp. 26–33.

Smith, W. K., Binns, A., and Tushman, M. L. 2010. 'Complex business models: Managing strategic paradoxes simultaneously.' *Long Range Planning*, 43 (2): pp. 448–61.

Smith, W. K., and Lewis, M. W. 2011. 'Toward a theory of paradox: A dynamic equilibrium model of organizing.' *Academy of Management*, 36 (2): pp. 381–403.

Smith, W. K., and Tushman, M. L. 2005. 'Managing strategic contradictions: A top management model for managing innovation streams.' *Organization Science*, 16 (5): pp. 522–36.

Sood, A., and Tellis, G. J. 2005. 'Technological evolution and radical innovation.' *Journal of Marketing*, 69 (3): pp. 152–68.

Sood, A., and Tellis, G. J. 2011. 'Demystifying disruption: A new model for understanding and predicting disruptive technologies.' *Marketing Science*, 30 (2): pp. 339–54.

Sosna, M., Trevinyo-Rodriguez, R. N., and Velamuri, S. 2010. 'Business model innovation through trial-and-error learning: The Naturhouse case.' *Long Range Planning*, 43 (2): pp. 383–407.

Spieth, P., Schneckenberg, D., and Ricart, J. E. 2014. 'Business model innovation—state of the art and future challenges for the field.' *R&D Management*, 44 (3): pp. 237–47.

Srinivasan, S., Pauwels, K., Silva-Risso, J., and Hanssens, D. M. 2004. 'New products, sales promotions, and firm value: The case of the automobile industry.' *Journal of Marketing*, 68 (4): pp. 142–56.

Szulanski, G. 1996. 'Exploring internal stickiness: Impediments to the transfer of best practice within the firm.' *Strategic Management Journal*, 17 (s2): pp. 27–43.

Szulanski, G., and Jensen, R. J. 2008. 'Growing through copying: The negative consequences of innovation on franchise network growth.' *Research Policy*, 37 (10): pp. 1732–41.

Takeishi, A. 2001. 'Bridging inter- and intra-firm boundaries: Management of supplier involvement in automobile product development.' *Strategic Management Journal*, 22 (5): pp. 403–33.

Taylor, A., and Helfat, C. E. 2009. 'Organizational linkages for surviving technological change: Complementary assets, middle management, and ambidexterity.' *Organization Science*, 20 (4): pp. 718–39.

Teece, D. J. 2007. 'Explicating dynamic capabilities: The nature and microfoundations of (sustainable) enterprise performance.' *Strategic Management Journal*, 28 (13): pp. 1319–50.

Teece, D. J. 2010. 'Business models, business strategy and innovation.' *Long Range Planning*, 43 (2): pp. 172–94.

Teece, D. J., Pisano, G., and Shuen, A. 1997. 'Dynamic capabilities and strategic management.' *Strategic Management Journal*, 18 (7): pp. 509–33.

Tellis, G. J. 2006. 'Disruptive technology or visionary leadership?' *Journal of Product Innovation Management*, 23 (1): pp. 34–8.

Tellis, G. J. 2012. *Unrelenting innovation: How to create a culture for market dominance.* New York: John Wiley & Sons.

Tessun, F. 2001. 'Scenario analysis and early warning systems at Daimler-Benz Aerospace.' In J. E. Prescott and S. H. Miller (Eds.), *Proven strategies in competitive intelligence: Lessons from the trenches*: pp. 259–73. New York: John Wiley & Sons.

Tikkanen, H., Lamberg, J. A., Parvinen, P., and Kallunki, J. P. 2005. 'Managerial cognition, action and the business model of the firm.' *Management Decision*, 43 (6): pp. 789–809.

Timmers, P. 1998. 'Business models for electronic markets.' *Electronic Markets*, 8 (2): pp. 3–8.

Totterdill, P., Dhondt, S., and Milsome, S. 2002. *Partners at work? A report to Europe's policy makers and social partners*. Nottingham: The Work Institute.

Tripsas, M., and Gavetti, G. 2000. 'Capabilities, cognition, and inertia: Evidence from digital imaging.' *Strategic Management Journal*, 21 (10/11): pp. 1147–61.

Tsai, K. H. 2009. 'Collaborative networks and product innovation performance: Toward a contingency perspective.' *Research Policy*, 38 (5): pp. 765–78.

Tsai, W. 2002. 'Social structure of "coopetition" within a multiunit organization: Coordination, competition, and intra-organizational knowledge sharing.' *Organization Science*, 13 (2): pp. 179–90.

Tushman, M. L., and Anderson, P. 1986. 'Technological discontinuities and organizational environments.' *Administrative Science Quarterly*, 31 (3): pp. 439–65.

Tushman, M. L., Anderson, P. C., and O'Reilly, C. 1997. 'Technology cycles, innovation streams and ambidextrous organizations: Organization renewal through innovation streams and strategic change.' In M. L. Tushman and P. C. Anderson (Eds.), *Managing strategic innovation and change*: pp. 3–23. New York: Oxford University Press.

Tushman, M. L., and O'Reilly, C. A. 1996. 'Ambidextrous organizations: Managing evolutionary and revolutionary change.' *California Management Review*, 38 (4): pp. 8–30.

Tushman, M. L., and O'Reilly, C. A. 2013. *Winning through innovation: A practical guide to leading organizational change and renewal*. Boston, MA: Harvard Business Press.

USA Today. 2015. 'Antonoff: How a struggling Netflix became the new Blockbuster.' USA Today. https://www.usatoday.com/story/money/2015/01/23/antonoff-column-video-streaming-netflix-blockbuster/22209273/

Uzzie, B. 1997. 'Social structure and competition in interfirm networks: The paradox of embeddedness.' *Administrative Science Quarterly*, 42 (1): pp. 35–67.

Vaccaro, I. G. 2010. *Management innovation: Studies on the role of internal change agents*. Rotterdam: Erasmus Research Institute of Management (ERIM).

Vaccaro, I. G., Jansen, J. J. P., Van den Bosch, F. A. J., and Volberda, H. W. 2012a. 'Management innovation and leadership: The moderating role of organizational size.' *Journal of Management Studies*, 49 (1): pp. 28–51.

Vaccaro, I. G., Volberda, H. W., and Van den Bosch, F. A. J. 2012b. 'Management innovation in action: The case of self-managing teams.' In T. S. Pitsis, A. Simpson and E. Dehlin, (Eds.), *The handbook of organizational and managerial innovation*: pp. 138–62. Cheltenham: Edward Elgar Press.

Van de Ven, A. H. 1986. 'Central problems in the management of innovation.' *Management Science*, 35 (5): pp. 590–607.

Van den Bosch, F. A. J. 2012. *On the necessity and scientific challenges of conducting research into strategic value creating management models*. Rotterdam: Erasmus Research Institute of Management (ERIM).

Van den Bosch, F. A. J., and Van Riel, C. B. M. 1998. 'Buffering and bridging as environmental strategies of firms.' *Business Strategy and the Environment*, 7 (1): pp. 24–31.

Van den Bosch, F.A.J.,Volberda, H.W., and De Boer, M. 1999. 'Coevolution of firm absorptive capacity and knowledge environment: Organizational forms and combinative capabilities.' *Organization Science*, 10 (5): pp. 551–68.

Van Doorn, S., Jansen, J. J. P., Van den Bosch, F. A. J., and Volberda, H. W. 2013. 'Entrepreneurial orientation and firm performance: Drawing attention to the senior team.' *Journal of Product Innovation Management*, 30 (5): pp. 821–36.

Van Driel, H., Volberda, H. W., Eikelboom, S., and Kamerbeek, E. 2015. 'A co-evolutionary analysis of longevity: Pakhoed and its predecessors.' *Business History*, 57 (8): pp. 1277–305.

Vanhaverbeke, W.,Van de Vrande,V., and Chesbrough, H. 2008. 'Understanding the advantages of open innovation practices in corporate venturing in terms of real options.' *Creativity and Innovation Management*, 17 (4): pp. 251–8.

Vargo, S. L., and Lusch, R. F. 2008. 'Service-dominant logic: Continuing the evolution.' *Journal of the Academy of Marketing Science*, 36 (1): pp. 1–10.

Vazquez Sampere, J. P. 2015. 'Zappos and the connection between structure and strategy.' *Harvard Business Review Digital Articles*: 2–4. https://hbr.org/2015/06/zappos-and-the-connection-between-structure-and-strategy.

Velu, C., and Stiles, P. 2013. 'Managing decision-making and cannibalization for parallel business models.' *Long Range Planning*, 46 (6): pp. 443–58.

Venkatraman, N., and Henderson, J. C. 2008. 'Four vectors of business model innovation: Value capture in a network era.' In D. Pantaleo and N. Pal (Eds.), *From strategy to execution: Turning accelerated global change into opportunity*: pp. 259–80. Berlin-Heidelberg: Springer-Verlag.

Voelpel, S. C., Leibold, M., Tekie, B., and Von Krogh, G. 2005. 'Escaping the red queen effect in competitive strategy: Sense testing business models.' *European Management Journal*, 23 (1): pp. 37–49.

Volberda, H.W. 1996. 'Toward the flexible form: How to remain vital in hypercompetitive environments.' *Organization Science*, 7 (4): pp. 359–74.

Volberda, H.W. 1997. 'Building flexible organizations for fast-moving markets.' *Long Range Planning*, 30 (2): pp. 169–83.

Volberda, H. W. 1998. *Building the flexible firm: How to remain competitive*. Oxford: Oxford University Press.

Volberda, H. W. 2003. 'Strategic flexibility: Creating dynamic competitive advantages.' In D. Faulkner and A. Campbell (Eds.), *The Oxford handbook of strategy, Volume II: Corporate strategy*: pp. 447–65. Oxford: Oxford University Press.

Volberda, H.W. 2017. 'Rethinking strategic renewal in the multidivisional firm: New paths, organizational forms and managerial roles.' *Long Range Planning*, 50 (1): pp. 44–7.

Volberda, H. W., and Baden-Fuller, C. 1999. 'Strategic renewal and competence building: Four dynamic mechanisms.' In G. Hamel, C. K. Prahalad, H.Thomas, and D. O'Neal (Eds.), *Strategic flexibility: Managing in a turbulent economy*: pp. 371–89. Chichester: Wiley.

Volberda, H. W., and Baden-Fuller, C. 2003. 'Strategic renewal processes in multiunit firms: Generic journeys of change.' In B. Chakravarthy, G. Mueller-Stewens,

P. Lorange, and C. Lechner (Eds.), *Strategy process: Shaping the contours of the field*: pp. 208–32. Oxford: Blackwell.

Volberda, H. W., Baden-Fuller, C. W. F., and Van den Bosch, F. A. J. 2001. 'Mastering strategic renewal: Mobilizing renewal journeys in multi-unit firms.' *Long Range Planning*, 34 (2): pp. 159–78.

Volberda, H. W., Foss, N. J., and Lyles, M. A. 2010. 'Absorbing the concept of absorptive capacity: How to realize its potential in the organization field.' *Organization Science*, 21 (4): pp. 931–51.

Volberda, H. W., and Heij, C. V. 2014. *Het nieuwe businessmodel in financieel advies: Van provisie naar waardecreatie*. Amsterdam: Mediawerf.

Volberda, H. W., and Lewin, A. Y. 2003. 'Co-evolutionary dynamics within and between firms: From evolution to co-evolution.' *Journal of Management Studies*, 40 (8): pp. 2111–36.

Volberda, H. W., Morgan, R. E., Reinmoeller, P., Hitt, M. A., Ireland, R. D., and Hoskisson, R. E. 2011. *Strategic management: Competitiveness and globalization*. London: Cengage Learning EMEA.

Volberda, H. W., Van den Bosch, F. A. J., Flier, B., and Gedajlovic, E. R. 2001. 'Following the herd or not? Patterns of renewal in the Netherlands and the UK.' *Long Range Planning*, 34 (2): pp. 209–29.

Volberda, H. W., Van den Bosch, F. A. J., and Heij, C. V. 2013. 'Management innovation: Management as fertile ground of innovation.' *European Management Review*, 10 (1): pp. 1–15.

Volberda, H. W., Van den Bosch, F. A. J., and Mihalache, O. R. 2014. 'Advancing management innovation: Synthesizing processes, levels of analysis, and change agents.' *Organization Studies*, 35 (9): pp. 1245–64.

Volberda, H. W., Van der Weerdt, N., and Van der Mandele, M. 2015. 'De noodzaak van businessmodel-innovatie in de accountancy.' *Maandblad voor de Accountancy en Bedrijfseconomie*, 89 (3): pp. 77–86.

Volberda, H. W., Van der Weerdt, N., Verwaal, E., Stienstra, M., and Verdu, A. J. 2012. 'Contingency fit, institutional fit, and firm performance: A metafit approach to organization-environment relationships.' *Organization Science*, 23 (4): pp. 1040–54.

Von Hippel, E. 1998. 'Economics of product development by users: The impact of "sticky" local information.' *Management Science*, 44 (5): pp. 629–44.

Von Hippel, E. 2009. 'Democratizing innovation: The evolving phenomenon of user innovation.' *International Journal of Innovation Science*, 1 (1): pp. 29–40.

Von Hippel, E. A. 1977. 'Has a customer already developed your next product?' *MIT Sloan Management Review*, 18 (2): pp. 63–74.

Vuori, T. O., and Huy, Q. N. 2016. 'Distributed attention and shared emotions in the innovation process: How Nokia lost the smartphone battle.' *Administrative Science Quarterly*, 61 (1): pp. 9–51.

Waddell, D., and Mallen, D. 2001. 'Quality managers: Beyond 2000?' *Total Quality Management*, 12 (3): pp. 373–84.

Walker, R. M. 2008. 'An empirical evaluation of innovation types and organizational and environmental characteristics: Towards a configuration framework.' *Journal of Public Administration Research and Theory*, 18 (4): pp. 591–615.

Ward, A., Liker, J. K., Cristiano, J. J., and Sobek, D. K. 1995. 'The second Toyota paradox: How delaying decisions can make better cars faster.' *Sloan Management Review*, 36 (3): pp. 43–61.

Weick, K. E. 1982. 'Management of organizational change among loosely coupled elements.' In P. S. Goodman and Associates (Eds.), *Change in organizations: New perspectives on theory, research and practice*: pp. 375–408. San Francisco: Jossey-Bass.

Weitzel, W., and Jonsson, E. 1989. 'Decline in organizations: A literature integration and extension.' *Administrative Science Quarterly*, 34 (1): pp. 91–109.

Whittington, R., Pettigrew, A., Peck, S., Fenton, E., and Conyon, M. 1999. 'Change and complementarities in the new competitive landscape: A European panel study, 1992–1996.' *Organization Science*, 10 (5): pp. 583–600.

Whittington, R., and Pettigrew, A. M. 2003. 'Complementarities thinking.' In A. M. Pettigrew, R. Whittington, L. Melin, C. Sánchez-Runde, F. A. J. Van den Bosch, W. Ruighok, and T. Numagami (Eds.), *Innovative forms of organizing: International perspectives*: pp. 125–32. New York: Sage.

Wilkinson, A., and Kupers, R. 2013. 'Living in the futures.' *Harvard Business Review*, 91 (5): pp. 118–27.

Winter, S. G., and Szulanski, G. 2001. 'Replication as strategy.' *Organization Science*, 12 (6): pp. 730–43.

Winter, S. G., Szulanski, G., Ringov, D., and Jensen, R. J. 2012. 'Reproducing knowledge: Inaccurate replication and failure in franchise organizations.' *Organization Science*, 23 (3): pp. 672–85.

Wirtz, B. W., Schilke, O., and Ullrich, S. 2010. 'Strategic development of business models: Implications of the web 2.0 for creating value on the internet.' *Long Range Planning*, 43 (2/3): pp. 272–90.

Wu, J., and Shanley, M. T. 2009. 'Knowledge stock, exploration, and innovation: Research on the United States electromedical device industry.' *Journal of Business Research*, 64 (4): pp. 474–83.

Wu, S., Levitas, E., and Priem, R. L. 2005. 'CEO tenure and company invention under differing levels of technological dynamism.' *Academy of Management Journal*, 48 (5): pp. 859–73.

Yoon, E., and Deeken, L. 2013. 'Why it pays to be a category creator.' *Harvard Business Review*, 91 (3): pp. 21–3.

Youndt, M. A., Subramaniam, M., and Snell, S. A. 2004. 'Intellectual capital profiles: An examination of investments and returns.' *Journal of Management Studies*, 41 (2): pp. 335–61.

Yukl, G. 1999. 'An evaluation of conceptual weaknesses in transformational and charismatic leadership theories.' *The Leadership Quarterly*, 10 (2): pp. 285–305.

Zahra, S. A., and Chaples, S. S. 1993. 'Blind spots in competitive analysis.' *Academy of Management Executive*, 7 (2): pp. 7–28.

Zahra, S. A., and George, G. 2002. 'Absorptive capacity: A review, reconceptualization, and extension.' *Business Horizons*, 55 (3): pp. 219–29.

Zahra, S. A., and Nambisan, S. 2012. 'Entrepreneurship and strategic thinking in business ecosystems.' *Business Horizons*, 55 (3): pp. 219–29.

Zhou, K. Z., and Li, C. B. 2012. 'How knowledge affects radical innovation: Knowledge base, market knowledge acquisition, and internal knowledge sharing.' *Strategic Management Journal*, 33 (9): pp. 1090–102.

Zhou, K. Z., and Wu, F. 2010. 'Technology capability, strategic flexibility, and product innovation.' *Strategic Management Journal*, 31 (5): pp. 547–61.

Zook, C., and Allen, C. 2011. 'The great repeatable business model.' *Harvard Business Review*, 89 (11): pp. 106–14.

Zott, C., and Amit, R. 2007. 'Business model design and the performance of entrepreneurial firms.' *Organization Science*, 18 (2): pp. 181–99.

Zott, C., and Amit, R. 2010. 'Business model design: An activity system perspective.' *Long Range Planning*, 43 (2): pp. 216–26.

Zott, C., Amit, R., and Massa, L. 2011. 'The business model: Recent developments and future research.' *Journal of Management*, 37 (4): pp. 1019–42.

Index